A GUIDE TO

PUBLIC ART

in Greater Boston
From Newburyport to Plymouth

Revised Edition

Marty Carlock

THE HARVARD COMMON PRESS
BOSTON, MASSACHUSETTS

Author's Comment

The initial intention of this guide was to produce a complete list of *all* the public works in the greater metropolitan area that centers on Boston, an area that stretches from Newburyport to Milford to Plymouth and includes such communities as Lowell, often considered demographically separate from Greater Boston. Two years' research revealed that "complete" was too large an order in a vital art scene that sees new works sited almost weekly. The author will welcome additions and corrections; readers are encouraged to write Marty Carlock, c/o Harvard Common Press, 535 Albany St., Boston, MA 02118. Please include a telephone number.

All photos are by the author except those otherwise credited.

Information contained in this guide may have been edited for style and space considerations. We apologize for any discrepancies resulting from these adjustments and regret any inconvenience caused by inaccurate information. Every effort has been made to ensure accuracy in the guide, but we cannot assume responsibility for any errors.

Sponsored by New England Sculptors Association,
50 Winchester St., Brookline, MA 02146.

The Harvard Common Press
535 Albany Street
Boston, Massachusetts 02118

Library of Congress Cataloging-in-Publication Data

Carlock, Marty.
   A guide to public art in greater Boston : from Newburyport to Plymouth / Marty Carlock. — Rev. ed.
      p.   cm.
   ISBN 1-55832-062-8 : $12.95
   1. Public art—Massachusetts—Boston Metropolitan Area—Guidebooks.   2. Boston Metropolitan Area (Mass.)—Guidebooks.
I. Title.
N8845.B67C37   1993
709'.744'61—dc20
                                                      93-34413
                                                      CIP

Front cover: *Samuel Eliot Morison* by Penelope Jencks
(*see* Boston [Commonwealth Avenue]). Penelope Jencks Photo.
Back cover: *Echo of the Waves* by Susumu Shingu
(*see* Boston [Waterfront]). Marty Carlock Photo.
Cover design: Joyce C. Weston.

ACKNOWLEDGMENTS

The author gratefully acknowledges the work of Joan Brigham, associate professor of art at Emerson College, and her students who in 1982 pounded the city's pavements to compile *What's Up?*—a booklet listing public art in the cities of Boston, Cambridge, and Chelsea—as well as the work of Netta Lynn Davis and Stephanie Berman in expanding that list under the auspices of Mary Shannon, executive director of the Boston Art Commission.

Other resources to whom this book owes a debt include UrbanArts, Arts on the Line, Cambridge Arts Council, the Artists Foundation, Lowell Historic Preservation Commission, the Massachusetts Art Commission, the Quincy Historical Society, the Brockton, Danforth, DeCordova, and Rose Art Museums, the Boston Museum of Fine Arts, the Boston Public Library, the Bostonian Society, the Essex Institute, the Museum of the National Center for Afro-American Artists, the Addison Gallery, the Massachusetts Historical Society, the Museum of Our National Heritage, Mount Auburn and Forest Hills Cemeteries; art specialists at Babson College, Boston College, Boston University, Harvard University, Massachusetts Institute of Technology, Framingham State College, Northeastern University, Pine Manor College, Tufts University, Wellesley College, Wheaton College; the Crabtree Trust, the staff of *Folio*, Massport, the Metropolitan District Commission, Milton Academy, Roxbury Latin School, Newton Arts in the Park, the Pilgrim Society, numerous arts lottery council chairpersons, many executives, executive secretaries, and public relations people, the artists themselves, and, most important, to countless reference librarians in public libraries for their willing assistance. Finally, not least, thanks to Prof. Bonnie Grad of Clark University for her helpful perusal of the manuscript, and to the New England Sculptors Association for its aid and sponsorship.

THIS PROJECT IS FUNDED IN PART BY THE

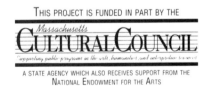

A STATE AGENCY WHICH ALSO RECEIVES SUPPORT FROM THE
NATIONAL ENDOWMENT FOR THE ARTS

This edition is made possible by the generosity of the Beacon Companies, of Irma Mann Stearns Strategic Marketing, Inc., and of Sonesta International Hotels and Royal Sonesta Hotel, Cambridge. This project is also supported in part by the local agencies listed below, by the Massachusetts Cultural Council, a state agency, and by the National Endowment for the Arts.

Arlington Arts Council
Concord Cultural Council
Hingham Cultural Council
Lawrence Cultural Council

Revere Cultural Council
Wellesley Cultural Council
Weston Cultural Council

Boston Neighborhoods

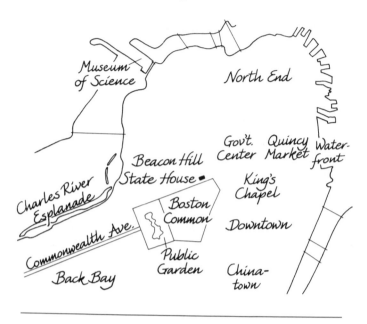

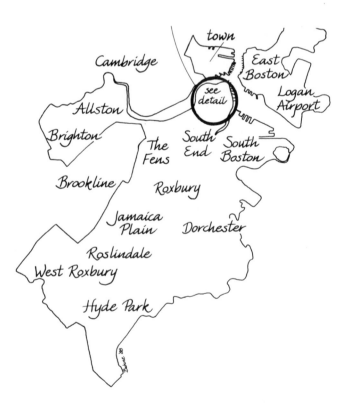

INTRODUCTION

Curious countercurrents affect Boston's attitudes about the visual arts. On the one hand, this metropolitan area is home to the Center for Advanced Visual Studies, an institution marching at the vanguard of techno/art, dedicating itself to the synthesis of art and scientific technology. On the other hand, the Boston Museum of Fine Arts, venerable arbiter of the city's visual art, spent most of this century ignoring contemporary work. A Department of Twentieth Century Art was established in 1971, but not until 1991 did it begin an assertive program of showing and acquiring cutting-edge works. The Institute of Contemporary Art has dedicated its resources to showing, not collecting, contemporary work, and owns no permanent collection.

Boston boasts the oldest arts commission in the country, yet if the connoisseur is looking for famous names Boston's public art takes a back seat to that of Philadelphia. Here monuments have been the mode. Walter Muir Whitehill commented in his book *Boston Statues* that the erectors of our public works, generally the Legislature or the Boston Art Commission, have never "shown great devotion to any abstract principles of selection."

The Commonwealth's Arts Lottery, now ten years old, injected new blood into the arts, and new thinking. But in the early 1990s the funds allotted to it were drastically reduced. Political problems and fiscal considerations forced Massachusetts' art entities into a series of incarnations: the Massachusetts Council on the Arts and Humanities (MCAH) and the Artists Foundation, threatened thrice with extinction, merged in 1991 into a pared-down Massachusetts Cultural Council (MCC). Legislation mandating one percent of the cost of state construction projects for art (with a maximum of $100,000) spawned a program called variously 1% for Art or the Massachusetts Art in Public Places Program; economic woes have terminated it.

Currently there are two schools of thought about public art, one tending toward site-integrated art, and one favoring "plop art." (Theorists work through a gradation from "site-dominant" to "site-adjusted" to "site-specific" to "site-determined" art, but for our purposes we can consider the two extremes.) "Plop," or site-dominant, art is a term given to works that were created independently of the site, usually by one of the stars of the international art world, and plopped down in some open space with varying degrees of acceptance and success. This method is rather out of fashion just now with those who commission public art. M.I.T. has a collection of very good plop art, some of which is accepted to the degree that it is routinely climbed on and sat upon; some of which is openly disliked and occasionally disfigured by the student body. To its credit, M.I.T. saw to it that its new List Arts Center integrated site-responsive art and architecture (perhaps too thoroughly—few would recognize the color tiles on the building as art by internationally known colorist Kenneth Noland).

Site-determined art is designed for a specific site, often with input from the neighborhood which will live with it. Local involvement sometimes even takes the form of hands-on creation, as in the children's tiles in the Davis Square subway station, the Rosenberg ceramics in Newton, Lynn, and at Villa Victoria housing project, and in the community mural in Chinatown. At times the neighborhood's opinions limit the artist's vision too strictly, diminishing the formal qualities of the art: North Cambridge's brickworker made of brick or, for example, Lechmere Canal Park's totem of faces. At times the art is so thoroughly integrated as to be invisible, like that of the List Center, or like Sennot Park's *Sun Arc*, indistinguishable from totlot climbing equipment.

When it works, site-specific art is wonderful: Harries' cast-bronze debris at Haymarket, Haas' architectural murals, Rosenberg's Puerto Rican *Betances Mural*, Dorrien's mock-architectural fragment in Cambridge's Winthrop Park, Biegun's cookie-cutter ceramic at a pre-schoolers' playground in Weston, Shaner's poetry underfoot on the Davis Square subway platform, the McKinnell-Singer sitework at Wellesley College. Its best quality is its wit, a quiet wry appropriateness that leaves the viewer surprised and a bit dazed to find something so perfectly suited to its place.

It occurs to most viewers to ask, "Who are these people, anyway?" Who are the artists who are privileged to place their concepts and visions into our daily lives, and who are the powers that have chosen them? More than most guides, this book lays out the artist's credentials for public inspection. When it is known, the person or institution which commissioned the work is listed. Who the people within those institutions are, the people who are choosing, commissioning, and shaping our aesthetic environment today, would have to be the subject of another book, and a fat one.

This book rejects the concept that "fine" art should have exclusive command of the viewer's attention. The trend toward participatory and community art can only be encouraged; from such beginnings artists and art audiences come. For the benefit of students of aesthetic history, the guide stars some works as "must see." (A star before a name indicates an artist of historical importance; a star before a title indicates the author's opinion that the work is worth seeing.) Lack of a star does not imply that the work or artist is inferior, however. Other than that, the author has endeavored in most cases (not quite all) to leave personal opinion aside and to content herself with explaining artists' intentions and concepts, describing the processes of making art, and researching the reasons for a particular work's presence on a particular site and the history of the persons or events commemorated.

CONTENTS

BOSTON

CAMBRIDGE

OTHER CITIES AND TOWNS

Boston

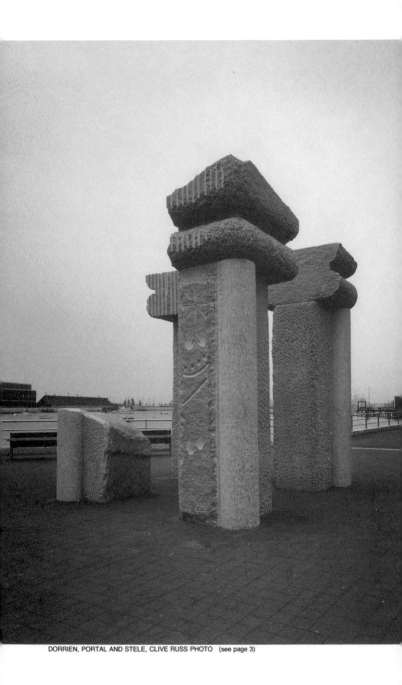

DORRIEN, PORTAL AND STELE, CLIVE RUSS PHOTO   (see page 3)

EAST BOSTON

At Logan Airport:

★ PORTAL AND STELE, 1985. Stone, four pieces, h. 6½'–14'.
Harborwalk, airport ferry landing (Maverick St.).
Carlos Dorrien (*see* Waltham [Bentley College]: *Portal*).

★ WINDWHEELS, 1982. Stainless steel with diffraction grating, h. 16'–20'
(varies as sculpture moves).
Harborwalk.
William Wainwright (1924–   ).

   Indiana-born, Wainwright attended Purdue, Cornell, and the Chicago
Institute of Design, then did graduate work at M.I.T. He is a
registered engineer and architect; among his mentors was modern-
design guru Buckminster Fuller. Now a resident of Brookline,
Wainwright has taught graphics and architecture at Harvard School of
Design and has been a visiting artist at Massachusetts College of Art.
   One of a dozen publicly sited Wainwright works in Greater Boston,
Windwheels employs diffraction grating that results in prismatic color
changes as kinetic parts move in the wind. Funded by friends of the artist and City Life, Boston.

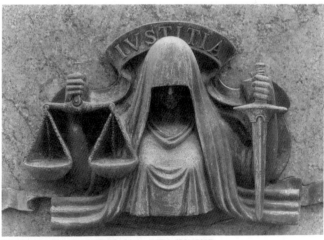

COLETTI, GEN. EDWARD LAWRENCE LOGAN   (DETAIL FROM BASE)

GEN. EDWARD LAWRENCE LOGAN, 1956. Bronze, larger than life.
Mall at entrance to airport.
Joseph A. Coletti (1893–1973).

Coletti's family emigrated to Quincy from Italy when the future sculptor was two years old. His father worked in the granite industry, and the son had a job as a tool sharpener for a time. He attended Massachusetts College of Art and Harvard; he assisted John Singer Sargent with the sculptural elements of his murals at Boston Public Library and in the rotunda of the Museum of Fine Arts. Coletti served for six years as chairman of the Massachusetts Art Commission.

Lawyer, judge, and soldier, the airport's namesake is portrayed in uniform. In civilian life he was a Boston city councilman, legislator, and municipal court judge; in his military role he saw duty in the Spanish–American War on the Mexican border, as a colonel of the 101st Infantry during World War I, and as lieutenant-general in the National Guard. Coletti's granite bas-relief carvings, art deco style, on the base are more interesting than the statue itself.

PASSING REFLECTIONS, 1986. Mirror arrays, h. 9' × 45'.
North and south ends of Terminal C, upper level.
James Seawright.

Seawright is director of the visual arts department at Princeton University. His intention with his reflective materials is to employ the passing scene as part of the work, the patterns of motion and color changing as people move by. Commissioned by Massport.

AUDIOKINETIC SCULPTURES, 1986. Multimedia, h. 7' × 9' × 9'.
Upper level, Terminal C.
George Rhoads (see Museum of Science: Archimedian Excogitation).

CLOUD THE TRAVELER, 1985. Polyester sailcloth, approx. 100 units each 34" square, spaced 14" apart.
Ceiling, upper level, Terminal C.
Susumu Shingu (see Waterfront [New England Aquarium]: Echo of the Waves).

The fabric units are suspended and balanced so that they move with the air stream from the air conditioning system.

LADIES PREPARING NEWLY WOVEN SILK, 1981. Photo replicas from Chinese scroll painting, h. each 6' × 3½'.
Terminal C, pier B corridor.
Emperor Hui Tsung (1082–1135).

Although this scroll is attributed to the emperor himself, it is thought to be a copy of an earlier work. Magnified thirty-one times, the photo replicas are taken from a Chinese handscroll in the Asiatic collection of the Boston Museum of Fine Arts, which houses an oversized Polaroid camera for fine-arts reproduction. Funded by Polaroid Corp. and the Boston Museum of Fine Arts.

BANNERS
Terminal E (International Terminal).

These banners were fabricated by sailmaker Ted Hood (formerly of Marblehead), known for his sails for world-class international competitions such as the America's Cup race.

NINE CERAMIC MURALS, 1990. Ceramic tile, varied sizes, approx. h. 4' × 8'.
Central garage, at elevators and walkways, and Terminals D and E.
Malou Flato (*see* MBTA [Orange Line]: Stony Brook Station).

Each mural is inspired by a locale or a generic landscape, such as Greece, Mexico, the Maine Coast, New Hampshire, and Boston itself. Commissioned by Massport.

WINDOWS OF LIGHT, 1991. Neon sculptures, from 5'8" square × 7" to 17' × 11'4" × 7".
Central garage, east and west stairwells.
Jane Haskell.

Pittsburgh sculptor Haskell took her B.A. from Skidmore College in 1944 and her M.A. in art history from the University of Pittsburgh in 1961. For the past seven years she has concentrated on environments with light; her work is owned by Amherst College, Carnegie Institute, and the Milwaukee Art Museum. Here her light sculptures provide a sense of place for travelers seeking their automobiles. Commissioned by Massport.

MADONNA QUEEN OF THE UNIVERSE, 1954. Bronze, h. 35'.
Atop Madonna Queen National Shrine, Don Orione Home, 111 Orient Ave.
Arrigo Minerbi.

When World War II began, Minerbi was already an established artist; his works included the doors of the cathedral at Milan and the tomb of the mother of the Italian politician and writer D'Annuncio. A Jew, Minerbi was hidden by the Don Orione fathers in Rome and survived the Holocaust. In gratitude, he offered to sculpt this figure; he based the face on studies of the shroud at Turin and the physiognomy of Jewish women. The original stands atop Mount Mario, Rome. When Don Orione fathers came to Boston in 1949 to establish a home for the aged, they proposed to have a copy erected here. Minerbi, who had become a convert to Catholicism, supervised the casting of this duplicate. It is set into a seven-story tower; the top floor is an observatory. Funded by individual donations.

TWIRLING, 1975. Bronze.
Mariana Pineda (1924–   ).
Heritage House, Sumner St. Elderly Housing, Maverick Sq.

One of the Bunting Institute's early fellows in the 1960s, Pineda has since taught sculpture at Boston University, Boston College, and

Newton College of the Sacred Heart. She studied sculpture at Cranbrook Academy, Bennington College, University of California at Berkeley, Columbia University, and in Paris. Pineda may be termed an
expressionist/realist whose figures contain strong emotional impact.
Among her public commissions is an eight-foot bronze of Lili'uokalani,
last queen of Hawaii, commissioned by that state for its capitol building. Funded by Boston Redevelopment Authority, 1% for Art.

COMMEMORATIVE RELIEF OF NODDLE ISLAND, 1975. Bronze, h. 8' × 4'.
Heritage House, Sumner St. Elderly Housing, Maverick Sq.
Ted Barbarossa (*see* Arlington: *Uncle Sam*).

What is East Boston today was once Noddle Island; this bas-relief re-
capitulates the area's history from its beginnings, including the era of
clipper ships, the early airport (Lindbergh is shown landing here), and
problems of the present day. Funded by 1% for Art.

CALLAHAN AND SUMNER TUNNEL MEMORIALS, 1956. Bronze relief.
Facades (west end, Callahan Tunnel; east end, Sumner Tunnel).
Joseph Coletti (*see* above: *Gen. Edward Lawrence Logan*).

It is certain that Coletti did the bas-reliefs on the Callahan Tunnel facade (he signed the portrait), and it is as good a guess as any that he
may also have done those on the earlier Sumner Tunnel; no records
have been found. Opened in 1961, the Callahan Tunnel paralleled the
much older Sumner Tunnel, dating from 1934 and named for Gen. William Sumner of Roxbury (1780–1861), adjutant general of Massachusetts 1818–35. The Callahan Tunnel is named in memory of the son of
William F. Callahan, chairman of the Massachusetts Turnpike Authority,
which took over the tunnels in 1959.

CHARLESTOWN

JOSEPH WARREN, 1857. Marble, larger than life.
Bunker Hill, inside the Park Service building.
★ Henry Dexter (1806–1876).

It is instructive to compare this rather old-fashioned marble statue, in
the style of the early 1800s, to Story's livelier *Prescott* outside. Known
early in his career as "the blacksmith sculptor," Dexter was apprenticed to that trade and practiced it, but was drawn to art. After some
mediocre attempts at painting, he discovered clay and a natural bent
for portrait modeling. He shortly became Boston's most popular portrait
sculptor, taking the likenesses not only of Bostonians but of visitors
such as Charles Dickens. In 1859 he undertook an ambitious journey
to visit every state and the Capitol, to portray the governor of each
state and the President, James Buchanan. In 1861 he exhibited the
fruit of the undertaking, thirty-two busts, in Boston, but his timing was
terrible: the Civil War eclipsed his achievement; the collection was donated to the National Museum and forgotten.
The most famous American casualty at the battle of Bunker Hill, Dr.
Warren is remembered by a better statue at Roxbury Latin School.
Commissioned by the Bunker Hill Monument Association for the 75th
anniversary of the battle.

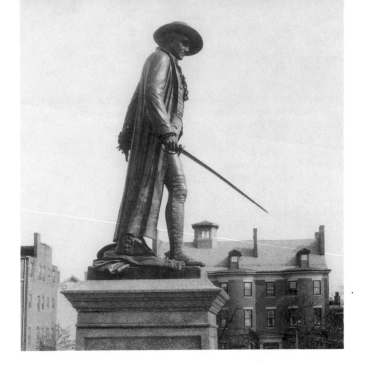

WILLIAM PRESCOTT, 1881. Bronze, larger than life.
Bunker (Breed's) Hill, Monument Ave. and High St.
★ William Wetmore Story (*see* Dorchester: *Edward Everett*).

The first major engagement between British and colonial American forces occurred on Breed's (miscalled Bunker) Hill in June of 1775. The entrenchments were dug overnight under the command of Col. William Prescott (1726–1795). As the fighting and the weather grew hot, the colonel shucked his uniform for a broadbrimmed hat and light coat, and is thus immortalized here. Commissioned by the Bunker Hill Monument Association.

MASSACHUSETTS KOREAN WAR MEMORIAL, 1993. Bronze on Korean granite base, h. 9′4″.
Charlestown Navy Yard.
Robert Shure, Moise Altshuler, and Skylight Studios (*see* Norwood: *Protectors of the American Way*).
Commissioned by the Massachusetts Korean War Veterans Committee.

RECLAMATION ARTISTS SITE #1, annual event.
Underneath Route 93 interchange, at end of Warren Ave.
Reclamation Artists.

Each Columbus Day weekend since 1990, twenty-five to thirty members of Reclamation Artists have unleashed their talents on this urban waste space as a political statement. Transforming debris and weeds, the artists intend to show how neglected spaces can be reclaimed, how art can help people see what is around them. This event is the antithesis of "plop" art (*see* Introduction); it enlarges the concept of what art is about. A loosely organized group of more than one hundred environmental artists, Reclamation Artists occasionally occupies other sites, but this is their favorite.

WIND SCULPTURE, 1978. Stainless steel, h. 25′ × 3′ × 3′.
   Charlestown High School.
   Michio Ihara (*see* Lowell: *Pawtucket Prism*).

BIRNHAM WOOD, 1970. Welded steel, h. 11½′.
   Fire station, 525 Main St., Sullivan Sq.
   Robert Amory (*see* Downtown: *Helion*).
   Funded by 1% for Art.

SUNDIAL, 1991. Bronze, three life-sized figures and thirteen bas-relief elements on granite sundial, h. 1½′ × diam. 10′.
   Hayes Sq., Bunker Hill and Moulton Sts.
   Lu Stubbs (*see* Brookline: *Three Women*).

   Craftspeople of colonial days are pictured on the face of the sundial. Funded by the Browne Fund.

UNTITLED, installation planned spring, 1994.
   Thompson Sq., Main St. and Dexter Row.
   Jeffrey Schiff (1952–   ).

   Jeffrey Schiff has drawn a good deal of critical attention for his collaborative performance and installation art, but he also makes permanent objects combining concrete, lead, stone, steel, and wood. Assistant professor of sculpture at Wesleyan, he is a graduate of Brown and holds a master's degree from UMass/Amherst. In 1985 he was awarded a Boston/Kyoto Sister City grant enabling him to study temples and tea houses in Japan. Among his fellowships have been three from the National Endowment for the Arts, three from the Artists' Foundation, and the Rome Prize from the American Academy in Rome. Schiff has also taught at Boston College, Massachusetts College of Art, Clark University, and Rhode Island School of Design. His work is owned by La Jolla Museum of Contemporary Art, UMass/Amherst, and the University of Connecticut. He now lives in Brooklyn, N.Y.
   This environment, combining granite, bronze, brick, and trees, will feature a double font which spills water into basins on both sides. Funded by the Browne Fund.

MUSEUM OF SCIENCE

FIVE CARVED STONE PANELS
   Exterior, river side.
   Theodore Barbarossa (*see* Arlington: *Uncle Sam*).

ARCHIMEDIAN EXCOGITATION, 1987. Steel, percussion instruments, billiard and bowling balls, h. 26′.
   Atrium stairwell.
   George Rhoads (1927–   ).

A multifaceted artist, George Rhoads has been a printmaker, ceramicist, muralist, advertising artist, medical illustrator, and toy designer. As an art student in Paris he developed the first innovation in centuries in the ancient Japanese art of origami (paper-folding); he folded an elephant, ears and all, from a single sheet of paper. Rhoads is a member of a generation of sculptors who began as engineers before turning to art. He attended engineering school at the University of Wisconsin while in the U.S. Army in 1943, but finished with a B.A. at the University of Chicago and moved on to the Art Institute of Chicago and then to studies in Paris. Rhoads now lives in Ithaca, N.Y.

Rhoads' audiokinetic (sound/motion) works use machinery to lift balls to the top of a system through which they travel by gravity. Several random distribution mechanisms along the track introduce variety into their action. This work is actually three separate systems stacked atop one another. The top two use candlepin bowling balls whose journeys through the maze activate pendulums and turn wheels and windmills, as well as creating sounds. The bottom system uses billiard balls. Rhoads' audiokinetic sculptures are installed in shopping centers in half-a-dozen cities in this country and Canada, at the Port Authority Bus Terminal in New York, and at Logan Airport's Terminal C.

★ SOUNDSTAIR, 1988. Mixed electronic media, one flight long.
Lobby, Omni Theater.
Christopher Janney (1950–   ).

As a fellow of the Center for Advanced Visual Studies at M.I.T., Janney developed *Soundstair* as part of his 1978 thesis—installing it on the Spanish Steps in Rome. It is now a permanent installation here, with a twin in Minnesota. Stair-climbers trigger musical synthesizer tones as they pass through electric eye beams. "I'm trying to make art more spontaneous, and music more physical," he explains.

Born in Washington, D.C., Janney earned a degree in architecture and visual arts at Princeton, attended the Dalcroze School of Music, then took a master's degree in visual studies at M.I.T. He teaches at Cooper Union in New York and has been artist-in-residence at Massachusetts College of Art and at M.I.T. He has developed interactive environments for such settings as the Paris Metro, Miami International Airport, and many art museums. He lives in Lexington.

HUMAN CONNECTIONS, 1987. Polarized light mural, h. $27' \times 25'$.
Lobby, Omni Theater.
Austine Wood-Comarow (1942–   ).

Daughter of a United Nations official, Austine Wood attended elementary school in Germany, high school and art school in Switzerland, and Swarthmore College before graduating from Indiana University in 1964. After beginning her work with polarization, she studied color with Eduardo Vilches in Chile and took a graduate degree (M.F.A.) at Syracuse University. She now maintains a studio in California and works under the name "Austine." Her Polage murals, some interactive with the viewer and some not, are located across the country, including three in the Kodak Pavilion at Epcot Center (Disney World) in Florida.

In 1967 Wood-Comarow invented the technique of Polage (a

trademark), or polarized collage, by sandwiching clear colorless cellu-
lose (cellophane) between polarized filters. Color is created by the
angle of one polarized layer to another, the filters acting as prisms to
break white light into its component colors. Thus some areas seem
white until a polarizing filter is rotated to the proper position; others,
completely light-blocked, appear black. Rather than an entire rainbow,
the interacting filters reveal a segment of the spectrum, a short range
of color cycles as the angle of polarization changes. Both hand-held
and mechanized filters are provided here so viewers can experiment
with color changes. The 140 disks hanging in front of the work form
what the artist calls "pixels" of visual information. For clear portions of
the mural, they provide the second polarized filter that creates color.
Wood-Comarow sees an analogy between Polage and music, because
it incorporates the dimension of time. This mural depicts the history of
our civilization in the context of communication. It is funded by Polaroid
Corp., the Boston company that invented the polarizing filter.

THE LOOP, 1986. Mixed media, h. 15′.
Wave Room.
Mayer Spivak (*see* South Station: *Musclebound for Miami*).

   Conceived as a kinetic artwork which illustrates wave motion, this interactive piece hangs from the ceiling of the Wave Room. Commissioned by the Museum of Science.

CHARLES RIVER ESPLANADE

GEN. GEORGE SMITH PATTON, JR., 1955. Bronze, heroic size.
Near Hatch Shell, west of Longfellow Bridge.
   ★ James Earle Fraser (1876–1953).

   Fraser lived for a time as a boy on the Dakota frontier, an experience that marked his art with a predilection for heroes and victims. A
pupil of Augustus Saint-Gaudens, Fraser was designer of the Buffalo
Nickel and of sculpture at the Supreme Court and National Archives
buildings in Washington. He is best known for *End of the Trail*, the
melodramatic portrayal of a defeated Plains warrior on an exhausted
pony. At Fraser's death *End of the Trail* was considered the best-
known sculpture in America. This work is a duplicate, the original being
at the U.S. Military Academy at West Point. Another copy is in Hamilton. Commissioned by the Commonwealth.
   Patton (1885–1945), colorful and eccentric commander of the American Third Army in Europe during World War II, was married to Beatrice
Ayer, daughter of wealthy Boston textile manufacturer Frederick Ayer.
(Their son George, also a U.S. Army general, was born in Boston and
retired to exurban South Hamilton.) Recklessly brave (and accident-
prone), Patton survived action against Pancho Villa's troops on the
Mexican border, in France in World War I, in North Africa, Sicily, and
Western Europe in World War II, only to die as the result of injuries suffered in a Jeep accident in Germany after the war.

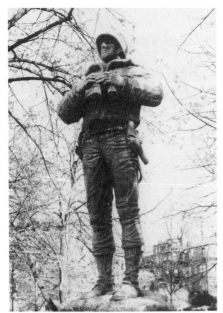

FRASER, GEN. GEORGE SMITH PATTON, JR.

DAVID IGNATIUS WALSH, 1954. Bronze, larger than life.
Near Hatch Shell.
Joseph A. Coletti (*see* East Boston/Logan Airport: *Gen. Edward Lawrence Logan*).

Lawyer and Democratic politician, Walsh (1872–1947) was elected lieutenant governor in 1913, governor in 1914, and U.S. Senator in 1919. The motto above his head, "Non sibi sed patriae," translates, "Not for self but for country." Commissioned by the Metropolitan District Commission.

GEN. CHARLES DEVENS, 1893–1896. Bronze, larger than life.
Near Hatch Shell.
★ Olin Levi Warner (1844–1896).

Connecticut-born Olin Warner made his way to Paris at the age of twenty-five, but within three years had to return to America because of political unrest in France. Lack of patronage and discouragement plagued him, although in time he was recognized for his sensitive portrait medallions. He was among the group that established the Society of American Artists in 1877. Commissioned to design bronze doors for the Library of Congress, Warner died in mid-task as a result of a bicycle accident in Central Park.

Devens (1820–1891), a Worcester lawyer who entered the Union Army as a major, won the brevet rank of major-general. Devens was later a judge in the state Supreme Judicial Court and U.S. Attorney General under President Hayes. Fort Devens in Ayer was named for him. Originally sited on Bowdoin St. behind the State House, this statue was displaced in 1950 by a parking lot. Commissioned by the Commonwealth.

MAURICE J. TOBIN, 1958. Bronze, life-size.
Near Hatch Shell.
Emilius R. Ciampa (b. 1896).

Ciampa came to Boston from Italy at the age of ten, studied at North
Bennett Street Industrial School and briefly at Massachusetts Normal
Art School. He served in France in World War I and later was in
charge of art projects for Northern Art Stone Corp. of New York. Living
and teaching in Medford after 1928, he executed a number of memorials and bas-relief portraits.

Tobin (1901–1953) was a protégé of the legendary mayor of Boston,
James Michael Curley. In the 1938 election, in what Curley forces
termed unprecedented treachery, Tobin ran against and defeated his
political mentor, winning the mayor's office and serving until 1944, between Curley's last two terms. Tobin was governor of Massachusetts
from 1946 to 1947; in 1948 he became Secretary of Labor under President Truman. The former Mystic River Bridge now bears his name.
Those who knew him say Tobin was imposing and "movie-star handsome"; if so, it is puzzling that this unimposing and unhandsome ren-
dering was accepted. Commissioned by the Commonwealth.

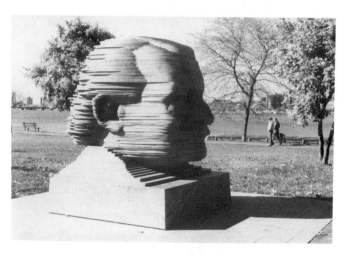

ARTHUR FIEDLER, 1984. Aluminum, h. 6′4″.
Ralph Helmick (1952–   ).

Cambridge sculptor Ralph Helmick earned a B.A. from the University
of Michigan in 1974 and an M.F.A. from the Boston Museum School in
1980. This monumental head is built up of cut-out layers of aluminum
in varying thicknesses, a distinctive technique originated by Helmick.

Famed and beloved conductor of the Boston Pops Orchestra for fifty
years, 1929–1979, Arthur Fiedler founded the free Esplanade concerts
still performed summer evenings at the nearby Hatch Shell. Funded by
contributions from Store 24, the Browne Fund, the Permanent Charity
Fund of Boston, David G. Mugar, J. F. White Contracting Co., the Al-
coa Foundation, and Bank of Boston.

LOTTA FOUNTAIN, 1939. Granite, h. 6'.
Dog sculpture above a tiled drinking basin for animals.
Katherine Lane Weems (*see* Fenway: *Rhinoceros*).

Legend persists that this is a memorial to a specific dog: a trick dog, a dog that rescued someone from drowning in the Charles River Basin, or one of the sled dogs who heroically took diptheria vaccine to Nome in 1925. In 1940, however, a year after its dedication, the writer of a column in the *Boston Herald* told a young reader that "it is not a memorial to a real dog."

The fountain is a bequest of actress and animal-lover Lotta Crabtree (1847–1924), who as a child was the Shirley Temple of the Golden West. Lotta had taken dancing lessons and done so well that the manager of a log theater in Rabbit Creek, Cal., persuaded the child's mother to let her appear onstage. Said to be petite and vivacious, with red-gold hair and brown eyes, "Little Lotta" was so engaging that the miners threw silver dollars and bags of gold dust at her feet, and her career was launched. She learned to play the banjo and began to act, earning enough money (which her mother shrewdly invested) that she died a wealthy woman. She owned racehorses late in life and was said to be "a ready contributor" to any cause to aid animals. She died in Boston; her trust still supports animal rescue efforts.

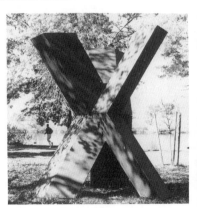

★ TRIMBLOID X, 1970. Cor-ten steel.
Esplanade at Clarendon St.
David Kibbey (1940–   ).

Vermont-born, Kibbey studied art at Boston University, Cummington School for the Arts, and Rhode Island School of Design. He has taught art at a number of colleges, including the University of New Hampshire, Windham College, and Hampshire College, and has been director of exhibitions at M.I.T. *Trimbloid X* is one of a series of geometric forms Kibbey fabricated while in Boston. He now designs and builds one-of-a-kind furniture in Oakland, Cal. Funded by Summerthing and Project '70.

NORTH END

★ WATER STAGE, 1986. Mixed media fountain.
Atrium, Tip O'Neill Bldg., Causeway St. (next to North Station).
Mary Miss (1944–   ).

Environmental artist Mary Miss was an "Army brat," moving frequently throughout childhood because of her father's military career. His interest in history led to visits to old forts, mines, and Indian sites in the American West, to castle ruins, medieval towns, and war ruins in Germany, all strong impressions for Miss. Her interests widened to include Japanese culture, Pueblo Indian structures, and Italian fortified hill towns. She studied sculpture at the University of California and at Colorado College, then moved to New York and began building room-sized structures. Her first exhibition was at the Whitney Museum in 1970, and in 1973 she was included in the Whitney Biennial. Her work is always designed specifically for the site: in 1986 she built a construct in the Fogg Museum at Harvard (temporary), and another in the entry of the Danforth Museum in Framingham (permanent). Although many of her installations are temporary, permanent ones such as this are increasingly commissioned.

HANGING CRYSTAL MOBILE, 1986.
Atrium, Tip O'Neill Bldg.
Jane Kaufman (1938–   ).

Born in New York City, Kaufman attended New York University and Hunter College, then taught in the city's public high schools for a decade. She won a Guggenheim Fellowship in 1974 and another from the National Endowment for the Arts in 1979. Kaufman has taught at Lehman College in the Bronx, Bard College, Brooklyn Museum Art School, and Queens College, and has been a visiting artist at Michigan State, Syracuse University, the University of Colorado, the Art Institute of Chicago, Cooper Union, and others.

PAINTERS PAINTING, 1978. Mural, h. approx. 12′ × 60′.
MBTA Elevated at Causeway and Canal Sts.
Miroslav Antic (1947–   ).

Born in Yugoslavia, Antic studied at the Academy of Fine Arts in Belgrade. He has been living and working here since the early 1970s; in 1980 he held a fellowship from the Artists Foundation. Funded by MBTA.

LEAVES 'N LINKS, 1978. Mural, h. 9′ × 70′.
MBTA Elevated at Causeway and Haverhill Sts.
Karen Moss (1944–   ).

Brookline artist Karen Moss studied painting at Rhode Island School of Design, then earned a master's degree from the Tufts/Boston Museum School program. She has held a grant from the Artists' Foundation and has taught at the Museum School, Massachusetts College of Art, Wheelock College, and Harvard summer school. Her paintings are owned by the Boston Museum of Fine Arts, Addison Gallery of American Art, Rose and DeCordova Museums, Vassar College, and many corporations. Funded by MBTA.

CALLAHAN TUNNEL MEMORIAL, 1956 (see East Boston/Logan Airport: *Callahan and Sumner Tunnel Memorials*).

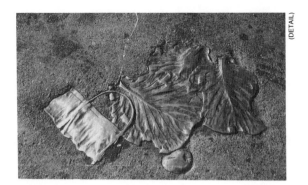

(DETAIL)

★ ASAROTON (Unswept Floor), 1976. Bronze pavement inserts, assorted
sizes, in area 55′ × 10′ × 9″ deep.
Pavement at Hanover and Haymarket Sts.
Mags Harries (*see* Chelsea: *Bellingham Square*).

Embedded in the asphalt at a busy outdoor market street crossing,
these cast bronze objects intrigue and puzzle tourists walking the Freedom Trail to the Revere House. Harries' bronze detritus is cast from
real garbage and items found in the street: fish, flowers, newspapers,
gloves, stepped-on strawberries, and squashed corn cobs. *Asaroton* refers to a Greco-Roman floor mosaic technique dating to 200 B.C. Commissioned to commemorate the U.S. Bicentennial.

CHILDREN'S MOSAICS, 1975. Ceramic tile.
Inside pedestrian underpass from Haymarket to Cross St.

These ceramic tile mosaics were designed, fabricated, and installed
by neighborhood children, as a project of Christopher Columbus Community Center.

★ GEORGE WASHINGTON, 1815. Marble.
Christ Church, Salem St.
Christian Gullager (d. 1827).

During his progress through New England in 1789, the general
paused in Portsmouth, N.H., to sit for two hours for Gullager, a Danish
artist who immigrated circa 1781. The resultant oil portrait is now
owned by the Massachusetts Historical Society. In 1790 Gullager produced a plaster bust, from which this bust is derived; its distinction is
that it appears to be the first Boston portrait work by a sculptor working
in America. Gift of Shubael Bell, senior warden of Christ Church.

PAUL REVERE, 1940. Bronze, equestrian, larger than life.
At Paul Revere Mall behind Old North Church, between Salem and
Hanover Sts.
★ Cyrus E. Dallin (1861–1944); (*see* Fenway [Boston Museum of Fine
Arts]: *Appeal to the Great Spirit*).

Paul Revere (1735–1818) owes his romantic image to a poem written by Longfellow more than fifty years after Revere rode out of Boston

in 1775 to rouse the militia for the battles of Lexington and Concord.
He was in fact caught by a British patrol and never reached Concord,
although his companion, Dr. Samuel Prescott, who joined him in Lexington and knew the local shortcuts, did. By profession Revere was a sil-
versmith, engraver, maker of copper ship hull sheathing, and owner of
a brass foundry (Revere bells still hang in the steeples of a number of
New England churches).

This is the final large work of Dallin, a sculptor better known for his
equestrian Indian statues, one of which stands in front of the Boston
Museum of Fine Arts. Funded by the George Robert White Fund.

WATERFRONT

COMPASS ROSE, 1989. Granite, diam. 60'.
  Pavement, Long Wharf, Atlantic Ave. at State St.
  Sasaki Associates.
  Funded by Boston Redevelopment Authority.

At Marriott Long Wharf Hotel, 296 State St.:

MURALS, 1989. Oil, h. 20' × 3'.
  Lobby.
  William C. Reynolds (1951–   ).

  As a student, Reynolds apprenticed to Jan Henryk de Rosen, son of
the last court painter of the Russian czars, then in his 90s. On his retirement from painting, de Rosen bequeathed his paints and brushes to
Reynolds.

  A native of Waterbury, Conn., Reynolds graduated from George
Washington University with a B.A. in graphics and continued in painting, earning an M.F.A. He also took courses at Franklin and Marshall
College, American University, and the Corcoran Museum. Reynolds
now lives in Arlington and maintains a studio in Waltham. His paintings
here depict Long Wharf when it was a working wharf, about 1915. Commissioned by the Marriott Hotel Corp.

BOSTON HARBOR SCENE, ca. 1821. Fresco, h. 7' × 15'.
  Lobby.
  Rufus Porter (1792–1884).

  Born in West Boxford, Mass., Porter probably traveled New England
and the Middle Atlantic States as an itinerant painter. He has been
credited with ten or so giant frescos like this one. In his time he was
known as an ingenious inventor and the author of several books. In
1845 he gave up painting and settled in New York City, where he
founded *Scientific American* magazine.

  This mural was restored by Christy Cunningham of Arlington, a graduate of the Boston Museum School and Central Institute of Restoration
in Rome. Consulting with her professors in Italy, Cunningham covered
the fresco with a clear, removable plastic "sandwich" and touched up

faded areas on top of it. Being reversible, the process preserves the integrity of the original.

Painted for the Prescott Tavern in East Jaffrey, N.H., this wall painting was salvaged when the building was torn down in 1950. Fresco technique involves painting on wet plaster so the pigment soaks in and becomes part of the wall; to salvage this fresco, the entire 400-pound plaster wall had to be saved. The Goyette Museum in Peterborough, N.H., where this work was stored, subsequently closed, leaving the mural to be rediscovered and rescued once more by the Marriott Long Wharf.

CEILING MURAL, 1989. Thirty-eight painted panels totaling 19′ × 230′.
Palm Garden, atrium.
Francoise Schein (1961–   ).

Trained as an architect in Brussels and at Columbia University in New York, Schein organized her geometric designs so as to reflect the thrust of the architecture. She maintains a studio in New York.

CHRISTOPHER COLUMBUS, 1979. Marble, life-size.
Waterfront Park, Atlantic Ave.
Artist unknown.

An unfortunate example of politics overriding aesthetics, this statue was erected at the behest of former city councilor Frederick Langone and his constituents. It was never approved by the city's Arts Commission. Produced in Carrara, Italy, possibly by a firm that makes garden statuary, it serves as an all-purpose memorial for a number of groups in the Italian community that occupies the nearby North End. According to advertisements in North End newspapers, it is still possible to have one's inscription added to the monument upon donation of several hundred dollars to the sponsoring group. This policy may explain the surprising amalgam of names carved here.

At New England Aquarium (Central Wharf, off Atlantic Ave. at Milk St.):

★ ECHO OF THE WAVES, 1983. Steel and fiber-reinforced plastic, h. 45′ at rest; 65′ with wings extended (see back cover photo).
Susumu Shingu (1937–   ).

Popularly called *The Whale*, this work is among the city's most impressive. Its majestic swimming motions imitate in an abstract but recognizable way the movements of nature's largest creatures, yet it moves for hours without repeating the same configuration. Although the wings are responsive to subtle movements of air, the artist has employed aerodynamic techniques to damp their motion in heavy weather.

An aesthetic idea new in this century is moving, or "kinetic," sculpture, introduced by a group that included Calder, Duchamp, and Tinguely. Working in the kinetic mode, the Japanese-born Shingu adds a dimension from his Asian heritage, a sensitivity to and a reverence for the rhythms of nature. The rhythms of each individual spirit, Shingu says, must grow and "change joyfully," and will do so best when intertwined with the rhythms of the natural world: streams flowing, grass swaying, the alternations of night and day. His works are "expressive conduits which connect us with the deeper life forces of nature," one associate comments.

Shingu studied at Tokyo University of the Arts and at the Academy of Rome. Beginning with an exhibition entitled "Wind" in 1967, he has investigated modern engineering and materials technologies to express space, time, and motion in his work. His major sculptures sited in Japan number more than twenty. This, his second work in the United States, was created in association with Cambridge Seven Associates, an architectural firm. Gift of Mr. and Mrs. David Bakalar.

DOLPHINS OF THE SEA, 1980. Bronze fountain.
Aquarium plaza.
Katherine Ward Lane Weems (*see* Fenway: *Rhinoceros*).

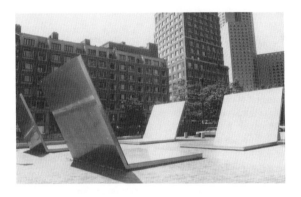

★ UNTITLED, 1972. Stainless steel. Four units, each h. approx.
15′ × 15′ × 17′.
Harbor Towers Plaza, India Wharf.
David von Schlegell (1920–   ).

Born in St. Louis, von Schlegell studied engineering at the University of Michigan and worked as an aircraft engineer before becoming an Air Force pilot in World War II. He studied painting at the Art Students League in New York, then began experimenting with wood, manipulating it by steaming and other boatbuilding techniques. In 1964 he began to work in aluminum, attempting to pare from his art the "excess of emotion" he saw in abstract expressionism. In earlier, more referential works critics saw a tension between engineering and love of nature, between a romantic sensibility and a coolly mechanistic art. Von Schlegell has taught at Yale, Cornell, the School of Visual Arts, and the University of California at Santa Barbara; museums owning his work include the Whitney in New York, the Hirschhorn in Washington, and those at Yale, Cornell, and Carnegie Institute.

Here von Schlegell has stripped his aesthetic to an engineering problem and has achieved a scale that, as he wished, relates to buildings, bridges, and the larger objects in our world. Funded by 1% for Art.

MILK BOTTLE, 1934. Wood and plaster, h. 40'.
Outside Children's Museum, Congress St. at Fort Point Channel.
Constructed by Arthur Gagner.

One of the first drive-in restaurants in the country, this milk bottle served for nearly half a century as a family ice-cream stand near Taunton. When it was finally closed, a private purchaser preserved it, recognizing it as an example of what is called urban archaeology. Its advocates wanted to site it on City Hall plaza—the idea was quickly rejected—but it was thought ideal as a "place marker" for this spot, near the Children's and Computer museums. It is again a snack stand. The bottle's theoretical capacity, 200,000 quarts, is lettered on its side. Refurbished by Hood Milk Co. and donated to the Children's Museum, 1977.

At Boston Harbor Hotel:

BOY WITH DOG, ca. 1905. Oil on canvas, 50" × 34".
Entrance foyer.
Charles W. Hawthorne (1872–1930).

A painter of portraits and figures, Hawthorne was raised in Richmond, Me. After studies with William Merritt Chase at Shinnecook, he founded the Cape Cod School of Art in Provincetown and taught there until his death.

THE CELLIST, ca. 1900. Oil on canvas, 45" × 31".
Main lobby.
★ Lilla Cabot Perry (ca. 1848–1933).

Painter, writer, and poet, Perry is credited with introducing Bostonians to the work of French Impressionist painters. She was one of the few American painters whose work was accepted in the Paris salons of the 1890s.

PORTRAIT OF MISS LA BARONNE DE R., ca. 1900. Oil on canvas, 46" × 29".
Main lobby.
Lilla Cabot Perry (*see The Cellist* above).

THE BREAKING WAVE, 1922. Oil on canvas, 25" × 30".
Entrance to Rowes Wharf Restaurant.
Soren Emil Carlson.

STILL LIFE. Oil on canvas, 29" × 36".
In hotel restaurant.
Severin Rosen.

BEACON STREET IN WINTER. Oil on canvas, 29" × 36".
Reception area.
A. C. Goodwin (1864–1929).

Born in Portsmouth, N.H., Goodwin was largely self-taught. He is considered a member of the Boston School, a group of realist/impressionists dating from the turn of the century to the present day.

THE U.S.S. CHESAPEAKE AND H.M.S. SHANNON, ca. 1815. Oil on canvas,
20″ × 32″.
In Harborview Lounge.
Thomas Buttersworth.

Thomas Buttersworth and his son James were both British marine
painters, and there is some uncertainty as to which one of them produced this painting, a chronicle of a naval battle that took place off Boston on June 1, 1813. It is usually attributed to the father because of the
early date and the distinctive technique.

The battle is one of the more famous in American history, the first
major loss of a U.S. warship in the War of 1812. The *Chesapeake*, suffering from a reputation as an unlucky ship, had just been put under
the command of Capt. James Lawrence and was refitting at Boston.
The *Shannon*, part of increased British blockading efforts, appeared off
the coast; in the quaint etiquette of the day, its captain, Philip Vere
Broke, sent Lawrence a written invitation for a one-on-one engagement
of the ships. Despite a green and somewhat mutinous crew—prize
money from their last voyage had not yet been distributed—Lawrence
set sail and courageously attacked. Throngs cheered his ship out of
the harbor, and people climbed the heights of Salem to get a distant
view of the brief and disastrous engagement. In the first exchange of
fire Lawrence was mortally wounded and his two officers disabled; the
disorganized crew was easy prey for the British boarding party. The
bloodiest battle in naval history to that time, it cost the British 84 casualties and the Americans 146.

NORMAN B. LEVENTHAL MAP COLLECTION. On display here, 48 maps.
Main lobby.

The largest private collection of maps of early Boston, this group
was assembled by Boston developer and art connoisseur Norman Leventhal, chairman of the Beacon Companies. It includes a map made by
Virginia explorer Capt. John Smith after a voyage to New England (previously called "North Virginia") in 1614 and used by the Pilgrims on
their voyage to the New World. A second printing of the same map in
1635 records the placename "Boston" for the first time. Reflecting the
earliest exploration of the Americas, some of this cartography dates
to the fifteenth century. Part of the collection is displayed at Hotel
Meridien, 250 Franklin St.

QUINCY MARKET

★ SAMUEL ADAMS, 1873. Bronze, heroic size.
In front of Faneuil Hall, Congress St.
Anne Whitney (1821–1915).

A native of Watertown, Anne Whitney in her thirties turned from writing poetry to modeling portrait busts of relatives and friends. Self-
taught, she progressed to idealized figures with so much success that
the Commonwealth awarded her the commission to carve Samuel Ad-

ams for the Statuary Hall at the federal Capitol. This is a replica of that
work, purchased by the city in 1880.

Adams (1722–1803), political writer and revolutionary firebrand, is
credited with being one of the principal shapers of the American Revolution. He was among the first to oppose Parliament's power to tax the
colonies, a stubborn opponent of compromise with the mother country,
and chief promoter of the Boston Tea Party. Second cousin to U.S.
President John Adams, Samuel Adams after the Revolution served as
lieutenant governor and from 1794 to 1797 as governor. Funded by the
Jonathan Phillips Fund.

WALTER MUIR WHITEHILL MEDALLION, 1976. Bronze.
Base of Samuel Adams statue.
From a drawing by Rudolph Ruzicka.

The dual-purpose memorial, perhaps a sample of New England fru-
gality, occurs more than once in Boston. Here the base of Sam Adams'
statue is employed to honor a citizen temperamentally and chronologi-
cally far removed from Adams. Whitehill (1905–1978), scholar, author
of popular regional histories, and long director of the Boston
Athenæum, was Boston's consummate cultivated man.

GRASSHOPPER WEATHERVANE, 1742. Sheet copper, gilt.
Atop Faneuil Hall.
Shem Drowne.

In colonial Boston, Drowne and his son Thomas were master tin-
smiths living and working in the North End.

★ RED AUERBACH, 1985.
Bronze, life-size.
Quincy Market mall, south
side.
Lloyd Lillie (*see* Government
Center and Environs: *James
Michael Curley*).

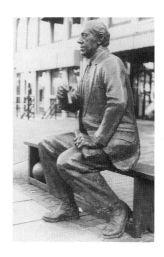

Longtime coach and man-
ager of the Boston Celtics bas-
ketball dynasty, Arnold "Red"
Auerbach is depicted in a characteristic moment: seated on
the bench at courtside, about
to light his victory cigar, an insouciant gesture indicating he
considers the game as good
as won.

THE SPIRIT OF BOSTON, 1982. Stainless steel, granite, h. approx. 12'.
Bostonian Hotel, North and Blackstone Sts.
David Lee Brown (1939–   ).

Brown has been an instructor in sculpture at Cranbrook and a professor of design at Pratt Institute. He studied at Cass Tech, North

Carolina School of Design, and Cranbrook; his work is at DeCordova Museum, the Hirschhorn, and Milwaukee Art Center. He lives on Long Island.

This fountain represents schematically the historic Boston waterfront.

Inside Faneuil Hall:

Access to this historic hall is gained via the middle door at the east end—the opposite end from where Samuel Adams stands. Sixteen portraits hang here, including that of Peter Faneuil himself, wealthy French Huguenot merchant who built the hall in 1742. Sculpture portrait busts include John Adams, John Quincy Adams, and Daniel Webster. Other works are:

WEBSTER'S REPLY TO HAYNE, 1851. Oil on canvas. $16' \times 30'$.
Over speakers' platform.
George Peter Alexander Healy (1813–1894).

In the U.S. Senate in 1830, Senator Daniel Webster of Massachusetts rose to debate Senator Robert Young Hayne of South Carolina on the issue of Nullification. Hayne contended that the Constitution was a compact among the states, and that states had the power to nullify any law of the federal government. Webster replied with a defense of the Union which, historians say, did more to unify the country than any single utterance of any other man. His ringing "Liberty and Union, now and forever, one and inseparable" resounded throughout the nation. (For more about Webster, *see* Marshfield: *Webster, the Farmer of Marshfield*.) In this hall Webster also delivered a famous eulogy of John Adams and Thomas Jefferson, who died within hours of each other on July 4, 1826.

Dealing loosely with history, Healy has included in the audience life portraits of more than one hundred men and women famous at the time. This work was commissioned by King Louis Philippe of France to be hung at Versailles, but he was overthrown before it was finished. Anonymous gift to the City of Boston.

EAGLE, 1798. Painted artificial stone.
On rear balcony.
Attributed to Daniel Raynerd.

This 250-pound bird was designed for an early bank building by Charles Bulfinch, architect of the New State House, who enlarged Faneuil Hall in 1806. When the bank was razed in 1824, the eagle was placed here. It is credited to Raynerd, Bulfinch's chief ornamental plasterer. The medium is pulverized marble, white sand, hair for binder, and lime putty.

MERCY OTIS WARREN, ca. 1763. Polaroid replica of oil painting, h. $51'' \times 41''$.
John Singleton Copley (1737–1815).

The outstanding portraitist of colonial America, Copley was born in Boston of Irish parents and self-educated. In 1774, despite success in his native city, he went first to Rome, then established himself permanently in London and was admitted to the Royal Academy. Less facile than his later work, Copley's American portraits are considered far stronger and more honest.

Playwright, poet, feminist, and political historian, Mercy Warren (1728–1814) was a controversial figure in her time. Sister of James Otis (*see* Downtown [Hotel Meridien]: murals), she received a thorough education by sitting in on her brother's classes. She married James Warren, a legislator; she and her husband were friends of John and Abigail Adams and other architects of the American Revolution. Her first published work was a satiric anti-British play in 1772; her best-known book was *History of the Rise, Progress and Termination of the American Revolution* published in 1805. An anti-Federalist pamphlet she wrote was wrongly attributed to Elbridge Gerry for a century. Warren feared that the new Federal Constitution would create another aristocracy and rob the people of their hard-won liberty; the quotation, "The origin of all power is in the people," is from her pen.

Because no woman's portrait hung in Faneuil Hall, a commission from the mayor's office was appointed to provide one to mark the bicentennial of the U.S. Constitution in 1987. Warren was chosen because of her political writings. The Copley original, owned by the Boston Museum of Fine Arts, was too valuable to lend; this fine-arts copy was produced by a room-size Polaroid camera at the museum.

GOVERNMENT CENTER AND ENVIRONS

JAMES MICHAEL CURLEY, 1980. Bronze double portrait statues, life-size.
Curley Memorial Park, Congress and North Sts.
Lloyd Lillie (1932–   ).

Lloyd Lillie has taken realism to its logical conclusion, bringing statues of public heroes down off their pedestals and placing them in naturalistic, accessible poses. Born in Washington, D.C., he attended the Corcoran School of Art there, won honors at the Boston Museum School, and was awarded a traveling scholarship with which he studied at the Accademia di Belle Arti in Florence. He is now a professor of sculpture at Boston University, where he has taught for twenty-nine years. His other life-size sculptures occupy sites in Washington, St. Louis, Hardy, Va., Falmouth, and Quincy Market in Boston. Here the two statues represent the two sides of Mayor Curley: standing, the powerful, egotistic public figure; sitting on the park bench, the folksy Irish friend to all.

Curley was four times mayor of Boston, never in consecutive terms. His education was cut short at age ten, when his father died and he went to work to help support his family. In 1904 he won election as alderman while serving a ninety-day sentence in jail for fraudulently taking a civil service exam for a friend; it was said he read everything in the prison library while there. He was successively alderman, councillor, legislator, twice Congressman, and governor (1935–36). His identity as mayor was indelible; his fourth term began in 1946. Funded by the Browne Fund.

NEW ENGLAND HOLOCAUST MEMORIAL, installation planned 1993.
Glass, granite, stainless steel, concrete, h. 55′.
Union Street Park, Union and Hanover Sts.
Stanley Saitowitz (1949–   ).

Professor of architecture at University of California at Berkeley since 1979, Saitowitz has also been an occasional visiting professor at Harvard Graduate School of Design. Born in Johannesburg, South Africa, he took his bachelor's degree from the University of Witwatersrand in that city and his master's in architecture from UCal/Berkeley. Much of his architectural practice involves California residences which are integrated with the landscape. His other public work was the design of nine structures for Mill Race Park in Columbus, Ind.

Each of the six towers here stands for one of the Nazi death camps: Auschwitz-Birkenau, Belzec, Chelmno, Majenek, Sobibor, and Treblinka. Etched on each tower are a million seven-digit numbers like the identification numbers tattooed on prisoners entering the camps; the architect intends that sunlight will cast shadows of the numbers, chillingly, on the bodies of passersby. Six feet deep in the pit beneath each tower, a gas flame burns. Dually symbolic, it reminds of the gas used in the killing, and it burns in perpetual memory of the dead. Commissioned by the New England Holocaust Memorial Committee.

★ THERMOPYLAE, 1966.
Bronze, h. approx. 15′.
City Hall Plaza, Cambridge
and New Sudbury Sts., outside
John F. Kennedy Bldg.
Dimitri Hadzi (*see* Brookline:
Primavera).

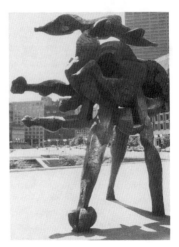

This work, like his *Elmo/MIT*, reflects Hadzi's interest in classical armor, history, and myth, stemming from his Greek heritage and his years working in Greece and Rome. The artist says the work was inspired by John F. Kennedy's book *Profiles in Courage*.

NEW ENGLAND ELEGY, 1966. Painting, h. approx. 6′ × 10′.
Overhead, entry corridor of John F. Kennedy Bldg.
★ Robert Motherwell (1915–1991).

A native of Washington state, Motherwell studied philosophy at Stanford and Harvard, then art history and archaeology at Columbia before deciding, at age twenty-six, to become a painter. Settling in New York City, he became associated with a cadre of abstract painters and with them founded a Greenwich Village art school called The Subjects of the Artist. His calligraphic shapes made him one of the elite of abstract expressionism; scarcely a contemporary museum in the country lacks an example. Motherwell taught at Hunter College. Funded by 1% for Art.

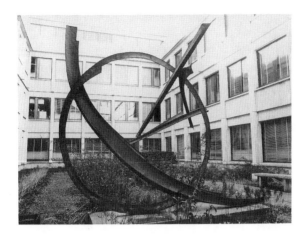

FULL CIRCLE, 1966. Welded copper and steel, h. 8'.
Courtyard, John F. Kennedy Bldg.
★ Herbert Ferber (1906–   ).

Despite a degree in dentistry from Columbia, Ferber began studying at the Beaux Arts Institute of Design and determined to become an artist. At first he carved directly in wood and stone; after the mid-forties he turned to welding techniques and soon enlarged them to architectural scale. Expanding the spatial possibilities of large works, in 1961 he developed entire rooms, which the viewer entered in order to explore the sculpture from within—an early version of environmental and installation art. He has been a leader of abstract expressionism in sculpture, attuned to the endless possibilities of nonobjective form. Funded by 1% for Art.

SPRING, 1986. Acrylic, 6½' × 30'.
City Hall lobby, balcony.
★ Maud Morgan (1903–   ).

The grande dame of Boston art, Morgan was born Maud Cabot in New York, attended Barnard College, studied art in Paris in the 1920s (where she became a friend of Hemingway) and with Hans Hofmann in Munich in the 1930s. She and her husband, Patrick Morgan, taught at Phillips and Abbot academies in Andover, numbering among their students painter Frank Stella and Minimalist Carl André. Although she never achieved the same international reputation, she knew and exhibited with such well-known names of the 1950s as Mark Rothko, Barnett Newman, and Jackson Pollock. She still works actively in her Cambridge studio.

This work is one of four, depicting the four seasons. Gift to the city from friends of the artist.

NANCY, A PASSAGE OF TIME, 1978. Cor-ten steel, h. 5'10".
Tremont and State Sts.
Rick Lee (1946–   ).

Lincoln resident Rick Lee earned a bachelor of science in art at the University of Wisconsin and a master's in design at Goddard College in Vermont. He taught for a time at Belmont Hill School. Gift of Bertram and Ronald Drucker.

THE JUDGES' BENCH, 1983. Limestone, h. 6′.
Pemberton Sq., between Suffolk County Courthouse (Somerset St.) and Center Plaza (on Cambridge St., facing Government Center).
Will Reimann (*see* Cambridge [Porter Square]: *Embroidered Bollards*).

This elaborate Ionic column, found in a junkyard, was salvaged from a downtown building. It has been hollowed out at the rear so it can be used as a speaker's rostrum; the idea was to bring activity to this often-deserted public space. Sponsored by Township Institute of Cambridge; funded by the Browne Fund.

BILL OF RIGHTS, 1992. Mosaic paving insert, 45′ × 5′.
Pemberton Sq.
Lilli Ann and Marvin Rosenberg (*see* Newton: *Five Concrete Mosaic Sculptures*).
Funded by the Browne Fund and a number of Boston law firms, whose names are noted on a plaque nearby.

RUFUS CHOATE, 1898. Bronze.
In Suffolk County Court House, Pemberton Sq.
★ Daniel Chester French (*see* Concord: *Minuteman*).

Choate (1799–1859), trained in the law, has been called one of the most scholarly of American public men. Born in Ipswich, valedictorian at Dartmouth College, Choate served in both houses of the Massachusetts legislature and in Congress before succeeding his friend Daniel Webster in the U.S. Senate. Gift of George B. Hyde.

MASSACHUSETTS ARTIFACT, 1975. Bronze, h. 30′ × 40′.
McCormack Bldg., 1 Ashburton Pl.
Alfred M. Duca (*see Computersphere* below and Back Bay: *Boston Tapestry*).

Its design influenced by a committee intent upon representing the diversity of the Bay State, this Duca bronze casting is less successful aesthetically than the *Boston Tapestry*. It is nevertheless intriguing as a treasure hunt. Interwoven with the seals of cities and towns are initials of eighty-nine of Massachusetts' most illustrious sons and daughters (all deceased at the time the sculpture was made)—from Tisquantum, "Tis," to the Plymouth Colony's most famous lovers, P.M. and J.A., to A.N.W. (philosopher), eec (poet), and L.F. (merchant founder of the world's most famous bargain basement). Further complicating the design are historic, cultural, ethnic, and institutional references, symbols of regional crafts, trades, and industries, animals both wild and domestic, and a few heroes and legends.

Among new art technology developed by Duca was foam vaporization casting, in which the artist carves an original in polystyrene foam, makes a sand mold around it, and pours in molten metal. Unlike other casting processes, this one permits the original to be left inside, because the styrofoam is vaporized and destroyed by the molten bronze. Duca devised another shortcut to carve the original: he drew his design on a block of styrofoam, then held it under a heat lamp; the dark drawing absorbed heat and melted enough to create an etched-out design, which was then cast in bronze by the foam vaporization process. Funded by 1% for Art.

HUMAN ELEMENT, 1981. Marble, h. 4' × 7' × 4'.
RKO General Bldg., New Sudbury St.
Gerald M. Sherman.
Funded by 1% for Art.

WALL RELIEF, 1973. Steel.
RKO General Bldg.
Anthony C. Belluschi and Craig D. Roney.
ICA open competition, funded by 1% for Art.

UPWARD BOUND, 1970. Brass, 30' × 18' × 15'.
Overhead, in portico outside Hurley Employment Security Bldg., Staniford and Cambridge Sts.
C. Fayette Taylor (1894–   ).

After a career as a professor of mechanical engineering at M.I.T., Fayette Taylor retired in 1965 and embarked on a new career in his former avocation, art. Through summer courses in Provincetown and Woodstock, a sojourn in Paris, and study with established artists in Boston and at M.I.T., Taylor had supplied himself with a complete art education, including life drawing, etching, and painting. After retirement, he began to draw upon his engineering skills to create sculpture in brass, steel, and stainless steel. A native of New York and a graduate of Yale, he has lived in Brookline, Rockport, and Weston.

MURAL, 1970. Plaster, painted, h. approx. 14'.
State Service Center, Hurley Employment Security Bldg.
Constantino Nivola (*see* Downtown: *Mural*).

This work and the one immediately below exemplify Boston's tendency, early in its public art renaissance, to seek second-tier New York artists in preference to local talent.

RICHARD CARDINAL CUSHING, 1981. Bronze bust, life-size.
Cushing Plaza, New Chardon and Cambridge Sts.
James Rosati (1911–1988).

On the faculty of Philadelphia Academy of Art until his death, Rosati also taught at Yale, Dartmouth, and the Vermont School of Art and had been a Guggenheim Fellow. In addition to portrait sculpture, he produced small- and large-scale abstractions. Gift of the clergy of the Archdiocese of Boston.

FALCON FORM VI, 1970. Cor-ten steel, h. 5'.
Jewish Family and Children's Services Center, 31 New Chardon St.
Herb Harrington.
Funded by 1% for Art.

COMPUTERSPHERE, 1965–67.
  Cor-ten steel, diam. 8'.
Government Center Post
Office, 25 New Chardon St.
Alfred M. Duca (*see* Back Bay:
Boston Tapestry).

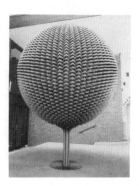

  The artist believes this may
be the first work ever done
from a computer-generated design. Funded by 1% for Art.

SUDDEN PRESENCE, 1971. Cor-ten steel, h. approx. 9'.
At Government Center Garage, New Chardon and Merrimac Sts.
  ★ Beverly Pepper (1924–   ).

  Born in Brooklyn, Beverly Pepper studied at Pratt Institute and the
Art Students League in New York, and in Paris. After working as art director for advertising agencies, she established herself in Rome in
1949 as an independent artist. Critics say her objects have an intrinsic
power that alters the environment in which they are situated. She has
spoken of the introspective nature of her work, "the inner reaches of a
geometric form. . . . My structures create a relationship that is not clear
to the viewer but is instead very private." Her sculpture is owned by
the Smithsonian, M.I.T., the Fogg Museum, Dartmouth College, and
the Hirschhorn. Funded by 1% for Art.

MURALS, 1990. Acrylic, h. six stories, four walls and ceiling.
  Atrium, 101 Merrimac St.
  Richard Haas (*see* Back Bay: *West Facade*).
  Commissioned by Howard Elkus of The Architects' Collaborative.

DOUBLE BOSTON VENUS, 1987. Bronze, h. 7½'.
  90 Canal St.
  ★ Jim Dine (1935–   ).

  One of the stars of the international art scene, Dine was born in Cincinnati, Ohio, and settled on his identity as an artist at an early age.
After earning a bachelor's degree in fine arts, he did graduate work at
Ohio University and later attended the Boston Museum School. He has
held guest and visiting artist positions at Yale, Oberlin, and Cornell
School of Architecture. In the 1960s Dine was associated with Pop Art
and was perhaps best known for his series of paintings of his bathrobe.
His work has also included printmaking and collage/assemblage paintings in which brushes, paint pots, and other accoutrements were left
attached to the canvas. In the 1970s Dine's work took a personal turn
and became more difficult to define; in the 1980s he began to produce

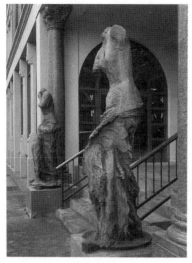

GREG HEINS PHOTO COURTESY THE GUND COLLECTION

bronze sculpture and to design variations on the Venus de Milo concept.

Architect Graham Gund, one of Boston's foremost collectors of contemporary art, commissioned these sculptures from Dine after Gund's firm converted the eighteenth-century Bulfinch Building here to office space. This is the only outdoor work by Dine in New England; another Dine *Venus* stands in a plaza in San Francisco.

MENORAH and ETERNAL LIGHT, 1972. Welded steel.
  Charles River Park Synagogue, Martha Rd.
  Richard Bertram.
  Commissioned by the congregation.

★ AFRICAN QUEEN, 1979. Oil on cotton duck, diptych, each unit h. 9′ × 8′.
  Main lobby, Massachusetts General Hospital, 55 Fruit St.
  John McNamara (1950–   ).

  Born in Cambridge, McNamara took a B.F.A. from Massachusetts College of Art in 1971, an M.F.A. in 1977, and began to garner a reputation as one of Boston's outstanding younger painters. Now a resident of Brookline, he has received three grants from the Massachusetts Council on the Arts and Humanities, an Award in the Visual Arts, and a fellowship from the National Endowment for the Arts. Gift of the artist.

BEACON HILL/STATE HOUSE

ARISTEIDES THE JUST and CHRISTOPHER COLUMBUS, ca. 1850. Stone.
  Louisburg Sq. (off Mount Vernon St.).

Garden ornaments rather than works of artistic merit, these two stand in one of the most-visited tourist locations on Beacon Hill. Aristeides (ca. 530–468 B.C.) was an Athenian statesman, several times elected strategus (something like a secretary of war) of the city. His sobriquet was probably derived from his fair assessment of taxes when a confederation of city-states, the Delian league, was formed. Legend persists that these statues were shipped from Italy as ballast in a ship owned by Joseph Iasigi, who lived at 3 Louisburg Square. Gift of Joseph Iasigi.

MUSEUM: Boston Athenæum, 10½ Beacon St. Incorporated in 1807, the Athenæum is a private museum/library, but offers tours to visitors. Of interest to connoisseurs of public art are the original plaster model of Ball's equestrian Washington, and a number of busts and sculptures by nineteenth-century sculptors who effected large outdoor pieces as well. A second-floor gallery open to the public exhibits contemporary art.

At the State House:

A catalogue, *Art in the Massachusetts State House*, published in 1986 by the Massachusetts Art Commission, may be purchased at the book store. Only the more prominent works are listed here:

THE BEACON HILL MONUMENT, 1898. Granite and bronze, h. 52′.
Bowdoin St., parking lot behind the State House.

This shaft is a re-creation of the 1790 original, the first monument in America to the War of Independence. In 1634 the General Court (legislative body) of the Massachusetts Bay Colony ordered a warning beacon erected atop the tallest of Boston's three hills (then sixty feet higher than it is now). In 1790 it was replaced by a Doric column topped with a gilt eagle and dedicated to the heroes of the American Revolution. The column was designed by Charles Bulfinch, America's first great architect, who next designed the "New" State House that still stands nearby as the front central portion of the vastly enlarged building. Bulfinch's monument was removed in 1811 when the top of the hill was cut down. The present version is a gift of the Bunker Hill Monument Association.

★ MARY DYER, 1959. Bronze, larger than life.
South lawn, near east wing.
Sylvia Shaw Judson (b. 1897).

A Chicagoan, Judson attended the Art Institute of Chicago and then studied in Paris under Bordelle, Rodin's pupil. Her work is owned by the Museum of Modern Art, the Metropolitan Museum, and the Philadelphia Museum of Art.

Mary Dyer and her husband were among those settling in Rhode Island with Anne Hutchinson, although they later broke off and resettled in Newport. During a trip to England, Dyer became a Quaker and, in an early act of civil disobedience, felt compelled to challenge the Boston colony's anti-Quaker laws enacted in the 1650s. Thrice jailed, once re-

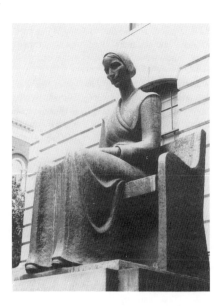

prieved on the gallows, Dyer returned yet again and was finally hanged in 1660, one of four Quakers executed in the Boston colony during this period. Their deaths impelled King Charles II to overturn the laws, but whipping of Quakers continued until 1665. Funded by legacy of Zenas Ellis of Fair Haven, Vt.

JOSEPH HOOKER, 1903. Bronze, equestrian, larger than life.
South lawn.
★ Daniel Chester French (*see* Concord: *Minuteman*) and Edward C. Potter (*see* Brookline: *Soldiers Monument*).

Maj.-Gen. Hooker (1814–1879) was commander of the Army of the Potomac defeated at Chancellorsville (thanks to Hooker's untimely caution) by Lee in 1863. Bostonians at first objected to the choice of Hadley native Hooker as an example of Union soldiery. But except for that disastrous lapse his military skills were enough to earn him the sobriquet "Fighting Joe"; he was twice wounded, and performed superbly as a subordinate commander for most of the war. French modeled the figure; Potter, the horse. Funded by an appropriation of the Commonwealth.

DANIEL WEBSTER, 1859. Bronze, larger than life.
South lawn, Beacon St.
★ Hiram Powers (1805–1873).

Young Hiram migrated to Ohio with his family about 1818 to escape a famine in Vermont. Working odd jobs, Powers became a supervisor at a Cincinnati museum, where he learned to model clay. He traveled East, soliciting portrait bust commissions so successfully that President Jackson, Calhoun, and Webster all sat for him. Armed with further commissions, he and his family relocated permanently in Florence, Italy, then the center for American sculptors. His *Greek Slave* (begun in 1843), so popular that he produced it in nine versions, brought him international fame.

The first Webster statue shipped from Italy was lost at sea; a second casting reached Boston and was erected in 1859. Webster (*see* Marshfield: *Webster, the Farmer of Marshfield*) was a New Hampshire-born orator, Congressman and Senator, proponent of the Union, and Secretary of State under Harrison and Fillmore. Funded by Webster Memorial Committee.

HORACE MANN, 1865. Bronze, larger than life.
South lawn.
★ Emma Stebbins (1815–1882).

Born in New York City, Stebbins first had a career as a painter; she was over forty when she went to Rome to study sculpture. Among her works is *Angel of the Waters*, a fountain in Central Park.

Horace Mann (1796–1859), best known for his educational theories, was first a lawyer and Massachusetts legislator. As president of the state Senate in 1836–37, he pushed for creation of a State Board of Education, then became its first secretary. Although the board had little power, Mann skillfully turned the state's regressive school systems into a model for other states. Congressman from 1848 to 1852, Mann accepted the presidency of newly formed Antioch College in Ohio, a liberal school where he was able to extend his theories favoring nonsectarian, nonsexist education. Funded by a collection from Massachusetts school children and teachers.

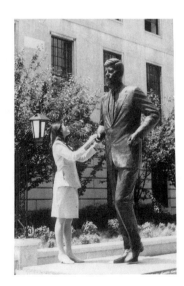

JOHN F. KENNEDY, 1988.
Bronze, h. 8′2″.
South lawn.
Isabel McIlvain (1943–   ).

Associate professor of art at Boston University, McIlvain was born in Westchester, Pa. Graduated from Smith College, she won a merit scholarship from the Art Students League, then earned a graduate degree from Pratt Institute. She lives in Sherborn.

McIlvain won the commission for the Kennedy memorial statue in intensive competition juried by the martyred president's family and former staff members. In portraying Kennedy, the sculptor had to contend with quarrels about whether JFK buttoned the top button of his suit jacket or not (photographs show he did) and whether there should be two or three buttons on it. Sere bronze oak leaves on the pedestal poignantly recall the dark November of his death.

John F. Kennedy (1915–1963) was the second son of a large and very political Boston Irish family; his maternal grandfather was Joseph "Honey Fitz" Fitzgerald, mayor of Boston early in the century. After the death of his eldest brother in World War II, Jack was designated by his family to seek political office. He was junior Senator from Massachusetts when he won the Democratic nomination for President in 1960, squeaking into office in a closely contested election.

His charisma and his vision of social reform and global responsibility kindled popularity, worldwide, for him and his wife, Jacqueline. Tragically, he was assassinated in Dallas in 1963. Funding from private sources raised by special legislative commission.

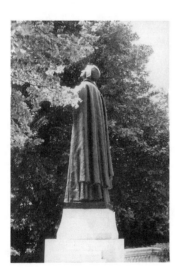

ANNE HUTCHINSON, 1922. Bronze, larger than life.
  South lawn, near west wing.
  ★ Cyrus E. Dallin (*see* Arlington: *Indian Hunter*).

Emigrating from England with her husband in 1634, Hutchinson became a leader among the women of the Massachusetts Bay Colony and shortly challenged its theocracy by advocating "a covenant of

grace," not "a covenant of works" (strict adherence to Biblical scripture). She had the support of Governor Vane (see Back Bay [Boston
Public Library]: Sir Henry Vane) and some of the clergy, but when
Vane was defeated in the election of the general court in 1637, she
was tried, excommunicated, and exiled. She and her husband founded
a colony of religious seekers in Rhode Island; after his death she
formed another on Long Island, where she was killed by Indians—an
event Boston Puritans ascribed to divine retribution. Funded by Anne
Hutchinson Memorial Association and State Federation of Women's
Clubs.

HENRY CABOT LODGE, 1932. Bronze, heroic size.
    South lawn, west end.
    Raymond A. Porter (see Somerville: Spanish War Memorial).

    The elder Lodge (1850–1924) was a Republican member of Con-
gress for thirty-eight years, more than thirty of them in the Senate. He
is remembered principally for his opposition to President Wilson and
the League of Nations. Commissioned by the Commonwealth.

STATE HOUSE CLOCK, 1990. Mixed media.
    Overhead, light court.
    Ronald M. Fischer (1947–   ).

    New York artist Fischer took a B.A. from Long Island University in
1971 and an M.F.A. from San Francisco Art Institute in 1973. His utili-
tarian art objects have been widely acclaimed and are held in such public collections as the Whitney Museum, the Dallas Museum of Art, and
the Tamayo Museum in Mexico City. He has been awarded grants
from the National Endowment for the Arts, the New York Council for
the Arts, and others.
    Commissioned by the Massachusetts Art in Public Places Program,
this $100,000 work raised a furor among politicians who called it an ex-
ample of waste of public money, although it was funded by 1% for Art
legislation. Public outcry about this and public artworks created at state
prisons was largely responsible for the termination of the Art in Public
Places Program.

GEORGE WASHINGTON, 1826. Marble, heroic size.
    Doric Hall.
    Sir Francis Chantrey (1781–1841).

    Chantrey, a British neoclassical sculptor, was chosen to execute this
work because no American sculptor was thought capable. The first sig-
nificant statue in Boston, it was commissioned to mark the fiftieth anniversary of American independence. Funded by a private committee.

JOHN ALBION ANDREW, 1871. Marble, larger than life.
    Doric Hall.
    ★ Thomas Ball (see Boston Public Garden: George Washington).

    Andrew (1818–1867) was governor of Massachusetts during the
Civil War, a friend of Lincoln's, and an effective supporter of the Union.
A graduate of Bowdoin College and a lawyer, he based his strong anti-

slavery stand on Unitarian religious convictions. Thanks to him, Massachusetts was the only northern state prepared for war; its troops were the first to go to the defense of the nation's capital. Andrew organized the first black regiments and fought successfully to have them paid on a par with white troops. Funded by public subscription.

WAR NURSES SCULPTURE, 1911. Bronze, heroic size.
Nurses' Hall, State House.
Bela Pratt (*see* Malden: *The Flag Defenders*).

WILLIAM FRANCIS BARTLETT, 1901. Bronze, larger than life.
Hall of Flags.
★ Daniel Chester French (*see* Concord: *Minuteman*).

Bartlett was twenty-one when the Civil War broke out; he volunteered, and rose to general by the age of twenty-four. He was urged to run for governor, but died at the age of thirty-six, before he had the opportunity to seek office. This statue was intended for the State House grounds, but on acceptance in 1903 it was placed in Memorial Hall with Civil War battle flags. Flags of other wars have since been added.

ROGER WOLCOTT, 1906. Bronze, larger than life.
Third floor, opposite main staircase.
★ Daniel Chester French (*see* Concord: *Minuteman*).

Governor during the massive addition to the State House by Brigham in 1898, Wolcott championed the preservation of the Bulfinch section, which now houses Doric Hall, the old and new Senate chambers, and executive offices.

BOSTON COMMON

★ ROBERT GOULD SHAW AND THE 54TH MASSACHUSETTS REGIMENT, 1897. Bronze bas-relief.
Beacon St. at Park St.
★ Augustus Saint-Gaudens (1848–1907).

A cobbler's son, born in Ireland but raised in New York, Saint-Gaudens began as a cameo-cutter, studied in Paris and Rome, and worked in New York and Cornish, N.H. Synthesizing vigorous naturalism and abstract ideals, he is best known for the enigmatic *Adams Memorial* in Washington, D.C.

Scion of a prominent and idealistic Boston family, the twenty-six-year-old Shaw, already a veteran of Antietam and Cedar Mountain, was offered command of the first black regiment (the 54th Massachusetts) to fight for the Union. His 900 troops, first of 180,000 blacks to enlist, were trained near Boston. Assigned to the siege of Fort Wagner, Col. Shaw and his men paraded down Beacon Hill toward their transport ships just as their bronze counterparts do now. Outnumbered two-to-one in an assault on Fort Wagner in July, 1863, the regiment was decimated; Shaw and his troops were unceremoniously buried by the

Confederates in a mass grave there. Some survived—Sgt. William Carney, thrice-wounded, snatched up the flag, rallied the regiment, and became the first black to receive the Congressional Medal of Honor.

Saint-Gaudens took fourteen years to complete the work, taking pains to portray the soldiers hidden behind the horse in as much detail as those readily seen. This work is thought to be the finest memorial in the city, and perhaps the finest war memorial anywhere. Although the names of the officers killed were engraved on the front of the monument from the beginning, the names of the sixty-two enlisted casualties were not added until 1982—and the only place there was room enough was on the obverse side. Funds raised by a citizens' commission.

BOSTON MASSACRE MONUMENT, 1888. Granite and bronze.
Tremont St.
Robert Kraus (1850–1902).

Records are oddly lacking regarding Kraus, who also sculpted the *Theodore Parker* now in Roxbury.

Names of the five Bostonians killed by British soldiers in the 1770 brawl are inscribed on the column behind a melodramatic Freedom, complete with flag, broken chain, eagle, and trod-upon British crown. One victim's hand, extending in high relief from the bronze plaque depicting the massacre, is kept polished by visitors who like to shake it. Many think they are shaking the hand of Crispus Attucks, famed as the first black to fall for this nation. But Attucks lies in the foreground, his protruding shoe toe also polished.

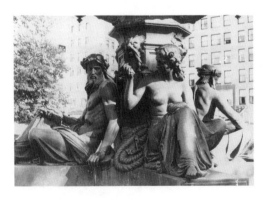

THE BREWER FOUNTAIN, 1855. Bronze, figures larger than life.
Near Tremont and Temple Sts.
Paul Lienard, French sculptor (d. 1900).

Brought home by Beacon Hill resident Gardner Brewer from the Paris Exposition of 1867, this is one of several castings from the 1855 original. Modeled in the Renaissance style, which seeks to portray the classic beauty of the human body, the mythological figures at the base are Greek god of the sea Poseidon, his wife Amphitrite, sea-nymph Galatea, and her lover Acis. Gift to the city from Gardner Brewer.

SOLDIERS' AND SAILORS' MONUMENT, 1877. Bronze and granite, h. 70'.
On Flagstaff Hill.
Martin Milmore (*see* Framingham: *Civil War Memorial*).

The four statues at the base represent Peace, the Sailor, the Muse
of History, and the Soldier; the bas-relief plaques (now grotesquely vandalized) between them depict the departure and return of the forces,
the Navy, and the work of the Boston Sanitary Commission. (In one
plaque, Longfellow with his great beard can be seen accompanying the
governor.) The figures at the base of the column represent the sections
of the country, North, South, East, and West. The Genius of America
stands at the top. The inscription was written by Harvard president
Charles W. Eliot. Funded by the Commonwealth.

THE PARTISANS, 1979. Cast metal, larger than life.
Near Charles and Beacon Sts.
Andrzei Pitynski (1947–   ).

Pitynski, born in 1947 in Ulanow, Poland, studied at the Academy of
Fine Arts and the Museum of Fine Arts in Cracow, becoming conserva-
tor of sculpture at Jagiellonski University Museum in that city. He emigrated to New York in 1974, studying at the New York Art Students
League and at Sculpture House. He shortly joined the Johnson Atelier/
Technical Institute in Princeton, N.J., where he is supervisor of the modeling, resins, and moldmaking departments.

One of the most popular of Boston's outdoor works, *The Partisans* is
technically here on temporary loan. A tribute to guerilla freedom fight-
ers everywhere, beaten but still persisting, it is realistic enough to intrigue viewers and enigmatic enough to provoke questions. Installation
sponsored by J. Seward Johnson, Johnson Atelier.

PARKMAN PLAZA, 1958–60. Three bronze statues, life-size, to Learning,
Religion, and Industry.
On Lafayette Mall, Tremont St. side of Boston Common.
Arcangelo Cascieri (1902–   ) and Adio di Biccari (1914–   ).

At the age of eighteen, Revere native Adio di Biccari was awarded a
scholarship to the Boston Museum School; upon graduation he snared
one of the school's top honors, a European traveling scholarship. For a
time he was employed in New Hampshire by the Works Projects Administration (WPA). His sculpture represented New England at the 1939
World's Fair in New York. In 1952 he formed a partnership with his
brother-in-law Arcangelo Cascieri, woodcarver and architect, for many
years dean of the Boston Center for Architecture. Compare the style of
the figures: *Labor* and *Education* were sculpted by di Biccari, *Religion*
by Cascieri.

In 1908 George Francis Parkman (1823–1908) left five million dollars to Boston's public parks, expressing a hope that the Common
would always remain one of them. Parkman was the son of the wealthy
banker Dr. George F. Parkman, who disappeared in 1849, victim of
one of Boston's most sensational murders; the perpetrator was found
to be a Harvard professor. Commissioned by the City of Boston.

THE FOUNDERS' MEMORIAL, 1930. Bronze bas-relief.
Near junction of Beacon and Spruce Sts.
John F. Paramino (*see* Fenway: *World War II Memorial*).

Boston's first settler, the recluse William Blackstone (he spelled it Blaxton), is shown greeting John Winthrop and his small band who had found Charlestown unsatisfactory and crossed to Shawmut, the peninsula that is now Boston. Distinguishable in the group are John Wilson, clergyman, and Ann Pollard, first white woman to step upon Boston's soil (who is not to be confused with the allegorical female figure symbolizing Boston). Inscription on the rear of the monument is a quote from Winthrop before the group debarked from the ship *Arabella* in 1630. Commissioned by the City of Boston to mark its 300th anniversary.

THE FAMOUS AUTHORS' FACES MURAL, 1992. Acrylic, h. 12' × 24'.
Side of Brattle Book Shop, 9 West St.
Jeffrey Hull (1961–   ) and Sarah Hutt (1961–   ).
With Harry Brock, Maggi Brown, Diane Darrow, Bob Ganong, Sarah Grimm, Anna Maria Hernado, Wayne Hopkins, Peter Hoyle, Debbie Kamy Hull, Shelley Loheed, Steve Mumford, Edie Read, Leon Robinson, Kathy Soles, Michael Wilson, Kathy Wysocki.

Collaborators since 1985 on projects to stimulate public awareness of the arts, Hull and Hutt have been at the forefront of a movement for subsidized housing for artists. Both painters are active as curator/organizers of art exhibitions.

Each artist chose to depict a favorite literary figure: James Baldwin, Gertrude Stein, T. Coraghessan Boyle, Gish Jen, Maya Angelou, Edith Wharton, Stephen King, Maria Elena Walsh, Thomas Bernhard, Leo Tolstoy, Virginia Woolf, Emily Dickinson, Esther Forbes, William Faulkner, Toni Morrison, Flannery O'Connor, Kurt Vonnegut, Franz Kafka. Underwritten by Kenneth Gloss of the Brattle Book Shop.

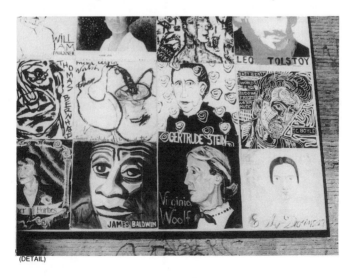

(DETAIL)

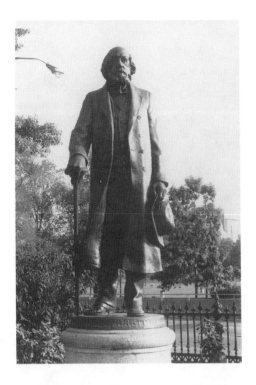

BOSTON PUBLIC GARDEN

★ EDWARD EVERETT HALE, 1913. Bronze, larger than life.
Near Charles St.
Bela Lyon Pratt (*seé* Malden: *The Flag Defenders*).

Pratt's naturalistic portrait of Hale was something of a departure for
the time: a statue out for a stroll in the garden, just like everyone else.

Hale (1822–1909), Unitarian minister (chaplain of the U.S. Senate)
and popular author, produced or edited more than sixty books of fic-
tion, biography, history, travel, and sermons. He edited several magazines and contributed copiously to others; he was author of *The Man
Without a Country*. His uncle was the orator Edward Everett; his great-
uncle, the martyred spy, Nathan Hale. Funded by subscription among
citizens.

TRITON BABIES, 1922. Bronze fountain, figures larger than life.
Anna Coleman Watts Ladd (1878–1939).

Born in Bryn Mawr, Pa., Anna Ladd studied in Paris in the studio of
Rodin and in Rome. She lived in Beverly Farms.

The title of this group is puzzling; the Triton of Greek mythology is a
merman, fish from the waist down. These two, although aquatically in-
clined, are totally human. Brought from the Panama Pacific Exhibit by
Mrs. Boylston Beal, a wealthy Beacon Street resident, this fountain was
placed across from her home in the spot now occupied by the George
Robert White Memorial. It was moved to this site in 1924.

BAGHEERA, 1986. Bronze, h. 2'.
Fountain near swan boats.
Lillian Swann Saarinen (1912–   ).

Lilli Swann left the Chapin School in New York in tenth grade to
study art at Hunter College. She also went to Cranbrook Academy in
Michigan, where she met and married Eero Saarinen, later one of the
foremost architects of the twentieth century. Her teachers included Carl
Milles, Heinz Warneke, and Alexander Archipenko. A portraitist and ani-
malist, she won the Anna Hyatt Huntington prize, among others. She
was one of five sculptors representing Michigan at the 1939 World's
Fair, and that same year she was a member of the first women's Olym-
pic ski team. She lived in Cambridge for many years.

This sculpture is named for the panther in Rudyard Kipling's *Jungle
Books*. It was placed here by friends of the sculptor through the offices
of Friends of the Public Garden.

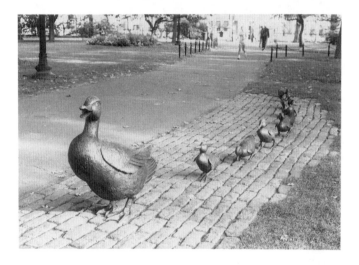

MAKE WAY FOR DUCKLINGS, 1987. Bronze, h. approx. 40″×35′.
Near Charles and Beacon Sts.
Nancy Schön (1928–   ).

Born in Boston, Nancy Schön took a bachelor's degree in sociology
from Tufts, then an M.F.A. and a fifth fellowship year from the Boston
Museum School. She has also held a fellowship from the Virginia Center for the Creative Arts. She lives in Newton.

Make Way for Ducklings, a children's book written by Robert McCloskey in 1941, won the Caldecott Medal (an award given annually for outstanding juvenile literature) in 1942. It quickly became a classic, going
through seventeen printings and selling more than 700,000 copies.
With his own drawings, McCloskey relates the tale of a pair of mallard
ducks looking for a nesting site in Boston. They find the perfect place
on an island in the Charles River Basin, but they remember the pea-
nuts fed them by visitors to the Public Garden. When the ducklings are

old enough, Mrs. Mallard and her progeny take an insouciant stroll up sidewalks and through traffic to the pond in the Garden. One of Boston's newer traditions is a children's parade in the spring, retracing the ducklings' route.

The ducklings' appeal has led to theft on three different occasions. One bird was quickly recovered; neighbors, including nearby bartenders who sold "Bring Back Mack" buttons, chipped in to replace the others and have campaigned for better lighting and security. Requests for replicas in other cities have been turned down by the sculptor because "it's a Boston story." She made exception when Russian First Lady Raisa Gorbachev asked her American counterpart Barbara Bush for a duplicate for Moscow; in 1991 a duck family was installed in Gorky Park.

Dedicated in the 150th anniversary year of the Public Garden, the sculpture is considered a tribute to McCloskey, whose drawings the sculptor followed closely. Given to the City of Boston by Friends of the Public Garden.

WENDELL PHILLIPS, 1915. Bronze, larger than life.
Boylston St. mall.
★ Daniel Chester French (*see* Concord: *Minuteman*).

Phillips (1811–1884) is best known as a masterly abolitionist orator; after the Civil War, he worked in other reform causes including women's suffrage, prohibition, and penal reform. Funded by appropriation from the Boston City Council.

THOMAS CASS, 1899. Bronze, larger than life.
Boylston St. mall.
Richard E. Brooks (1865–1919).

The granite industry in Quincy is credited with kindling the sculptural interests of Brooks, a native of nearby Braintree. He first set up shop as a commercial sculptor, modeling terra cotta panels for buildings and private homes. Commissioned to do a bust of Governor William E. Russell, Brooks was inspired to go to Paris to study; there he achieved some success. He became a follower of the Symbolist movement, which departed from strict realism to convey impressions by suggestion. This work, reverting to realism, was awarded a gold medal at the Paris Exposition of 1900.

A native of Ireland, Col. Cass was killed at Malvern Hill in July, 1862, at the head of his "Fighting Ninth" Massachusetts Regiment, a unit he organized entirely of Irish immigrants. Funded by the Jonathan Phillips Fund.

TADEUSZ KOSCIUSZKO, 1927. Bronze, larger than life.
Boylston St. mall.
Theo Alice Ruggles Kitson (*see* Malden: *The Hiker*).

Rallying to the American cause for idealistic reasons, Kosciuszko, a thirty-year-old Polish army captain, became Washington's adjutant and a colonel of artillery; he distinguished himself at the battles of New York and Yorktown. He had less success defending his homeland against Russian and Prussian invaders, but is remembered as a states-man advocating absolute liberty and equality before the law. Commissioned by Boston Polish organizations to commemorate the 150th anniversary of Kosciuszko's joining the Continental Army.

CHARLES SUMNER, 1878. Bronze, larger than life.
Boylston St. mall.
★ Thomas Ball (*see* Downtown: *Josiah Quincy*).

When Anne Whitney's proposal for a Sumner statue was rejected because of her gender (*see* Cambridge [Harvard Square]: *Sumner*), Thomas Ball was the sculptor given the commission. This work is the result.

Uncompromising advocate of emancipation and free speech, Sumner (1811–1874) served in the U.S. Senate for twenty-two years. His oratory opposing the Compromise of 1850 (which allowed slavery to expand into new territories) provoked an attack on the Senate floor from a cane-wielding Southern Congressman, who injured Sumner severely. During the three years it took Sumner to recover, Massachusetts reelected him and let his vacant seat speak for him. Commissioned by the Commonwealth.

GEORGE WASHINGTON, 1869. Bronze, equestrian, larger than life.
★ Thomas Ball (*see* Downtown: *Josiah Quincy*).

On horseback at the west end of the Public Garden, Washington (1732–1798), Revolutionary commander-in-chief and first President, looks down Commonwealth Avenue. The plaster study for this work is at the Boston Athenæum. Washington's sword has been broken so often by vandals that he is now equipped with a weapon of replaceable fiberglass. Funds raised by the sculptor's friends and an appropriation from the city.

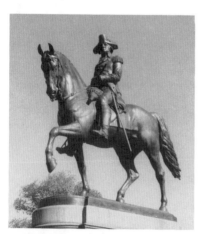

BOY AND BIRD, 1934, recast 1977. Bronze fountain, life-size.
On *Washington*'s (see above) left.
Bashka Paeff (1893–1979).

Paeff was born in Russia; she studied in Paris and at the Boston Museum School under Bela Pratt.

SMALL CHILD. Bronze fountain, life-size.
On *Washington*'s (see above) right.
Mary E. Moore (1887–1967).

Another of Bela Pratt's students, Moore taught at Beaver Country Day School in Brookline. She was born in Taunton. Given to the City of Boston by Mrs. Alfred Tozzer.

GEORGE ROBERT WHITE MEMORIAL, 1924. Bronze, larger than life.
Beacon and Arlington Sts.
★ Daniel Chester French (*see* Concord: *The Minuteman*).

In his day, French was famous for his sculpted angels. As a boy on his father's farm in Concord he became interested in animals and birds; his biographer daughter recounts that he had a collection of birds' wings that must have inspired his winged figures. French's original title for this statue was *The Spirit of Giving*; the allegorical figure is casting bread upon the waters.

Having accumulated a fortune in the wholesale drug business, White (1847–1922) became one of Boston's foremost philanthropists. His five-million-dollar legacy to the city provided funds for clinics and for art, including $50,000 for his own memorial.

THE ETHER MONUMENT, 1867. Granite and red marble.
Near Arlington St.
★ John Quincy Adams Ward (*see* Newburyport: *George Washington*).

The miracle of pain-free surgery was first realized at Massachusetts General Hospital in Boston in 1846: Dr. William G. Morton, a dentist who found ether useful in his practice, assisted Dr. J. C. Warren in removing a tumor from the neck of a patient named Gilbert Abbot. Claim to the discovery was disputed by Dr. Charles T. Jackson, and Ward resolved the dilemma by neither depicting nor naming the pioneers of anesthesia; the solicitous figure he carved is meant to be the Good Samaritan. (Oliver Wendell Holmes quipped that the monument was a memorial "to ether—or either.")

WILLIAM ELLERY CHANNING, 1902. Bronze, life-size.
Opposite Arlington St. Church, Arlington and Boylston Sts.
Herbert Adams (*see* Woburn: *Col. Loammi Baldwin*).

A gentle and much-loved clergyman, advocate of spiritual and intellectual freedom, Channing (1780–1842) was minister of the Federal Street Congregational Church in Boston from 1803 until his death. Following a sermon in 1819 he became known as "the apostle of Unitarianism," although he objected to the term. He wrote and spoke in opposition to slavery, but rejected enforced abolition as too radical; he thought an enlightened public conscience would end slavery. His thinking on war and peace, the education of children, and separation of church and state would be liberal in our own day. Funded by legacy of John Foster.

COMMONWEALTH AVENUE

ALEXANDER HAMILTON, 1865. Granite, larger than life.
On the mall between Arlington and Berkeley Sts.
Dr. William Rimmer (1816–1879).

William Rimmer's father, spirited out of France as a boy and raised
genteelly in England, had reason to believe he was Louis XVII, the lost
Dauphin of France. There were some forty other contenders, so for his
own safety Thomas Rimmer emigrated to the New World and altered
his name. Although the father worked as a cobbler, William was raised
in an intellectual and culture-conscious home and encouraged in his
pursuit of art as a profession. He had little success, pursuing a variety
of odd trades until, in his thirties, his interest in anatomy led to self-
taught medical study; he practiced in Randolph and East Milton for a
few years. At the age of forty-five he turned to sculpture full-time, with
mixed results; this statue was controversial. Rimmer knew so little
about technique (he failed to use an armature) that parts kept falling
off; nevertheless, powered by creative energy, he completed the clay
model for *Hamilton* in eleven days. He later taught art anatomy at
Cooper Union in New York and in Boston, and wrote a comprehensive
book on the subject.

A native of the West Indies, Hamilton (1757–1804) emigrated to the
colonial mainland and threw himself into the American rebellion, becoming Gen. Washington's aide and private secretary. His financial genius
(he had been in charge of a counting-house on St. Croix at the age of
thirteen) mandated his appointment as first Secretary of the Treasury.
His political thought was strongly Federalist, advocating a propertied oli-
garchy and an elected monarch who would rule for life. Hamilton's bril-
liance was marred by his penchant for intrigue; he schemed against
John Adams, hoping to deprive him of the Presidency. Another feud
with Aaron Burr brought about the duel that cost him his life. Gift of
Thomas Lee.

GEN. JOHN GLOVER, 1875. Bronze, larger than life.
Between Berkeley and Clarendon Sts.
Martin Milmore (*see* Framingham: *Civil War Memorial*).

Glover (1732–1797) led perhaps the most unusual regiment of the
American Revolution, an "amphibious" regiment composed largely of
Marblehead fishermen who supplied aquatic transportation for Washington's army. Born in Salem, Glover became one of the "codfish aristocracy"; he was a fish merchant and owner of a fishing fleet. His
regiment of small boats saved Washington's army after the Battle of
Long Island, ferrying 9,000 men to New York, and it was he and his
men who rowed the general and 2,400 troops across the Delaware on
Christmas night, 1776, braving snowstorm and river ice, to attack and
rout the Hessian mercenaries at Trenton.

ANGELS FRIEZE, 1872. Carved stone, copper trumpets.
Bell tower, First Baptist Church, Clarendon St. and Commonwealth Ave.
Frederic Auguste Bartholdi (1834–1904).

It has been said that if Bartholdi had not created the Statue of Liberty, he would be totally forgotten today. Architect H. H. Richardson, famed for his brownstone Romanesque public buildings, designed this as the Brattle Square Church in 1872. He commissioned the French sculptor Bartholdi to cut the decorative frieze to terminate its flat-topped Italianate bell tower. The bas-reliefs on the four sides represent baptism, communion, matrimony, and death. Thanks to the angels sounding trumpets on the four corners, the building was nicknamed the Church of the Holy Bean Blowers. Some of the angels may look familiar: Bartholdi used the faces of Lincoln, Emerson, Longfellow, Hawthorne, and Garibaldi.

PATRICK ANDREW COLLINS, 1908. Bronze bust and supporting figures.
Commonwealth Ave. between Clarendon and Dartmouth Sts.
Henry Hudson Kitson (*see* Lexington: *The Minuteman*) and Theo Alice Ruggles Kitson (*see* Malden: *The Hiker*).

Mayor of Boston from 1902 to 1905, Collins (1844–1905) died suddenly in office. By trade an upholsterer, he became a lawyer, state legislator, member of Congress, and consul general in London. Originally farther down Commonwealth Ave. at Charlesgate West, Collins' monument was relocated in 1968. The figures represent Columbia and Erin. Funded by public subscription.

WILLIAM LLOYD GARRISON, 1886. Bronze, larger than life.
Between Dartmouth and Exeter Sts.
★ Olin Levi Warner (*see* Charles River Esplanade: *General Devens*).

The Garrison family hated this likeness and commissioned Anne Whitney to do a small, more personable one. (For Garrison's biography, *see* Newburyport: *William Lloyd Garrison*.) Funded by public subscription.

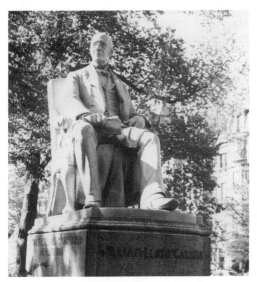

★ SAMUEL ELIOT MORISON, 1982. Bronze, larger than life (*see* cover photo).
On the mall between Exeter and Fairfield Sts.
Penelope Jencks (*see* Chelsea: *Chelsea Conversation*).

One of America's foremost maritime historians, Morison (1887–1976) twice won the Pulitzer Prize, for *Admiral of the Ocean Sea* and for *John Paul Jones*. An able sailor, Morison researched Columbus' life in the libraries of Spain and then personally retraced the great explorer's route in a sailboat, following the entries in his log. He also wrote the definitive *History of U.S. Naval Operations in World War II*. Commissioned by the Back Bay Federation with funds from the George B. Henderson Foundation.

DOMINGO FAUSTINO SARMIENTO, 1973. Bronze, heroic size.
Commonwealth Ave. between Gloucester and Hereford Sts.
Ivette Compagnion.

Compagnion is an Argentine sculptor.
The bulky, brooding figure of Domingo Sarmiento (1811–1888) seems misplaced on Commonwealth Mall; it is hard to guess that the subject was a famed political leader: writer, legislator, founder of his country's educational system, minister to the United States, and President of Argentina. He stands here because his admiration for Horace Mann led him to model Argentine educational programs on Boston's school system. A monument to Sarmiento in Boston was first proposed in 1913, but not realized until 1973. Gift of the Argentine Republic.

LEIF ERIKSSON, 1887. Bronze, life-size.
Commonwealth Ave. at Charlesgate.
★ Anne Whitney (*see* Quincy Market: *Samuel Adams*).

The legendary Norse explorer was memorialized here at the behest of Eben N. Horsford, a patent medicine maker, who believed that Vineland was located on the Charles River. This statue once overlooked the river; filling and highway-building have left Leif with a view of nothing much but traffic. Gift of Eben N. Horsford.

BACK BAY

BOYLSTON PLACE GATEWAY, 1988. Forged, colored galvanized steel, forged bronze, h. 19′ × 24′ × 6′.
Boylston St. end of pedestrian walkway linking theater district (via Transportation Bldg.) to Boston Common.
Dimitri Gerakaris (*see* Cambridge [Harvard Square]: *Longfellow Memorial*).

Celebrating Boston's midtown cultural district, Gerakaris' arch is festooned with lyres, masks, pianos, and musical notes. Characters from the children's tale *The Animal Musicians of Bremen* are greeted by swans and ducklings, denizens of the Public Garden across the street. The bear is the symbol of the Tavern Club, a formerly male-only bastion with quarters nearby. Funded by the Browne Fund, the Henderson Fund, and Massachusetts 1% for Art.

EMANCIPATION GROUP, 1877. Bronze, larger than life.
Park Sq., Charles and Stuart Sts.
★ Thomas Ball (*see* Boston Public Garden: *Washington*).

Commissioned by the Freedman's Memorial Society, the original version of this work stands in Lincoln Park in Washington, D.C. Charlotte Scott, a freedwoman from Virginia, originated the idea for this statue the day after Lincoln was shot, and its $17,000 cost was paid entirely by freed slaves. The head of the slave is modeled on that of Archer Alexander, the last person recaptured under the Fugitive Slave Act. This duplicate casting was given to the city by Moses Kimball in 1877.

GALLERY: Artists Foundation Gallery, in Transportation Bldg., Charles and Stuart Sts. Exhibitions featuring contemporary regional artists, particularly winners of Artists Foundation Fellowships.

MURAL, early 1970s.
Top facade of Josiah Quincy School, visible from east end of Mass. Pike.
Maria Termini.

Termini, a maker of serigraph prints and teacher at Brookline Arts Center, designed this mural with input from students at Quincy School. She earned her B.A. and M.F.A. at Catholic University in Washington; she has taught at the Art Institute of Boston and at the Cambridge Center for Adult Education. Executed by The Architects Collaborative.

GREEK KEY, 1969-70. Cor-ten steel, h. 6′ × 40′.
Howard Johnson Complex, 200 Stuart St.
Alfred Duca (*see* Back Bay: *Boston Tapestry*).

This welded sculpture weighs eight tons. Funded by 1% for Art.

BENCH, untitled with selections from TRUISMS, 1987. Marble, 17″ × 54″ × 25″.
10 Newbury St.
Jenny Holzer (1950–   ).

Holzer won a spot on the international art scene with blinking linear messages, like those that crawl across buildings high above Times Square—except that instead of conveying news headlines, Holzer's electronic billboards twist platitudes into philosophic messages meant to evoke puzzlement and reflection. She grew up in Lancaster, Ohio, and attended Duke University before taking her B.F.A. at Ohio University. While working on her M.F.A. at Rhode Island School of Design, she first used words in her paintings. Enrolled in the Whitney Museum's independent study program, Holzer began posting *Truisms*, her altered bromides, throughout Manhattan. Meanwhile she trained and worked as a typesetter. In 1982 the Public Art Fund invited her to display *Truisms* on the electronic Spectacolor Board in Times Square. For exhibition, she often combines sarcophagi and benches like this one with electronic signs. She now lives in Hoosick Falls, N.Y.

The artist made six versions of benches this size, covered with multiple messages, in editions of three. Gallery owner Barbara Krakow ordered one, but through some miscommunication with Holzer's dealer all three were sold elsewhere. A fourth was made for Krakow, with the proviso, in order to retain the value of the three-work edition, that it cannot ever enter the art market and must eventually be destroyed. Krakow has a five-year lease as of 1993, and says that the bench will be here as long as her gallery is here.

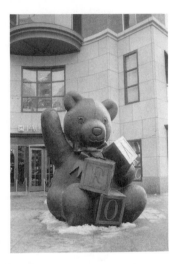

TEDDY BEAR, 1991.
Bronze, h. 12'.
Boylston and Berkeley Sts.
Robert Shure (1948–   ).

Born in New York City, Shure studied at New York Institute of Technology and at the Boston Museum School, earning an M.F.A. from Boston Museum School/Tufts in 1970. He became an assistant to Cascieri and di Biccari (*see* Boston Common: *Parkman Plaza*), and continues their traditional style of commission sculpture with his Skylight Studios in Woburn. He lives in Burlington. Commissioned by F.A.O. Schwarz toy store and Advanced Animations.

DORIC RESURRECTION, 1991. Painted ceramic, h. 11' × 20' × 2'.
399 Boylston St.
David Judelson (*see* Cambridge [Lechmere]: *Flag Fragments*).

An abstraction of a Greek temple site, this piece was commissioned by Copley Real Estate Advisers.

JOHN WINTHROP, 1880. Bronze, life-size.
At First and Second Church, 66 Marlborough St.
★ Richard Saltonstall Greenough (*see* Cambridge [Harvard University]: *Governor John Winthrop*).

Greenough's marble Winthrop is one of the state's two allotted statues in Statuary Hall in the U.S. Capitol in Washington. This bronze replica was placed in Scollay Square (now the site of Government Center) in 1880, moved here in 1903, and damaged in a 1968 fire that gutted the church.

Winthrop (1588–1649), English lawyer and strict Puritan, was first governor of the Massachusetts Bay Colony, later Boston. Between the settling in 1630 and his death he was elected governor a dozen times and is credited with staving off Parliamentary interference with the colony more than once. It was his re-election as governor, opposing the more tolerant Sir Henry Vane, that initiated the expulsion of Anne Hutchinson and subsequent persecution of non-Puritans.

SUSPENDED SCULPTURE, 1985. Brass, gold-plating, h. 7' × 3' × 2½'.
Interior, First and Second Church, 66 Marlborough St.
Michio Ihara (see Lowell: Pawtucket Prism).

THE NEWBURY STREET MURAL, 1991. Acrylic, h. five stories.
Newbury and Dartmouth Sts.
Joshua Winer (1956–   ).

While a painting major at Yale (B.A., 1978), Winer studied fresco painting one summer at Skowhegan (Maine) School of Painting and Sculpture. In 1986 he earned a master's degree in architecture at Harvard Graduate School of Design. A practicing architect, he has lectured and taught mural painting at such diverse venues as Skowhegan, the Brockton Art Museum, and the state correctional institute at Bridgewater. He lives in Arlington.

This trompe l'oeil mural contains more than fifty characters from Boston history, from the chief Massasoit to art patron Isabella Stuart Gardner to baseball great Babe Ruth to computer mogul An Wang. A key to the people (and the famous works of art replicated) is available at Du Barry Restaurant, on whose wall it is painted.

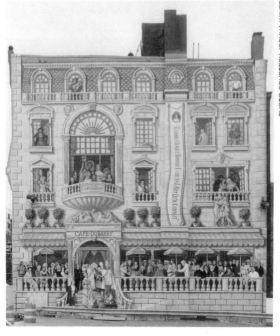

PHOTO COURTESY JOSHUA WINER

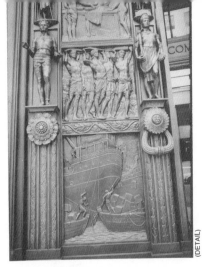

(DETAIL)

★ SALADA TEA DOORS, 1927. Bronze, marble doorframe, h. 12'.
330 Stuart St.
Henry Wilson (1864–1934).

Architect, sculptor, metalworker, and jeweller, British artist Henry
Wilson taught at the Royal College of Art. These doors, which cost half
a million dollars to produce, won a silver medal at the Paris Salon in
1927. A generation ago, when possibilities for juvenile entertainment
were less spectacular than they are today, parents used to bring their
children into Boston to see the exotic bronze and marble carved reliefs
depicting the growing and shipping of tea. The building is no longer occupied by the tea company.

JOHN HANCOCK, 1950. Bronze with gold patina, heroic size.
Lobby of old John Hancock Bldg. (the Berkeley Bldg.), 200 Berkeley St.
★ Paul Manship (*see* Andover: *Armillary Sphere*).

For Hancock biography, *see* Quincy: *John Hancock*.

THE DAY OF DECISION, 1950. Mural, over doorway.
Lobby, old John Hancock Bldg.
Barry Faulkner (b. 1881).

A native of Keene, N.H., Faulkner became associated with the Mo-
nadnock School of painting grouped around Abbott Thayer in nearby
Dublin, N.H. He went on to work in New York and study at the Art Students League and at the American Academy in Rome. His murals at
the National Archives in Washington illustrate the signing of the Declaration of Independence and the Constitution.

Here Faulkner depicts the moment on July 2, 1776, when Benjamin
Harrison of Virginia has resolved "that these United Colonies are, and
of right ought to be, free and independent states." John Hancock, president of the Congress, sits in the president's chair.

PHILLIPS BROOKS, 1910. Bronze, larger than life.
North of Trinity Church, Copley Sq., Boylston and Clarendon Sts.
★ Augustus Saint-Gaudens (*see* Boston Common: *Shaw Memorial*) and
Francis Grimes. Canopy by Stanford White.

Completed by Saint-Gaudens' students during the sculptor's final illness, this work falls short of the sculptor's best. The Brooks head was among partially completed clay works saved from a disastrous fire in the Cornish, N.H., studio, in 1903. Saint-Gaudens' first version of a Christ head, bare, its eyes closed, exists in Cornish; the final hooded version here, its hand on Brooks' shoulder, was done by Grimes under the master's supervision. It inspired a comment from a contemporary wit that the group ought to be called "The boys want to talk to you down at the station." Saint-Gaudens did not live to see the work unveiled.

Brooks (1835–1893), former rector of Trinity Church and briefly Episcopal bishop of Massachusetts, is depicted preaching. A charismatic speaker, he routinely packed the house for sermons delivered at a machine-gun pace reaching 213 words a minute. A bachelor, Brooks balanced his religious fervor with worldly predilections: art, literature, fast horses, fishing, billiards, and food. At 6'4", he weighed 300 pounds. Another image of the famous rector can be found on the opposite side of the building; when the porch was added in 1925, Brooks, to the consternation of some, was included in the row of saints above the columns. A century ago his sermons were widely read; he is now best remembered as author of "O Little Town of Bethlehem." Funded by Trinity Church congregation.

THE TORTOISE AND THE HARE. *See* Hopkinton.

At Boston Public Library:

More detailed descriptions may be found in the Handbook to the Art and Architecture of Boston Public Library, *for sale at the library's business office. A partial listing follows:*

★ ART and SCIENCE, 1911. Bronze, larger than life.
Dartmouth St. entrance, facing Copley Sq.
Bela Lyon Pratt (*see* Malden: *The Flag Defenders*).

Architect Charles McKim specified lavish use of art and sculpture for the 1895 Boston Public Library. Saint-Gaudens was commissioned to do the exterior sculpture but, a procrastinator, he had only preliminary models at the time of his death in 1907. Pratt completed these allegorical female figures, and the master's brother, Louis Saint-Gaudens, carved the Sienna marble lions on the main staircase inside. The three heraldic seals above the entrance are by Saint-Gaudens.

KNOWLEDGE AND WISDOM, TRUTH AND ROMANCE, MUSIC AND POETRY, 1902. Paired bronze doors.
Dartmouth St. entrance.
★ Daniel Chester French (*see* Concord: *Minuteman*).

Commissioned by the library's architect, Charles McKim, French's doors embodied a new idea in bronze door-making: instead of many narrative panels, there is one low-relief allegorical figure on each. The sculptor's daughter relates that she asked him the difference between wisdom and knowledge; French said, "Knowledge is proud that she hath learned so much—Wisdom is humble that she knows no more."

SIR HENRY VANE, 1893. Bronze, life-size.
Dartmouth St. entrance.
★ Frederick MacMonnies (1863–1937).

Although he was born in New York City and died there, MacMonnies spent much of his career working in Paris. While studying at the Art Students League and at the National Academy of Design in New York, he assisted Augustus Saint-Gaudens. After winning the Prix d'Atelier, MacMonnies found commissions from America flowing into his studio and subsequently did important sculpture for the cities of New York and Denver, the Library of Congress, and the Columbian Exposition of 1893. World War I forced his return to this country.

Son of an English secretary of state, Vane the younger (1613–1662) emigrated in 1635 to Massachusetts in order to practice his strong Puritan views. A spokesman for toleration, he served one year as governor in 1636 but was defeated in 1637 by Winthrop; under the latter, Anne Hutchinson and her free-thinking followers were expelled from the Bay Colony, and Vane returned to England in disgust. Although he opposed the execution of King Charles I, Vane served Cromwell until the Puritan dictator forcibly dissolved Parliament. After the king's restoration Vane, despite his advocacy of tolerance, negotiation, and compromise, was accused of high treason and executed. Gift of Dr. Charles Goddard Weld.

TIFFANY EMBEDMENTS, 1893. Brass, various sizes up to 20″ × 28″.
Main entrance hall, McKim Bldg., Dartmouth St. entrance.
Tiffany Studios, design possibly by John Maynard.

These signs of the zodiac were originally made for the New York State pavilion at the Chicago World's Fair of 1893, a structure designed by the architects McKim, Mead and White, who also designed this library. When the fair closed, these intarsia were embedded here in the lobby's marble floor. Worn featureless by a century of foot traffic, they were restored by Greg LeFevre (*see* Boston University: *Untitled*) in 1989–93. Because the original drawings were lost in a long-ago studio fire, LeFevre had to reconstruct the initial stylistic ideas. He believes the designs were by Maynard, a prominent New York sculptor.

THE MUSES OF INSPIRATION WELCOMING THE SPIRIT OF LIGHT, and eight allegorical murals, 1895–6. Oil on canvas, large mural, h. 20′ × 40′.
Main staircase.
★ Pierre Puvis de Chavannes (1824–1898).

The paintings in the stairwell are by France's greatest muralist, who did them immediately after completing acclaimed work at the Hotel de Ville in Paris. The eight panels in the upper arches represent science, poetry, and philosophy, subdivided into categories similar to library catalogue classifications: on the right are pastoral, dramatic, and epic poetry; on the left, history, astronomy, and philosophy; and on either side of the window, chemistry and physics.

QUEST OF THE HOLY GRAIL, 1895. h. 8′.
Delivery room (research circulation desk).
Edwin Austin Abbey (1852–1911).

An outstanding Victorian-era illustrator, Philadelphia-born Abbey was obsessed with the romance of English medieval legend. In this narrative set of scenes Sir Galahad is always clad in red; the Biblical figure in white is Joseph of Arimathea, from whom Galahad was traditionally descended. Abbey lived in England at this time and was a member of the Royal Academy.

JUDAISM AND CHRISTIANITY, 1893–1919.
Third floor corridor, atop main staircase.
★ John Singer Sargent (1856–1925).

Enormously celebrated in his day, Sargent fell into eclipse as twentieth-century modernism flourished. Descended from a Gloucester family, the painter was born in Italy, where his cosmopolitan parents had gone for a change of scene. Although he traveled often to this country, his was a continental life; he lived for forty years in London. Tall, handsome, socially well-connected, Sargent never in his career had to seek a commission; he painted English nobility and American nouveau riche with equal honesty and facility. In 1910, at the height of his fame, he found himself bored and renounced what he called "paughtraits," turning to watercolor and to commissions such as this one, which he considered the crowning achievement of his life work. Biographers describe Sargent as an omnivorous reader, a passionate musician, an excellent host, and an artist oblivious to critical comment, generous to students and fellow artists. He is buried in St. Paul's Cathedral, London.

Although Sargent traveled to Egypt and Palestine to absorb authenticity, and spent thirty years on the project, this series looks embarrassingly dogmatic today. On the north "pagan" wall are the children of Israel under their oppressors and a frieze of prophets; on the south, the Christian dogma of redemption. On the west wall seven swords representing the seven sorrows pierce the heart of the Virgin, and opposite are the Synagogue, represented as blind and dethroned, and the Church, triumphant. The chauvinistic attitude of these works is an enigma; Sargent's biographers present him as a man who neither evidenced nor practiced any particular religious convictions.

BACCHANTE AND INFANT FAUN, 1896. Bronze, h. 7'.
Courtyard.
★ Frederick MacMonnies (*see Sir Henry Vane above*).

A study in Boston attitudes toward aesthetics and morality, this work is newly reinstalled (1993) after being banished for almost a century. Made when MacMonnies was studying in Paris and given to architect McKim, MacMonnies' benefactor, the nude shocked the Victorian sensibilities of the press and the city's newly formed Art Commission. McKim plucked it out of the Boston Public Library courtyard and gave it to the more worldly Metropolitan Museum of Art in New York. In 1901 MacMonnies made a cast of the work for the Boston Museum of Fine Arts, where it evoked less criticism. During a $21-million library restoration in 1992–3, Boston asked New York to send the original back but was refused; this copy was made from the MFA copy instead.

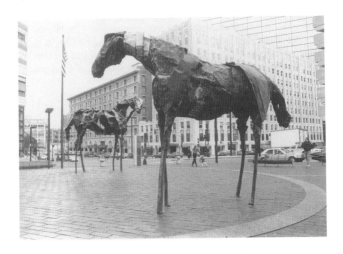

★ PAINT and HENRY, 1987. Welded sheet copper on cast bronze armature, h. 86″ and 89″.
Exterior plaza, Copley Place, Dartmouth and Stuart Sts.
Deborah Butterfield (1949–   ).

Butterfield's horse sculptures are portraits, in a style that has earned her widespread recognition, of the animals she and her husband raise on their ranch in Montana. A Californian, Butterfield received a B.F.A. and an M.F.A. from the University of California at Davis. Her work is owned by such museums as the Hirschhorn in Washington, the Whitney and Metropolitan in New York, by museums in Chicago, Cincinnati, and Jerusalem, and by several corporations.

The artist is also a dedicated dressage rider; her love of her animals and knowledge of their forms and postures enable her to create the unmistakable concept, "horse," in an abstract way (she always leaves the interior armature showing) and with unlikely mediums. For interior spaces, she constructs horses of such found materials as branches, burlap, straw, mud, and corrugated iron. Purchase of Urban Investment and Development Co.

FOUNTAIN, 1985. Granite, travertines, marble, h. three stories by 140′.
Second-floor atrium, Copley Place.
Dimitri Hadzi (see Brookline: *Primavera*).

The verticals here form "symbolic welcoming gates," the artist says. Color and forms were inspired by local architecture such as nearby Trinity Church.

PEOPLE IN THE PARK, 1983. Bronze, six pieces, h. 4′.
In Boylston Park Cafe, Sheraton Boston Hotel, 39 Dalton St.
Richard Duca (see Cambridge [Mount Auburn Cemetery]: *Knoll Garden Sculpture*).

WINGED CARYATIDS, 1990. Pre-cast concrete reliefs, two panels, each h.
12′ × 5′.
Thirteenth floor, flanking the circular window, 116 Huntington Ave.
Syma (1944–   ).

Hingham artist Syma (a.k.a. Marsha Gordon Komarin; her working
name is Hebrew for "rejoice") took a B.S. in psychology at University
of Pittsburgh. She also studied art there, as well as at the Art Students
League in New York, the University of Paris, Mass/Art, N.Y.U., Columbia, and Haystack. She has held a National Endowment for the Arts sti-
pend and numerous artist-in-residence grants, working extensively with
children. She does some pottery and small sculpture she describes as
"inward explorations," but the thrust of her current work is large-scale
brick or concrete reliefs designed in collaboration with architects. (*See
also* Symphony Road Town Houses below, and Somerville [Davis
Square].) Commissioned by JMB/Urban Development Co.

★ BOSTON TAPESTRY, 1962. Cast iron and stained glass, h. 20′ × 60′,
weight five tons.
South Lobby of Prudential Bldg.
Alfred Duca (1920–   ).

A native of Milton, Duca was trained at Pratt Institute and the Boston
Museum School and became active on the Boston art scene during the
years of Boston Expressionism, the 1950s. As a young painter, he
evolved a new artists' medium by hand-grinding pigments into polyvinyl
acetate solvents; he is considered the inventor of polymer tempera
paint. Invited to M.I.T. to experiment with new casting methods, Duca
used them in producing this sculpture for the then-new Prudential Center, at that time the tallest building in New England.

Sand-casting, a traditional means of reproducing forms in metal, ordi-
narily requires a master object made in some other material, such as
plaster, clay, or wood. The master is packed into a mold filled with

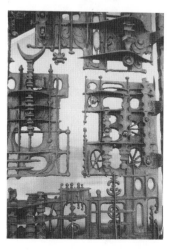

(DETAIL)

hardened foundry sand (sodium silicate stabilized with carbon dioxide gas); the object is then removed, and molten metal is poured into the negative hollows, reproducing the original faithfully. For this work Duca omitted what appears to be the essential step, the original object. Working at an ordinary industrial foundry in Waltham (a firm that customarily cast stoves and manhole covers), he pioneered an innovative method: from full-scale drawings, he carved negatives directly into the sand-packed molds. The pouring then produced an object that had not existed before. To install the eighty-three components, he camped out in the lobby of the unfinished building, casting the Sandwich glass "jewels" and installing them on the spot. Vandals have pried out and stolen many of these over the years. The huge screen with its variety of images evokes, the sculptor says, the multiplicity of Boston, its historic three hills, "the vitality of its people, the boldness of their lives, their culture and artifacts." During recent renovations to this high-rise complex, the Prudential Co. considered removing the screen. Public outcry encouraged it to change its mind and restore the work instead. In reinstalling the piece, the Pru has placed it on a wall where the glass inserts are out of reach of prying hands. The unfortunate trade-off is that the effect of daylight shining through gemlike glass is lost.

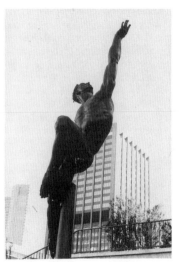

QUEST ETERNAL, 1967. Bronze, heroic size.
Boylston St. side of Prudential Center.
Donald De Lue (*see* Lexington: *George Washington*).

★ WEST FACADE, 1977. Mural, h. seven stories × one block wide.
Boston Architectural Center, 320 Newbury St.
Richard Haas (1936–   ).

Wisconsin-born, Haas was inspired by Frank Lloyd Wright's work there and thought of becoming an architect. He studied art instead, taught printmaking at Bennington College in Vermont for eleven years, then moved on to New York. After some printmaking (a series of New York's cast-iron buildings), Haas painted his first huge tongue-in-cheek mural in 1976 on a facade at Prince and Green Streets in Soho. Perhaps his best-known work is a re-creation of the 1905 New York Times building, demolished in 1965, on the blank shaft of a structure that replaced it. More recently Haas has produced spatial illusions for the underground corridors at the new Smithsonian museums in Washington.

Haas' command of architectural concepts is evident in this trompe l'oeil cutaway drawing of a classic dome-and-buttress structure. Visible from the Massachusetts Turnpike Extension as cars approach the Prudential/Copley exit, Haas' sophisticated satire occupies the entire west wall of the Boston Architectural Center's contemporary concrete structure. Funded by City Walls, New York, and the New York and Boston Architectural Centers.

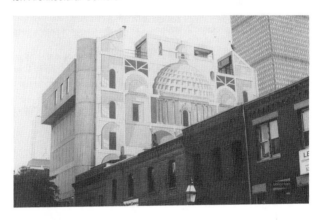

TRAMONT, 1981. Mural on steel panels, h. 18′ × 45′.
354 Newbury St.
Morgan Bulkeley (1944–   ).

Morgan Bulkeley grew up in the remote Berkshires mountain town of Mount Washington, population thirty-two. Educated at Yale, he still summers in Mount Washington, carving wooden sculptures from trees he personally has felled. In winter he occupies a studio in Boston, painting. Bulkeley employs a personal imagery that flirts with surrealism, yet has something in common with the dreamlike concepts of Henri Rousseau and René Magritte. Here, on a building that was once a trolley turn-around station, his iconography mingles with images from Boston history.

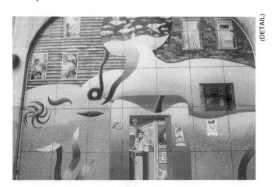

(DETAIL)

ANGEL, 1983. Bronze, h. 5'9".
  At Church Court condominiums, Mass. Ave. and Beacon St.
  Gene Cauthen (*see* Cambridge: *Four Figures*).
  Commissioned by Graham Gund.

CLASSICAL STATUES, c. 1900. Plaster, sixteen statues, heroic size.
  Above upper balcony inside Symphony Hall.
  Reproductions cast by Pietro Caproni.

   As Symphony Hall neared completion at the turn of the century, the architects, McKim Mead and White, and their acoustical advisor, Prof. Wallace C. Sabine, realized the blank wall surfaces above the balconies would create dissonorities. Sabine theorized that concave niches could solve the problem, and that he could also conceal some unsightly experimental acoustic materials in the niches if statues were placed there.

   A committee of civic benefactors selected and donated casts of well-known sculptures from antiquity, all of which can still be seen in European museums. Most were chosen because of some relation to the arts.

   On the audience's right, beginning nearest the stage, the sculptures are:
Faun with Infant Baccus (original at Naples)
Apollo Citharoedus, god of music and poetry (Rome)
Girl of Herculaneum (Dresden)
Dancing Faun (Rome)
Demosthenes, Athenian orator (Rome)
Sitting Anacreon, chief Greek poet of love and wine (Copenhagen)
Euripedes, Greek tragic dramatist (Rome)
Diana of Versailles, goddess of the hunt (Paris)

   From the left, beginning at the stage:
Resting Satyr of Praxiteles (Rome), the inspiration for Hawthorne's novel
   The Marble Faun
Amazon (Berlin), reputed to be the Greek sculptor Polyclitus' winning
   entry in a sculptors' competition for the Temple of Artemis at
   Ephesus, where the legendary female warriors took refuge from
   Dionysus in mythic times
Hermes Logios, messenger and god of science, commerce, travel,
   eloquence, and cunning (Paris)
Lemnian Athena, said to be the greatest work of the fifth-century Greek
   sculptor Phidias (torso at Dresden, head at Bologna)
Sophocles, Athenian tragic poet (Rome)
Standing Anacreon (Copenhagen)
Aeschines, Athenian orator and political opponent of Demosthenes
   (Naples)
Apollo Belvedere (Rome)

BEETHOVEN, 1855. Bronze, larger than life.
  Corridor to Brown Hall, New England Conservatory, 290 Huntington Ave.
  Thomas Crawford (*see* Cambridge [Harvard University]: *James Otis*, and
  Peabody: *Soldiers and Sailors Monument*).
  Presented by Handel & Haydn Society, 1951.

PANELS, 1986. Hand-cast brick, sixteen panels.
  Above windows, all four facades, Symphony Road Town Houses, 47
  Symphony Rd.
  Syma (*see Winged Caryatids* above).

These decorative architectural panels represent the spirit of Boston, with Back Bay (including the Prudential Building) rising out of the waters; a star goddess; Bacchus, god of wine, music, and feasting; swans (symbol of the Public Garden); and art nouveau motifs existing in the area. The artist hand-carved the molds and hand-cast the thirteen to twenty-one bricks that form each panel. Commissioned by architects Strekalovsky & Hoyt.

FENWAY

The Fenway, a green park created by the eminent landscape designer Frederick Law Olmsted, is part of the "Emerald Necklace" of greenery linking Boston Common with Franklin Park.

TENT BAY, 1987. Aluminum, h. 12′ × 34′.
Harry Ellis Dickson Park, Westland Ave. and Edgerly Rd.
Taylor McLean (1943–   ).

A native of Jersey City, N.J., McLean studied at the Art Students League in New York, then earned a degree in art history and a master's in education from Harvard. In the 1960s he apprenticed to sculptor Mirko Basaldella at Harvard's Carpenter Center. McLean is also a jazz percussionist, dancer, and filmmaker; when not making art, he works with children and performs as an accompanist to dance classes.

Although some observers read hints of musical imagery here, the sculptor says the spiral is based on Fibonacci numbers, which describe mathematically the Golden Mean of art, the spirals of the galaxy, and patterns of seashell and plant growth. The title honors McLean's father, who was born in Tent Bay, Barbados. This park is dedicated to Harry Ellis Dickson, longtime associate conductor of the Boston Pops Orchestra and founder of the Boston Symphony Youth Concerts. Funded by the Fund for the Arts.

JOHN BOYLE O'REILLY MEMORIAL, 1896. Bronze and stone.
East end of Fenway and Boylston St.
★ Daniel Chester French (*see* Concord: *Minuteman*).

O'Reilly (1844–1890), Irish-born, was one of the few convicts ever to escape the English penal colony of Australia. He had been a British soldier but, because of Irish nationalist sympathies and/or activities, was accused of treason. A sympathetic priest recognized his promise and arranged his escape: he had to swim to an American ship waiting a mile offshore. Settling here, he became a naturalized Bostonian, poet, and editor of the Catholic publication *The Pilot*. He faces the city, back-to-back with an allegorical Erin flanked by her sons Courage and Poetry. Carvings on the background stone are Celtic calligraphy.

JAPANESE TEMPLE BELL, 1675. Bronze, h. 3'.
Cast under supervision of Suzuki Magoemon.

    This bell was thought to have been donated to the Japanese war effort during World War II but somehow spared. It was "liberated" from a scrap heap in Yokosuku, Japan, in 1945 by sailors from the *U.S.S. Boston* and presented to the city. In the 1950s a group of Bostonians asked whether Japan might like the antique bell back; in reply, the former enemy country donated the bell to Boston as a symbol of world peace. The inscription declares "Priest Koyu states that the bell was dedicated to the Bishamondo at Sendai by Priests Yusho and Sonsai in 1675."

WORLD WAR II MEMORIAL, 1947–49. Bronze and granite, heroic size.
Between Agassiz Rd. and Fenway rose garden.
John Paramino (1889–1956).

    Boston native John Paramino attended North Bennett Street Industrial School; later he was a pupil of Bela Pratt and assisted both Pratt and Saint-Gaudens. Beginning as a designer of commemorative medals and plaques, Paramino cornered the market on plaque production in Boston under Mayor Curley. In 1931 he was accused by a city councillor of running a monopoly and of charging twice the going rate, but his supporters defended him successfully. Many of the city's bronze historical markers are signed with his name.

    This granite ellipse with a winged victory commemorates Boston's World War II dead. Memorial tablets bearing the names of Bostonians killed in Korea and Vietnam were added in 1989.

JOHN ENDECOTT, 1937. Stone, larger than life.
Forsythe Way, near the Museum of Fine Arts.
C. P. Jennewein (*see* Plymouth: *The Pilgrim Mother*).

    One of the six "joint adventurers" who purchased a strip of land (sixty miles wide and extending westward to the Pacific Ocean) from the Plymouth Company, Endecott led settlers of the Massachusetts Bay Colony to join Roger Conat in Salem. He was governor until the arrival of John Winthrop and again after Winthrop's death. Oddly, although he was a member of Roger Williams' congregation at Salem and defended Williams in his difficulties with the colony, Endecott displayed great bigotry and harshness toward Quakers; he was governor at the time Mary Dyer (*see* Beacon Hill/State House: *Mary Dyer*) and others were executed in Boston.

At Boston Museum of Fine Arts (465 Huntington Ave.):

Boston's Museum of Fine Arts, the grande dame of New England art museums, dating from 1870, is said to be second in this country only to the Metropolitan Museum in New York. Superlatives are commonly applied to its collections: finest collection of Chinese and Japanese art in the Western world, examples of Indian painting greater than any in India, Old Kingdom Egyptian sculpture second only to that in Cairo, dozens of renowned "household-word" Impressionist works. Its weakness has been twentieth-century work, a lack for which it has been criticized and which it has tried, by fits and starts, to rectify.

★ APPEAL TO THE GREAT SPIRIT, 1908. Bronze, heroic size.
Huntington Ave. entrance.
Cyrus E. Dallin (*see* Arlington: *Indian Hunter*).

This emotional, perhaps sentimental, work won a gold medal for Dallin at the 1909 Paris Salon. Visitors sometimes express surprise at its presence here; the subject is clearly a Plains Indian. Although he was born in Utah, Dallin lived and taught here, principally at what is now Massachusetts College of Art, for forty years.

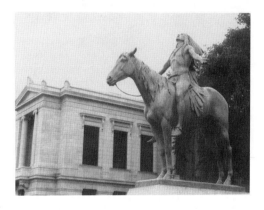

★ TENSHIN-EN, Japanese garden, 1987. 100′ × 120′.
Fenway side of Museum.
Kinsaku Nakane.

Because of its extensive Asiatic collections, the MFA has a long-standing interest in bringing to Boston examples of Japanese art and culture. This garden is a *karensansui*, or "dry mountain water landscape." Its creator, Prof. Kinsaku Nakane, is considered Japan's leading landscape architect, having built more than 300 gardens throughout the world. The name *Tenshin-En* translates, "Garden in the Heart of Heaven." Funded by Yosoji Kobayashi, former president of Nippon Television Network.

RHINOCEROS, installed 1987. Polyester resin, bronze powders, life-size.
Courtyard, Boston Museum School, 230 The Fenway.
Katherine Ward Lane Weems (1899–1989).

A graduate of the Boston Museum School, Weems has animal sculptures at other sites in Greater Boston, including a school of dolphins at the Aquarium, a pair of rhinos at Harvard, and a dog on the Esplanade. Her father was Gardiner Martin Lane, president of the Museum of Fine Arts during construction of the Huntington Avenue building in the early 1900s.

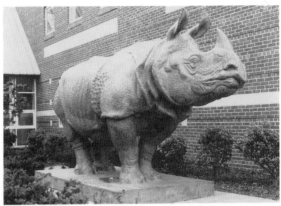

WEEMS, RHINOCEROS

GALLERY: Grossman Gallery, west wing, Museum School.

GALLERY: Massachusetts College of Art, North Hall Gallery, 621 Huntington Ave., entrance on Tetlow St.

GALLERY: Simmons College, 300 The Fenway. Rotating exhibits of Boston-area painters and photographers.

MUSEUM: Isabella Stewart Gardner Museum, 280 The Fenway. Completed in 1903, this Venetian-style palace houses the collection of the nouveau-riche and socially controversial Mrs. Jack Gardner (1840–1924). It is worth visiting simply for the ambience of the atrium courtyard, but it also houses Mrs. Jack's personal collection, acquired with the guidance of Bernard Berenson, which ranges from Greco-Roman through the portraits of John Singer Sargent, not omitting Reubens, Rembrandt, Raphael, Titian, Holbein, Botticelli, Piero della Francesca, Fra Lippo Lippi, Vermeer, Whistler, and early Matisse.

SKY COVENANT, Louise Nevelson, Cor-ten steel facade; ETERNAL LIGHT, George Arons, bronze candelabra and sculpture; ETERNAL LIGHT, Harris Barron, wooden arc door and brass sculpture; STAINED GLASS WINDOWS, Jack Duvas; all 1973. FOUNTAIN, C. Fayette Taylor, 1976. At Temple Israel, 260 The Riverway. Commissioned by the congregation.

At Northeastern University (360 Huntington Ave.):

CY YOUNG, installation planned 1993. Bronze, h. 5.5′. In front of Churchill Hall, off Forsythe St. Robert Shure (*see* Back Bay: *Teddy Bear*).

Boston's first baseball park stood on this site, and sports historians have calculated what are believed to be the exact locations of home plate (reproduced in granite) and the pitcher's mound. On the mound is the immortal Boston Pilgrims pitcher Dalton True "Cy" (for "Cyclone") Young (1867–1955), winningest pitcher in major league history (511 games). In twenty-two seasons with Cleveland, St. Louis, and Boston, he won more than twenty games fourteen times; five times he won thirty or more. His record of 7,377 innings pitched is still unbroken. Poised to begin his windup, Young peers toward the plate as he did in the first World Series in 1903—when he won twice to help Boston defeat the Pittsburgh Pirates. Commissioned by Northeastern University and the Yawkey Foundation.

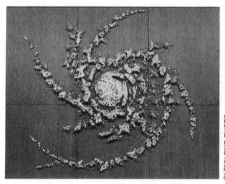

GLENN PIKE PHOTO
COURTESY NORTHEASTERN UNIVERSITY

GALAXY, 1985. Brass on steel frame, h. 64″ × 78″.
   Chapel.
   C. Fayette Taylor (*see* Government Center and Environs: *Upward Bound*).

   Taylor exploits carefully controlled "accidental" effects in this work, melting brass on brass to produce ragged forms.

TERRA COGNITA, 1974. Brass and gold leaf on steel, diam. 44″ on 24″ base.
   Library.
   C. Fayette Taylor (*see* Government Center and Environs: *Upward Bound*).

MOTHER AND CHILD, 1931. Bronze, h. 40″.
   Mugar Life Sciences Bldg.
   Amelia Peabody (1890–1984).

   Peabody maintained a studio in Dover.

HUSKY, no date. Bronze, larger than life.
   Ell Bldg., outside Alumni Auditorium, and at Parsons Field, Brookline.
   Adio di Biccari (*see* Boston Common: *Parkman Plaza*).

CIRCULAR FOUNTAIN, 1984. Granite, h. 9'.
  School of Law.
  Edward P. Monti (*see* Quincy: *Constitution Common Sculpture*).

GALLERY: Northeastern University Art Gallery, 213 Dodge Library.

At Children's Hospital Medical Center (300 Longwood Ave.):

SUNDIAL, 1976. Bronze.
  In Prouty Garden.
  Lu Stubbs (*see* Brookline: *Three Women*).

FOUR SEASONS, 1987. Ceramic mosaic bench, length 126'.
  Winter garden.
  Joan Wye (see MBTA [Davis Station]: *Children's Tile Mural*).

NURSE AND TODDLER, 1988. Bronze, life-size.
  Outdoor courtyard.
  Patricia L. Verani (1927–   ).

  Upon graduation from the Boston Museum School, Verani was awarded the Hunt Scholarship for a year of study in Europe. Although much of her work is in numismatics, in 1979 she won the competition to sculpt the eight-foot Fighting Black Bear for the University of Maine at Orono. A native of Long Island, she now lives and works in New Hampshire. Commissioned by Boston Children's Hospital School of Nursing Alumnae.

DOUBLE SPIRAL, 1990. Bronze, h. 7'.
  Blanche Berenberg Garden.
  Richard Duca (*see* Cambridge [Mount Auburn Cemetery]: *Knoll Garden Sculpture*).

  This abstraction suggests the unfurling of growth and life, the artist says. Commissioned by Children's Hospital.

A GARDEN, 1987. Painted silk, twenty-five banners, each h. 6', various widths from 1' to 8'.
  Lobby, new wing.
  Norman Laliberte (1925–   ).

  Laliberte's work is owned by some sixty corporate, public, and museum collections in this country and Canada. Designer, teacher, muralist, banner-maker, painter, and printmaker, he was born in Worcester of French-Canadian parents and grew up in Montreal. He studied at Illinois Institute of Technology, Chicago Institute of Design (B.S., 1951; M.S. in art education, 1954), the Montreal Museum of Fine Arts, and Cranbrook Academy. As either author, designer, or illustrator, Laliberte has been involved in the production of thirty-five books. His teaching stints include Notre Dame in Indiana and the Rhode Island School of Design.

MR. FROG, 1990. Bronze, h. 32".
  Lobby fountain.
  Lu Stubbs (*see* Brookline: *Three Women*).

FOLK TALES FROM THE FOUR CORNERS OF THE EARTH, 1987. Fabric,
  h. 6' × 10'.
  Entrance, new wing.
  Clara Wainwright (1936–   ).

  Wainwright is originator of two of Boston's favorite festivals, First
Night—the New Year's Eve city-wide arts festival—and the Great Bos-
ton Kite Festival. She attended Winsor School and the University of
North Carolina; in 1986 she was a Bunting Fellow.

MURALS, 1976–87. Mosaic, four units, various sizes.
  Judge Baker Clinic, 295 Longwood Ave., exterior and first and second
  floors.
  Lilli Ann Killen Rosenberg (*see* Newton: *Five Concrete Mosaic Sculp-
  tures*).
  Commissioned by Judge Baker Clinic.

RAIN ON WATER, ROLLING FIELDS, and TREES IN WIND, 1989. Stained
  glass, three windows, each h. 7' × 11'.
  Research Laboratory Auditorium, Binney St. and Longwood Ave.
  Dan Dailey (1947–   ).

  Daily teaches at Massachusetts College of Art, where he originated
the glass program. After earning a B.F.A. at Philadelphia College of Art
and an M.F.A. at Rhode Island School of Design, he won a Fulbright
scholarship to study at Murano, a glass center near Venice. For five
years he was a fellow of the Center for Advanced Visual Studies at
M.I.T.; among his awards are a fellowship from Rhode Island School of
Design and grants from Massachusetts Council on the Arts and the National Endowment for the Arts. He maintains a studio in Kensington,
N.H.

BRIGHAM TRIPTYCH. Wall hangings, three quilts, each approx. 2½' × 3½'.
  Lobby, Hematology-Oncology Division, third floor, Brigham and Women's
  Hospital, 75 Francis St.
  Rhoda Cohen (*see* Natick: *Fiber Revival*).

BANNER, 1982. Appliqued felt, 6' sq.
  Lobby, Dana Farber Institute, 44 Binney St.
  Norman Laliberte (*see* Fenway [Children's Hospital]: *A Garden*).

SCREEN, 1977.Triptych in brass, steel, 72" × 84".
  Lobby, Beth Israel Hospital, 330 Brookline Ave.
  C. Fayette Taylor (*see* Government Center and Environs: *Upward
  Bound*).

  This sculpture was originally made for Brookline Hospital, which is
now closed.

At Boston University:

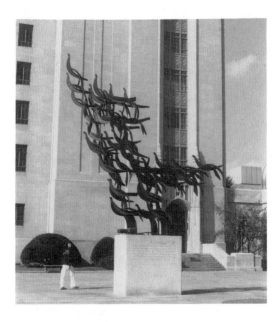

★ FREE AT LAST, 1975. Cor-ten steel, h. 20′.
Marsh Plaza, 740 Commonwealth Ave.
Sergio Castillo (1925–   ).

   A distinguished Chilean artist, Castillo was visiting professor of sculpture at B.U. in 1975, at which time he produced this memorial to Martin
Luther King, Jr. He has more recently been an adjunct professor here
(*see Explosion* below), as well as a visiting professor at the University
of California at Berkeley. Although he maintains a home and studio in
Spain, he has been a professor of sculpture at the University of Chile
for twenty years. Among his forty-five or more public works world-wide
are seven in the United States.

   The Rev. Martin Luther King, Jr. (1929–1968) was the charismatic
spokesman for the Civil Rights movement in the late 1960s, seeking
equality for blacks. He was assassinated by a sniper in Memphis,
Tenn., in 1968.

FOUNTAIN, 1976. Granite, h. 15′.
   Hearst Plaza, in front of B.U. School of Communications.
   Edward P. Monti (*see* Quincy: *Constitution Common Sculpture*).

   Funded by the Hearst Foundation and Robert Bergenheim, alumni
trustee.

EXPLOSION, 1987. Welded stainless steel, h. 24'.
   In front of Metcalf Science Center, 590 Commonwealth Ave.
   Sergio Castillo (*see Free at Last* above).

   Called "the big bang" by the student body, this work was created on
site by Castillo while teaching here. A campus story relates that architects and engineers who saw Castillo's model said it wouldn't work; the
sculpture would have to be held up by guy wires. But the physics department said it could, and the physics faculty has worked with the
sculptor on the project. Commissioned by Dr. Arthur G. B. Metcalf,
chairman of B.U. board of trustees.

COUNTERPOINT, 1983. Stainless steel, h. 12' × 14' × 9'.
   Storrow Dr., behind Marsh Chapel (735 Commonwealth Ave.).
   Russell Jacques (1943–   ).

   Vermont-born, Jacques is a Boston University alumnus who now
lives in Northampton. He describes this work as "an interplay of lyrical
and energetic rhythms."
   Placed on the embankment overlooking the Charles River that is often called "B.U. Beach," this work was intended for the courtyard of
the George Sherman Union. On the day of installation, the crane opera-
tors opined that it was too risky to place it there; this site, perhaps temporary, is a substitute. The material is surgical-quality stainless steel.

MOBALLIZATION, 1992. Mixed media, width 12'.
   Lobby, Engineering Research Bldg.
   George Rhoads (*see* Museum of Science: *Archimedian Excogitation*).
   Gift to the college from the College of Engineering Alumni Association.

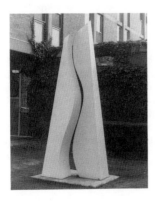

UNTITLED, 1974. Epoxy over ferrocement, h. 8'.
   140 Bay State Rd.
   Gregg LeFevre (1946–   ).

   Gregg LeFevre's parents opposed his boyhood choice of art as a profession, so he took pre-medical courses at St. Lawrence University,
then philosophy at Columbia and B.U., from which he graduated cum

laude. As an alternative to military service he taught in a tough South Bronx school. He and his students combed the streets for materials to make assemblage sculpture, a project so successful he wrote a classroom manual, *Junk Sculpture*. Working in Boston since 1974, LeFevre has evolved a specialty of making detailed bronze maps of cities for pavement inserts; he has created some thirty large-scale works for public and corporate spaces, including NASA, the U.S. State Department, the cities of Boston, Chicago, San Francisco, and Richmond, Va., and the town of Brookline. He also maintains a studio in New York.

PROVINCETOWN WHEELS. Steel, h. $7' \times 12' \times 20''$.
121 Bay State Rd.
George Greenamyer (*see* Marshfield: *Webster, The Farmer of Marshfield*).

UNTITLED, 1974. Epoxy and urethane paint over ferrocement, h. 10′.
Behind Student Union and Mugar Library.
Gregg LeFevre (*see Untitled* above).

ALLSTON/BRIGHTON

BRECK GARDENS PLAQUES, 1990. Ten bronze plaques, $10.5'' \times 34''$.
MEDALLION, 1990. Bronze, diam. 5′.
Oak Sq., Washington and Tremont Sts.
Kate Burke (1952–   ).

A St. Louis native, Burke studied at the Art Institute of Boston and has lived in Boston and Provincetown for the past twenty years. She recently completed for the city of Minneapolis a hundred bronze castings of eighteen designs for public-art manhole covers.

When this little-used square was renovated, neighbors urged Burke to include images from a historic engraving: the schoolhouse once here and the ancient oak tree, which had a hollow that would hold ten kids.

The plaques commemorate the location of the long-gone Breck Gardens at this site. For her cornucopias and eighteen flower cameos, Burke was inspired by Victorian drawings and stylistic motifs from the famous Breck seed catalogs. Medallion commissioned by the Browne Fund; plaques by the Henderson Fund.

MURAL, 1971.
MBTA power station, Washington St. at Oak Sq.
Maria Termini (*see* Back Bay: *Mural*).
Funded by Summerthing.

FAMILY GROUP, 1988. Bronze, h. 6′.
At Veronica Smith Senior Center, 20 Chestnut Hill Ave.
Nick Edmonds (1937–   ).

An associate professor at Boston University School for the Arts, Edmonds earned a certificate from the Boston Museum School in 1962. In

1976 he was a Fulbright Scholar to Japan, studying the reconstruction of a 600-year-old temple and gate.

To create this group of grandparents and grandchildren, Edmonds drew on Japanese wood lamination techniques. In a departure from customary methods, in which figures to be cast in bronze are molded in clay or wax, the sculptor carved the figures in wood and made bronze-casting molds from the wooden prototypes. Scallops from his gouges can be seen if the work is examined closely. Commissioned by the Browne Fund.

WALK IT DOWN, 1985. Varnished Okawara paper, bamboo, leather lacing, cotton cord, h. 12 stories.
Atrium wall, Guest Quarters Suite Hotel, 400 Soldiers Field Rd.
Susan Singleton.

SFERA, 1983. Bronze, h. 3'.
Lobby, Guest Quarters Suite Hotel, 400 Soldiers Field Rd.
★ Arnaldo Pomodoro (*see* Downtown [Hotel Meridien]: *Awakening City*).

At Harvard Business School:

★ PRISMS and TIME-PIECE TOWER, 1992.
Class of 1959 Chapel, Harvard Business School.
(*See* Cambridge [Harvard University].)

KING'S CHAPEL AND OLD CITY HALL

At King's Chapel (Tremont and School Sts.):

SHIRLEY MONUMENT, 1754. Marble.
Peter Scheemakers (1691–1781).

Scheemakers was a native of Antwerp working in London between 1716 and 1771; fourteen of his portrait busts adorn Westminster Abbey. This is his only work in North America, and is likely the first public sculpture erected in Boston.

Shirley, royal governor of Massachusetts Bay Colony (1741–56), erected this plaque alongside his pew in memory of his wife Frances and their married daughter, Frances Bollan, both of whom had died in the previous decade. It is not known which Frances is depicted, but the fulsome Latin inscription extolls the virtues of both.

APTHORP MEMORIAL, 1758. Marble.
Henry Cheere (1703–1781).

A London portrait sculptor, Cheere executed works for William III and Queen Caroline, and was eventually knighted and created a baronet.

The cherub, urn, and plaque commemorate Charles Apthorp (1698–1758), a prosperous merchant and provisioner of the army, who with Governor Shirley was one of the donors who made possible the building of King's Chapel in 1750–54.

SAMUEL VASSALL, 1766. Marble.
   William Tyler (d. 1801), member of the Royal Academy.

   This portrait bust was sent by Vassall's great-grandson Florentius,
who had contributed ten guineas toward the construction of King's
Chapel. Jamaican settler Vassall (1586–1667) refused to pay royal mercantile taxes in 1628 and was imprisoned and ruined financially. He
was later elected to Parliament and awarded damages by that body.
Seeing his ancestor as a predecessor of American colonial protest,
Florentius paid to have a pew removed so the bulky memorial could fit
here.

At Old City Hall (School St. near Tremont St.):

★ BENJAMIN FRANKLIN, 1856. Bronze, larger than life.
   In front of Old City Hall.
   Richard Saltonstall Greenough (*see* Cambridge [Harvard University]: *Gov-
   ernor John Winthrop*).

   This may be Richard Greenough's finest work; here he understood
that Bostonians wanted their "very own" Franklin, not an abstraction.
The Massachusetts Historical Society provided a suit of Franklin's
clothes, and the sculptor labored to render Franklin, he said, as
"thoughtful, dignified, of kindly expression, and un(self)conscious." Two
of the bas-reliefs on the pedestal (scenes from Franklin's life) are by
Greenough; the other two, the signing of the Declaration of Independence and the Treaty of Paris, were Thomas Ball's first public commission.
   Franklin (1706–1790), most famous scientist, inventor, journalist, philosopher, and ambassador of colonial America and the young Republic,
was born on Milk St. in Boston. He apprenticed here to his brother
James, publisher of *The New England Courant*, sometimes called "the
first sensational newspaper in America." At age seventeen he left for
Philadelphia. Funded by public subscription.

★ JOSIAH QUINCY, 1879. Bronze, larger than life.
   In front of Old City Hall.
   Thomas Ball (1819–1911).

   Son of a Charlestown house and sign painter, Ball began his career
as a self-taught portrait painter. It did not go well, and he found other in-
come as a church choir soloist. Turning to portrait busts, Ball found success with images of Jenny Lind and Daniel Webster, later mass-
duplicated for public sale. At age thirty-five Ball went to study sculpture
in Florence, returned to Boston for eight years during which he constructed the equestrian *Washington* for the Public Garden and other
works, then settled in Florence for the next thirty years, dean of the expatriate American artistic community.
   Josiah Quincy (1772–1864), third of at least six generations to bear
that name, lawyer and author, served in the Massachusetts Senate, the
U. S. Congress, as mayor of Boston (1823–29), and finally as president of Harvard College. Before the century was out his son and great-
grandson, also Josiah Quincys, served as mayors of Boston.

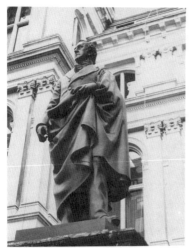

BALL, JOSIAH QUINCY

CITY CARPET, 1983. Ceramic, brass, and stained concrete, 25′ sq.
In front of Old City Hall.
Lilli Ann Killen Rosenberg (*see* Newton: *Five Concrete Mosaic Sculptures*).

It was on School St. that Boston Latin School, with its unique concept of free education (for boys only, however), was established in 1635. Although it has long since moved, Boston Latin remains a prestigious public school and the oldest educational institution in the country, antedating Harvard by a year. Rosenberg's "carpet" is a hopscotch diagram, but details within its borders recall old-fashioned games and Boston traditions. Latin's motto, beneath its image, translates "Work conquers all—Opportunity for all." Commissioned by Townscape Institute.

BOSTON: THE SHAPING OF A CITY, 1993. Acrylic, four walls, each 18′ × 15′, and ceiling, 15′ × 15′.
School St. lobby.
Joshua Winer (*see* Back Bay: *Newbury Street Mural*).
Campari Knoepffler (*see* Cambridge [Harvard Square]: *Harvard Square Theater Mural*).
Olga Voronina (1960–   ).

Built in 1865 in elaborate Second Empire style, Old City Hall served the city until the development of Government Center in 1968. In rehabilitating the structure, the new owners were required by city fire codes to gut the interior. The mural on the wall facing the entrance was painted in 1984 by Winer and his original partner, Knoepffler. Along with fool-the-eye architectural detail, the names of Boston's mayors are inscribed in typestyles reflecting the eras in which they served. The rest of the vestibule has been decorated by Winer and Voronina, a Russian-born artist trained at Leningrad Academy of Art.

MURAL.
  Inside Old City Hall, Court St. entrance.
  Elizabeth Carter (*see* Cambridge [Central Square]: *Floating Down Mass. Avenue*).

·DOWNTOWN·

GIANT BOSTON LANDMARK CHESS SET, 1991. Balsa wood composite, plywood, metal, h. 5′, board 29′ × 29′.
  The Games Project/Chess Makes Kids Smart and the Boston Society of Architects.

  Listed here only because BSA headquarters are downtown, this work is likely to be found in any part of the city—a giant portable chess set, it goes wherever there are kids and festivals. The concept of activist and psychiatrist Dr. Michael Cherney, who was familiar with similar giant public sets used in Europe, this set was created largely with in-kind donations and volunteer labor. Architects Joseph Mamayek and Mark Moeller of Jung Brannen designed the pieces: an "old" side painted brick red whose king is the Custom House and pawns are Beacon Hill row houses, and a "new" steel-blue side with a Prudential Center king and triple-decker pawns. Other pieces are the new State House, Old North and Trinity churches, the Longfellow Bridge, the Grain Exchange, and Park Plaza Castle (all red); and the Hancock Tower, 75 State Street, 125 High Street, Tobin Bridge, the Federal Reserve Bank, and new City Hall (all blue). Funded by private donations and given to the City of Boston.
  A predecessor of this set, still sometimes seen, is a yellow-and-red cardboard set designed by William Hubbard, professor of architecture at M.I.T., at Cherney's request.

TAPESTRIES, 1979.
  Boston Five-Cent Savings Bank, 10 School St.
  Jane Bell, Fritz Stewart, and Edward Fields.
  Commissioned by Boston Five-Cent Savings Bank.

COURTYARD GATE, 1987. Wrought iron, h. 9½′ × 10′.
  Washington and Milk Sts., entrance to Orange Line State St. Station.
  Albert Paley (1944–   ).

  Born in Philadelphia, Paley lives in Rochester, N.Y., where he is a professor at New York State University College at Brockport. He received a B.F.A. (1966) and an M.F.A. (1969) from Tyler School of Art, Temple University. His interest in the handmade object, both wood and metal, has led to film and video documentaries. Before coming to Brockport in 1972, he taught at the School for American Craftsmen at Rochester Institute of Technology. Paley has styled this one-of-a-kind gate in the Art Nouveau tradition of the early twentieth century.

VIEW OF BOSTON HARBOR FROM PEMBERTON HILL, 1829. Tempera
on canvas, 95″ × 180″.
Lobby, One Boston Pl., Washington and State Sts.
★ Robert Salmon (ca. 1775–ca. 1846).

Probably self-taught, Robert Salomon exhibited his marine paintings
in England and Scotland until 1828, when he emigrated to Boston and
simplified his name. To establish his reputation here, he began work on
several large-scale panoramic views, exhibiting this and eighty other
works in 1829 in the newly built Quincy Market. He gained the patronage of collectors and philanthropists (a number of his works are at the
Boston Museum of Fine Arts and at Peabody Museum, Salem) and
worked here for fourteen years. At one time he exhibited alongside Gilbert Stuart, Asher Durand, and John James Audubon; he is considered
an important influence on what is now called the Luminist School, painters of light-in-landscape. He returned to Europe and died, possibly in
Italy; his last works are dated 1845.

The painting is on long-term loan from its owner, the Society for Preservation of New England Antiquities, to Equitable Real Estate, which donated funds for its restoration.

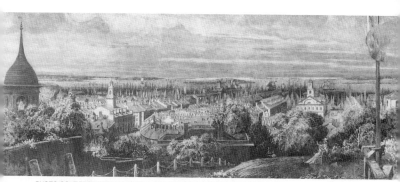

PHOTO COURTESY EQUITABLE REAL ESTATE INVESTMENT MANAGEMENT, INC.   (DETAIL)

GALLERY: The Vault Gallery, 1 Boston Pl., at Washington and State Sts.
An exhibition space new in mid-1987, this gallery is located at The
Boston Company/Boston Safe Deposit and Trust. It focuses on new
regional talent. Open business days only.

MILK STREET MURALS, 1986. Painted wall, h. two stories × approx. 12′.
31 Milk St., near Broad St.
Richard Haas (*see* Back Bay: *West Facade*).
Commissioned by Windsor Building Associates.

HUNGARIAN MONUMENT, 1988. Bronze, h. approx. 20′.
Liberty Sq., Milk and Kilby Sts.
E. Gyuri Hollosy (1946–   ).

Hungarian artist Gyuri Hollosy is associate professor of sculpture
and drawing at Bethany College, Lindsborg, Kan. He received a B.F.A.

from Ohio University and a master's from Tulane University. He has done three other major memorials, in Ohio and Louisiana.

In 1956 a student-led anti-Communist uprising in Hungary gave that iron-curtained nation an illusive week of freedom. Soviet tanks crushed the revolt and reimposed the repressive regime, and 200,000 refugees fled the country, many to the Boston area. The thirtieth anniversary of the short-lived revolt was marked in Boston by the dedication of this sculpture. Sponsored by the Hungarian Society of Massachusetts, with funding from the Browne Fund, Liberty Square Park Associates, and private donations.

GALLERY: Concourse Gallery, 225 Franklin St., at State Street Bank and Trust Co. Rotating exhibits; open business hours.

★ *At Post Office Sq., Milk, Pearl, Congress, and Franklin Sts.:*

THE CREATURE POND, 1982. Bronze, granite, diam. 14′.
Collaboration: Lowry Burgess, Donald Burgy, John Cataldo, Carlos Dorrien, Robert Guillemin, David Phillips, Sydney Roberts Rockefeller, William and Clara Wainwright.

Site of the first post office in America in 1639, this square had been occupied by a horse fountain and memorial to Dr. George Thorndike Angell, founder of Massachusetts Society for the Prevention of Cruelty to Animals. By 1975 it was severely neglected. Citizen advocates raised funds and recruited artists to revive the square in a collaborative effort. The artists wanted to continue the animal theme set by the Angell memorial; to forestall vandalism, they tried to make the work as "lovable" as possible. Funded by the Browne Fund.

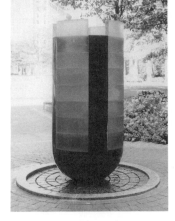

INSTALLATIONS WITH FOUNTAINS, 1992. Cast glass, bronze, granite. South Plaza fountain, h. 5′, diam. 30″; North Plaza fountain, h. 11′, diam. 9′, diam. granite seating walls 29′.
Howard Ben Tré (1949–   ).

Ben Tré's signature style, aqua-tinted glass cast in large translucent chunks, has caught the imagination of the art world and rapidly carried his career to prominence. After studying ceramics at Portland (Me.)

State University (B.S.A., 1978), Ben Tré concentrated in sculpture glass at Rhode Island School of Design (M.F.A., 1980). He has twice been awarded fellowships from the National Endowment for the Arts and the Rhode Island State Council on the Arts, among others; his work is owned by major international collections. He lives in Providence, R.I.

The unsightly parking garage that occupied this site was banished below ground in 1988 and the 1.7-acre space remade by interested citizens and abutters working with the city government. Twenty firms and individuals formed Friends of Post Office Square, Inc., and raised a million dollars to launch the project; proceeds from the public/private venture are earmarked for the city's neighborhood parks. The project has won several awards, most notably from the American Institute of Architects in 1991.

Although Ben Tré's style is more readily recognized in the smaller fountain, the concept is his: to create two intimate spaces, independent yet in dialogue with each other. His classical forms refer to Boston's characteristic architecture; the sculptures, functioning as garden ornaments, reinforce the feeling of the park as an oasis in the urban desert. The sculptor planned the fountains without any pools to stand empty during the winter, but a misguided contractor installed the ring seen in the photo; it is to be removed. Funded by Friends of Post Office Square.

DANCING TRELLIS—TRANSFORMING LIGHT INSTALLATION, 1992. Computerized lighting system, 143′ long.
In trellis.
Ross Miller (1953–   ).

One of the more innovative of Boston's public artists, Miller has been involved in Reclamation Artists (*see* Charlestown: *Site #1*). It was his idea to have forty artists make art tables at The Loading Zone restaurant, and his Christmas-light designs sparkle in season over Harvard Square and Downtown Crossing. A native of Cambridge, England, he took a degree in environmental visual studies at Harvard.

Among works of art unlikely to be identified as such is Miller's installation here. The trellis is draped with lights run by a computer mechanism; they seem quite ordinary except that every five to seven minutes they go crazy, spiraling, blinking and jumping in unpredictable ways, leaving the viewer wondering what was seen. Commissioned by Friends of Post Office Square.

ORNAMENTAL FENCE, 1990. Cast iron, h. 1.5′ to 3.5′, total length 631′.
FORTY ORNAMENTAL DRAIN GRATES, 1990. Cast bronze.
Richard Duca (*see* Cambridge [Mount Auburn Cemetery]: *Knoll Garden Sculpture*).
Commissioned by Friends of Post Office Square.

TELEPHONE KIOSKS, LIGHT FIXTURES, FLAGPOLE HOLDERS, ENTRY CANOPY AND "BEACON," GRANITE PAVING, PLANTERS, 1990–92.
Mixed media, varying dimensions; "beacon" h. three stories.

New England Telephone & Telegraph Co., 185 Franklin St.
Ann Sperry and Goody, Clancy & Associates.

A native of the Bronx, Sperry attended the High School of Music and
Art in New York before earning a B.A. at Sarah Lawrence College. In
addition to her sculpture, which is owned by public collections in Europe, Israel, South Africa, and the U.S., she has done theater set and
costume design, video art, and artists' books. Sperry has executed
civic commissions in Seattle and in Lausanne, Switzerland, in addition
to this one.

This spruce-up of an aging building was cited in 1993 by the Boston
Society of Architects as a particularly successful "seamless" collaboration between artist and architect.

At Hotel Meridien (250 Franklin St.):

AWAKENING CITY, 1962. Brass, h. 6'.
★ Arnaldo Pomodoro (1926–   ).

Pomodoro's feel for intricacy and detail is attributed to his early career with his brother Gio as a jewelry-maker, largely self-taught.
Arnaldo later worked in Milan as a stage designer, a profession that
added a sense of drama to his art. He has taught in California.

Pomodoro's gleaming forms, their flawless exterior skins eroded to
reveal complex inner detail, gained international popularity a quarter-
century ago. In 1964 Pomodoro won the grand prize for sculpture at
the Venice Biennial. Commissioned by The Beacon Companies.

HAGAR IN THE DESERT, 1947–57. Bronze, h. 30".
★ Jacques Lipchitz (*see* Cambridge [M.I.T.]: *The Bather*).

EXODUS, 1982–84. Mixed media, framed.
Edward Giobbi (1926–   ).

Giobbi has been a Guggenheim Fellow and Ford Foundation grant
recipient. His works are owned by the Boston Museum of Fine Arts, the
Whitney, and the Art Institute of Chicago; he has been artist-in-residence at Dartmouth College. A native of Connecticut, he now lives in
Katonah, N.Y.

ABRAHAM LINCOLN AND SALMON P. CHASE; GEORGE WASHINGTON,
ALEXANDER HAMILTON, AND ROBERT MORRIS. Murals, each 8' × 8'.
N. C. Wyeth (*see* Needham: *Wyeth Paintings*).

Done when this building was the Federal Reserve Bank, these two
murals depict important figures in United States financial history. (For
Hamilton biography, *see* Commonwealth Avenue: *Alexander Hamilton*.)
Morris (1734–1806) was a prosperous Philadelphian businessman, con-
servative enough to oppose the Declaration of Independence at first.
He did sign it, as a member of the Continental Congress, and became
the chief finance officer of the Revolution. Scraping together requisi-
tions from the states, loans from the French, his own private credit, and
money from his own pocket, Morris provided the means for Washington's army to move to Yorktown for the decisive final battle of the war.

He was offered the office of Secretary of the Treasury by Washington but deferred to Hamilton and was elected to the Senate. Speculation in Western land eroded his fortune, and ironically the man whose credit was once better than the government's spent three years in debtor's prison.

Lincoln's Secretary of the Treasury during the early years of the Civil War, Chase accomplished two great innovations: establishment of a national banking system, and issue of legal tender paper currency. A lawyer and early opponent of slavery, he argued that slavery laws were local and could not be established by the Constitution; he became known in Ohio as "attorney general of fugitive slaves." He served in the Senate, failed to secure the Republican nomination for President in 1860, and in 1864 was appointed Chief Justice of the Supreme Court, an office he held until the end of his life.

NORMAN B. LEVENTHAL MAP COLLECTION, 30 pieces (*see* Waterfront, Boston Harbor Hotel).
Julien Bar and other locations.

MARITIME SCENES, 1924. Oil on canvas, four units, each h. 15' × 12'.
Lobby, Bank of Boston, 100 Federal St.
N. C. Wyeth (*see* Needham: Wyeth Paintings).

Although he spent most of his career in Pennsylvania, Wyeth returned to his birthplace, Needham, for two years and painted this series at about that time for the original First National Bank building. A pictorial marine history, these four paintings depict important eras: the first maritime traders of the Mediterranean, the age of galleons, the age of clippers, and the age of steam. A fifth work from the series is at the Peabody Museum. Temporarily removed for an asbestos abatement program, the murals are to be rehung in July 1994. The lobby is open from 7 a.m. to 6:30 p.m.

GALLERY, 36th floor, Bank of Boston. Open to the public during business hours, this corridor displays changing exhibitions from Bank of Boston's collection. It is closed at the noon hour because the area doubles as an executive dining room. The gallery will be closed from January 1994 to January 1995 for asbestos abatement.

CROSSING, 1975. Painting on canvas, h. 12½' × 15'.
Lobby, Shawmut Bank, 1 Federal St.
Friedel Dzubas (1915–   ).

Teacher of painting at the Boston Museum School, Dzubas was born in Berlin but fled Germany in 1939. In the 1960s he held two Guggenheim fellowships and another from the National Council on the Arts. He has been visiting artist at Cornell, New York University, Dartmouth, Sarah Lawrence, and University of Pennsylvania. Widely collected, his work is owned by two dozen museums, including the Metropolitan, Guggenheim, and Whitney museums in New York, Boston Museum of Fine Arts, the Phillips Collection in Washington, and Yale, Brandeis, and Cornell universities.

This painting is representative of Dzubas' "staining" technique, an innovation of the 1950s. The painter leaves the canvas unprimed and thins his paint to a stain, so the fibers absorb the pigment; instead of resting on the surface, the color becomes visually part of the canvas.

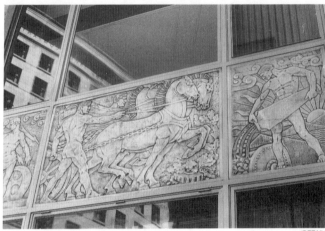

(DETAIL)

★ ART DECO PANELS, 1930. Bronze.
75 Federal St., surrounding exterior of the building.
Paul Fjelde (b. 1892).

When H. N. Gorin Associates renovated this building in 1987, cleaning the decorative exterior bronze panels was not part of the original plan. Someone decided to do it anyway, and the results were stunning; the bronze looked like gold leaf. The metal has been sealed and the owners say they plan to maintain it. The panels are grouped into six themes: Finance, with a beehive representing thrift, an owl for wisdom watching a clerk record investment in a ledger, and a family receiving the benefits; Architecture and Sculpture (the sculptor carves a griffin, which represents the arts); Trades essential to building (carpenter, mason, blacksmith); Transportation; Power (horse, water, and electric); and the three basic industries, agriculture, manufacturing, and mining.

Of Norwegian extraction, Fjelde was born in Minnesota, attended Minneapolis School of Art and the Art Students League in New York, then taught at Pratt Institute. He was a member of the Society of Beaux-Arts Architects, dedicated to promoting the traditional Beaux-Arts principles. His architectural sculpture was commissioned in Norway as well as in this country.

ROBERT BURNS, 1917. Bronze, larger than life.
Winthrop Sq., junction Otis and Devonshire Sts.
Henry Hudson Kitson (*see* Lexington: *The Minuteman*).

Burns (1759–1796), considered the greatest of Scottish poets, author of "Auld Lang Syne," among hundreds of other songs and poems, is depicted walking with his collie dog. Originally intended for the Public Garden, this statue was shunted to the Fens and stood there in obscurity for fifty years; it was relocated downtown in 1975. Presented to the city by Burns Memorial Association.

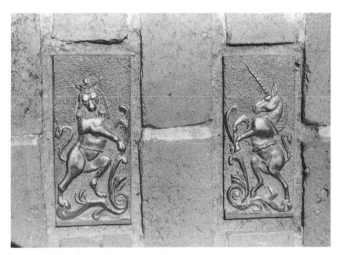

(DETAIL)

BOSTON BRICKS, 1985. Bronze, more than one hundred brick-sized units.
Winthrop Lane, off Winthrop Sq. between Arch and Otis Sts.
Gregg LeFevre (*see* Fenway [Boston University]: *Untitled*) and Kate Burke (*see* Allston/Brighton [Oak Square]).

HELION, 1975. Molded polyethylene, aluminum, h. 26′, diam. 16½′.
Cabot, Cabot & Forbes Bldg., 100 Summer St.
Robert Amory (*see* Burlington: *Windhover*).

This work is from a series that Amory calls "windflowers"; mounted on ball bearings, the twenty-four orange disks move in the wind, as does the entire "flower head." It is popularly called the Lollipop Sculpture. Funded by 1% for Art.

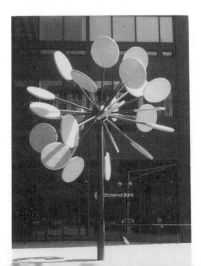

MURAL, 1973. Plaster, carved and painted, h. approx. 8' × 10'.
At Provident Institution for Savings, 30 Winter St.
Constantino Nivola (1911–   ).

   Born in Sardinia, Nivola learned such skills as masonry, plastering,
stucco work, and woodcarving from his father. He studied art in Milan,
worked as art director for the Olivetti Co., then migrated to the United
States in 1939. His work draws upon the terra cotta traditions of his
birthplace. After a stint at *Interiors* magazine, he became director of the
Design Workshop, then a visiting professor at Harvard and at Harvard
Graduate School of Design. He has taught at Columbia, International
University of Art in Florence, the University of California at Berkeley,
and has been artist-in-residence at the American Academy in Rome.
Commissioned by the Provident Institution for Savings.

At Federal Reserve Bldg. (Atlantic Ave. and Summer St.):

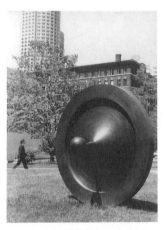

LIFE FORCE, 1989. Bronze,
   h. 7'9" × 4',
   #1 in edition of 6.
   Plaza south of
   Federal Reserve Bank.
   David Bakalar (1924–   ).

   A high-tech entrepreneur turned sculptor, David Bakalar studied physics at Harvard before entering M.I.T. to earn a doctorate in physical
metallurgy. Briefly a consultant for the Marshall Plan and then a Bell
Telephone Laboratories engineer working on transistor development,
he founded his own company, Transitron Electronic Corp., in 1952. At
the age of sixty he retired to devote himself to sculpture. All his work
has roots in his technological background. Anonymous donation.

ZAG FOUR, 1968. Stainless steel.
   Lobby.
   Beverly Pepper (*see* Government Center and Environs: *Sudden
   Presence*).
   On indefinite loan.

TIMELESS COLUMN. Marble.
   Lobby.
   Colette Perazio-Itkin.

_ bla

OMINOUS IKON SERIES VIII, 1977. Steel h. 8'.
Lobby.
Dennis Kowal (*see* Wellesley [Babson College]: *Ominous Icon #6* and *Yaddo Study*).
Gift of Rita and Samuel Robert.

MURALS, 1968. Acrylic on cotton duck.
Lobby.
Hugh Stubbins.

Stubbins, a Cambridge architect, also designed this building.

GALLERY, Federal Reserve Bank, 600 Atlantic Ave., across from South Station.
Curated exhibits, often featuring Boston-based arts organizations; open business hours.

CHINATOWN

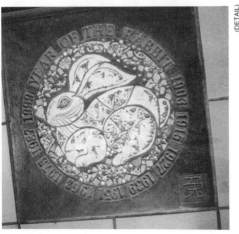

(DETAIL)

CHINESE ZODIAC, 1986. Mosaic walkway, twelve floor panels each 2' sq., and wall mural h. 4' × 5'.
First floor interior, China Trade Center, Washington and Boylston Sts.
Lilli Ann Killen Rosenberg (*see* Newton: *Five Concrete Mosaic Sculptures*).

The Chinese calendar assigns to each year in its twelve-year cycle an animal, whose characteristics determine the traits of those born in that year. The floor panels identify the years of this century associated with each animal; the mural outlines the character traits associated with each sign. Commissioned by the Bay Group.

CHINA GATES, 1982. Ceramic.
Beach St.
Jung/Brannen Associates.
Funded by the Browne Fund.

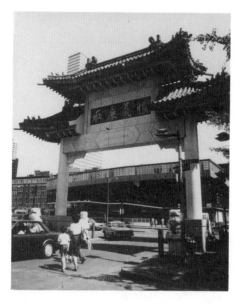

MURAL, 1970.
Chinese Merchants' Association Bldg., Hudson and Beech Sts.
Dan Hueng and Bob Uyeda.
Funded by Summerthing.

BRITA, 1988. Bronze, life-size.
New England Medical Center, 750 Washington St., Breast Health Center, Biewend Bldg., sixth floor.
Lu Stubbs (*see* Brookline: *Three Women*).

Funded by donations in memory of Mary Ann Deterling, wife of former chief of surgery Ralph Deterling.

CONFUCIUS, ca. 1984. Bronze, h. approx. 30″.
At Chinese-American Civic Association, Tyler St., near Oak.
Taiwanese artist, name unknown.

The sage whose thinking permeates China's cultural traditions, Confucius (551–479 B.C.) was born to an impoverished noble family. His clan name was K'ung; the boy was called Ch'in, meaning hill, because of the prominent bump on his forehead. His literary name is Chung-ni, but he is referred to as K'ung Fu-tzu, or Grand Master K'ung. He was supervisor of parks and herds for another noble clan;

then at the age of twenty-two began a school for those who wished to be instructed in the principles of right conduct and government. For a time he was influential in the government of Lu. Centuries before Christianity, he expressed the Golden Rule in negative form: "What you do not like when done to yourself, do not do to others." Gift to the Chinese Consolidated Benevolent Association of Boston from the government of Taiwan.

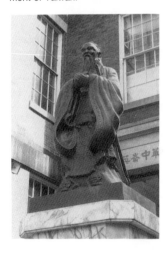

UNITY-COMMUNITY, 1986. Paint on masonry, h. 40'.
34–36 Oak St.
David Fichter (*see* Lawrence: *Bread and Roses Mural*) and Wen-ti Tsen (1936–   ).

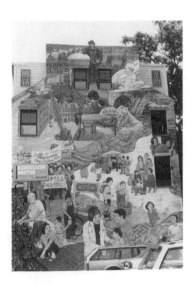

Wen-ti Tsen grew up in China, moved to Europe, and now lives and works in Cambridge. After art studies in London and Paris, he earned a diploma at the Boston Museum School and was awarded a traveling scholarship to study in Pakistan. He has taught at the Boston Museum School and, for three years, in Lebanon. Interested in using art for progressive purposes, he has created comic-strip books about social problems, in addition to a sophisticated body of painting and installation work.

Community residents, children and adults alike, were invited to help paint this mural depicting the history of Chinese immigration into Boston. The story begins with laborers brought here as contract workers for the construction of the old telephone exchange building; it continues through other trades and segues into contemporary life in Chinatown. Funded by Massachusetts Council on the Arts and Humanities; sponsored by Quincy School Community Council.

SOUTH END/ROXBURY

At Roxbury Community College, 1234 Columbus Ave.:

NYAME BIRIBI WO SORO, 1991. Mahogany, copper, porcelain enamel, 10′ × 5′.
Resource Library, second floor, Academic Bldg.
Napoleon Jones-Henderson (1943–   ).

A native of Chicago, Jones-Henderson earned a certificate from the American Artists and Student Center at the Sorbonne in Paris, graduated from the Art Institute of Chicago in 1970, and took a master's degree at Northern Illinois University. He is executive director of the Research Institute for African and African Diaspora Art and of the Edward Everett Hale House. The title of these ceremonial doors translates, "God There Is Something in Heaven."

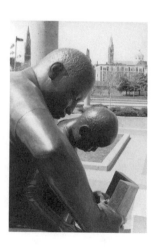

FATHER AND CHILD, 1990.
  Bronze, h. 7′.
  Plaza between Media Center
  and Administration Bldg.
  John Wilson
  (*see* South End/Roxbury:
  Eternal Presence).

THREE FIGURES, 1965. Cor-ten steel, h. 8′.
    Courtyard, Castle Sq. Project, 438 Tremont St.
    Alfred M. Duca (*see* Back Bay: *Boston Tapestry*).

    This work is cut entirely from 1″ steel plate.

. UNTITLED, 1988. Four stained-glass windows, each h. 1′ × 2′.
    Entrance doors, Rosie's Place, 889 Harrison Ave.
    Linda Lichtman (*see* Cambridge [Central Square]: *Untitled*).
    Commissioned by Rosie's Place.

WORCESTER SQUARE GROUP, 1989. Bronze, h. 8.5′.
    Worcester Sq., off Washington St.
    Gene Cauthen (*see* East Cambridge: *Four Figures*).

    To evoke the era in which the bowfront houses around this square
    were built, Cauthen's figures hint of Victorian women and children out
    for a walk. Commissioned by the Worcester Square Neighbors Associa-
    tion; funded by the Henderson Fund.

WEST CANTON STREET CHILD, 1992. Bronze, h. 27″.
    West Canton St. and Warren Ave.
    Kahlil Gibran (1922–   ).

    Inventor as well as artist, Gibran attended the Boston Museum
    School but did not graduate. A tripod he designed was recently bought
    by the Museum of Modern Art in New York for its collection; he also
    holds a patent on an energy furnace that burns a combination of met-
    als called thermite, yielding heat plus water and oxygen as by-prod-
    ucts.
    This sculpture is a gift of the artist in memory of James and Anne
    Hayes, recognizing their contribution to the neighborhood.

GROUND RELIEF, 1982. Stone and concrete.
    Roxbury Youthworks, 135 Dudley St.
    Susan Hoenig.

THE UNITED STATES OF MIND, 1970. Acrylic on masonry, h. 15′ × 50′.
    Roxbury Comprehensive Clinic, Tremont and Lenox Sts.
    Collaboration: Paul Chin, Paul Goodnight (*see* MBTA [Ruggles Station]:
    Mural), Periwinkle, Gary Rickson (1942–   ).

    Rickson says his philosophy about art is, "put it outside, where the
    people are. It's like music on the radio; they'll absorb it, and it will
    come back out of them, like music." A life-long Roxburian, Rickson was
    an active organizer of neighborhood mural production in Roxbury in the
    early 1970s. He was a minister at twenty-one, then for ten years a ra-
    dio personality on WHRB, Harvard University radio. Rickson studied
    painting technique with Don Berry of Roxbury; he has held a National
    Endowment for the Arts fellowship. More recently he has become a
    landscape contractor and is in charge of campus maintenance at Rox-
    bury Community College. Of the other muralists, Periwinkle is a Gay
    Head Indian; Chin was simply a young man living in the neighborhood
    at the time.

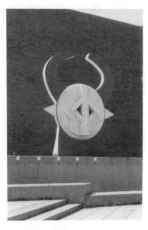

THE JUDGE, 1990. Painted steel, h. 12.5'.
　At Roxbury Municipal Court, Warren and Dudley Sts.
　Vusumuzi Maduna (1940–　　).

　　Born Dennis Didley, Maduna was given his African name ("Keeper of the Culture") by South African friends almost a decade ago. He grew up in Cambridge and graduated from the Museum of Fine Arts School in 1967. Co-founder of the gallery specializing in work of black artists at Harriet Tubman House in the South End, he was for a time guidance counselor and art teacher at UMass/Boston. For the past fifteen years he has devoted himself to his art, which draws profoundly on his African-American heritage. His work was included in the landmark traveling exhibition "Black Art: Ancestral Legacy" originated by the Dallas Museum of Fine Art. In this piece Maduna captures the geometric strength of the art of the Dogon people of East Africa. Commissioned by the Browne Fund.

THE BRIDGE, INC., 1972. Acrylic mural, 5' × 8'.
　At The Bridge (community center), 537 Mass. Ave., interior.
　Gary Rickson (*see The United States of Mind* above).
　Gift of the artist.

BEN'S CIRCULAR TOWER, installation planned 1994. Granite, glass, solar-powered light, h. 10' × 22' diam.
　McLaughlin Park, Parker Hill Ave.
　Mags Harries (*see* Chelsea: *Bellingham Square*).

　　As a memorial to Ben Beland, a leukemia victim, Harries has designed a ruined castle turret with a child-sized reading area inside. Centerpiece and counterfoil to the 180-degree view is a glass rock that will store solar rays during the day and glow at dusk, to represent the boy's spirit. Commissioned by the Browne Fund.

MURAL, 1991. Enamel on copper, h. 40" × 16'.
　Youth and Family Services Bldg., Dimock Community Health Center, 1800 Columbus Ave.
　Napoleon Jones-Henderson (*see* Roxbury Community College: *Nyame Biribi Wo Soro*).
　Commissioned by Dimock Community Health Center.

CHILDREN ARE OUR FUTURE, 1991. Acrylic, h. 30' × 20'.
Atrium wall, Youth and Family Services Bldg., 1800 Columbus Ave.
David Fichter (*see* Lawrence: *Bread and Roses Mural*).
Commissioned by Dimock Community Health Center.

VIVA MOZART PARK, 1987. Mural on masonry, h. 7' × 180'.
Mozart Park, Mozart and Bolster Sts.
Bayardo Gamez (1951–   ) and Baltazar Gutierrez (1959–   ).

As part of a cultural exchange program, these two Nicaraguan artists, chosen by the National Center for Popular Culture in that country,
were brought to Boston to paint this community-participation mural.
Sponsored by Arts for a New Nicaragua.

AFRICA IS THE BEGINNING, 1969, and AMERICA IS OUR BEGINNING
THRU MEDITATION, 1975. Exterior murals, each approx. 30' × 50'.
Roxbury YMCA, 401 Warren St. at Martin Luther King Blvd.
Gary Rickson (*see The United States of Mind* above).
Funded by Summerthing.

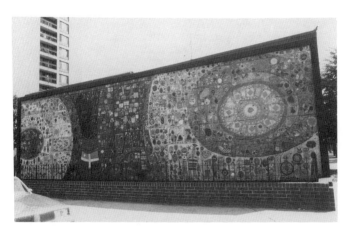

★ BETANCES MURAL, 1977–78. Ceramic, h. 14' × 45'.
Courtyard, Villa Victoria housing project, Aguadilla St.
(formerly West Newton St.), south of Tremont St.
Lilli Ann Killen Rosenberg (*see* Newton: *Five Concrete Mosaic Sculptures*).

When Villa Victoria project was built, a pre-existing electric power station remained like a sore thumb in one of the courtyards. An activist
group at the project thought its wall would be a prime site for a mural
and sought out Rosenberg, who was teaching at the South End Settlement House. Together they wrote a funding proposal that Boston Edison accepted. More than 300 children and residents made clay pieces
which Rosenberg organized into this colorful collective statement. The
portrait of Betances was sculpted in cement by Rosenberg, a process
calling for speed and a sure hand. Into the wet concrete she mixed ad-
ditives including iron oxide, which gives the work its reddish color plus

greater plasticity; nevertheless, she had to complete the sculpture in less than three hours.

Dr. Ramon E. Betances (1827–1898) is called "the Abraham Lincoln of Puerto Rico"; he freed his own slaves and was exiled after causing several abortive uprisings against the Spanish colonial government. The inscriptions read, "Let us know how to fight for our honor and our liberty," "The clay in this mural was made by neighbors and groups from Villa Victoria," and "a gift from the Hispanic community to this and future generations." Sponsored by Casa del Sol and the Emergency Tenants Council; funded by Boston Edison Co.

VIVA VILLA VICTORIA, 1989. Acrylic, h. 13′ × 30′.
Exterior, Jorge Hernandez Cultural Center, 85 West Newton St.
David Fichter (*see* Lawrence: *Bread and Roses Mural*).

Tracing the history of Villa Victoria, this mural fills what was once a window of a church; Fichter's design hints of stained glass. Funded by the Browne Fund and Boston University Hospital.

IN PRAISE OF HANDS, 1976. Ceramic mural, h. 7′ × 4′.
Exterior, Charles E. Mackey Middle School, 90 Warren St.
Mackey students and Lilli Ann Killen Rosenberg (*see* Newton: *Five Concrete Mosaic Sculptures*).

I'VE BEEN TO THE MOUNTAIN TOP, 1982. Acrylic on plywood.
Martin Luther King School, Laurence Ave.
Dana Chandler (*see Knowledge Is Power* below).
Funded by Martin Luther King School.

KNOWLEDGE IS POWER/STAY IN SCHOOL, 1972.
Warren Ave. and Zeigler St.
Dana Chandler (1941–   ).

A graduate of Massachusetts College of Art, Chandler was born in Lynn, lives in Newton, and now is a professor at Simmons College. He was founder and is director of the African American Master Artists in Residency Program at Northeastern.

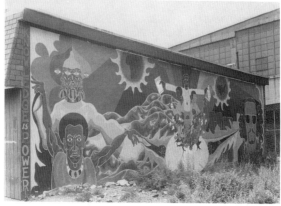

DANA CHANDLER PHOTO

VALUE LIFE, 1974. Acrylic on masonry, h. three stories.
Braddock Park, West Newton and Carleton Sts.
Gary Rickson (*see The United States of Mind* above) and VALUE students.
Funded by ICA VALUE program.

BLACK WOMEN, 1970. Mural, acrylic on masonry, h. three stories.
Columbus Ave. and Yarmouth St.
Sharon Dunn.

Although the mural itself is in fair condition, the upper courses of
brick are deteriorating. Funded by Project '70 and Summerthing.

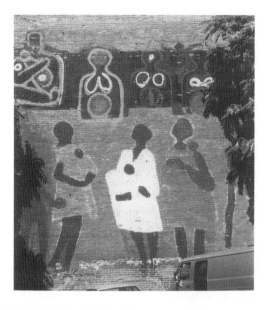

FREDERICK DOUGLASS, 1976.
1002 Tremont St.
Arnold Hurley and Gary Rickson (*see The United States of Mind* above).

Rickson painted the background for this mural, but to do the figure
he recruited Hurley, a portrait painter in the African American Master
Artists in Residency Program at Northeastern.
Douglas (1817–1895), born into slavery as Frederick A. W. Bailey,
was secretly taught to read and write by the wife of a family he served
in Baltimore. Apprenticed as a ship caulker, he made his escape to
New York masquerading as a sailor. For greater safety he went on to
New Bedford, Mass., and changed his name to Douglass. In 1841 he
created a sensation with an extemporaneous speech in Nantucket, was
appointed an agent of the Massachusetts Anti-Slavery Society, and began to speak extensively for the cause of abolition. Accused of being
an imposter, he responded by writing his autobiography, *Narrative of
the Life of Frederick Douglass, an American Slave*. Fearing his

recapture, his friends sent him to England on a two-year lecture tour, and during his absence raised funds to buy his legal freedom. He published an anti-slavery weekly, *The North Star*, continued to lecture even after the Civil War, and late in life served as consul-general to the Republic of Haiti.

BEAUTIFUL PEOPLE COMING TOGETHER IS TRUTH, 1971. Mural, 8′ × 10′.
William Monroe Trotter School, 135 Humbolt Ave.
Gary Rickson (*see The United States of Mind* above).

SELF DISCIPLINE/FAMILY DISCIPLINE, 1971. Mural, 60′ × 50′.
Interior, Lena Park Community Center, 150 American Legion Hwy.
Gary Rickson (*see The United States of Mind* above).

The fifteen-foot figure here is Jubal, in African myth the first storyteller.

CITYSCAPE III, 1984. Painted steel h. 7½′ × 7′ × 2½′.
West Concord St. Park, at Shawmut and West Concord Sts.
Miriam Knapp (1934–   ).

Brookline sculptor Miriam Knapp was born in France, educated at Bennington College, Columbia University, and the Boston Museum School. Her steel sculpture appears minimalist but is not; it is a landscape (or cityscape) drawing in space. Knapp calls this series of works "landscapes of the mind." Sited by HOME, Inc., Rutland Housing Associates, and West Concord Street Homeowner's Association with funding from the City of Boston and the Browne Fund.

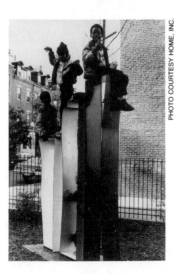

PHOTO COURTESY HOME, INC.

MARCUS GARVEY, 1980. Acrylic on masonry.
Exterior, Marcus Garvey Center, Roxbury and Shawmut Sts.
Bra Sharihed and James E. Newton.

Garvey (1887–1940), born in Jamaica, was founder of a black nationalist movement advocating self-help, race purity, and social separation. He founded the Universal Negro Improvement Association, a militant newspaper, *Negro World*, and the Black Star steamship line intended to link black communities in the United States and the Caribbean. In dealings with its stock, he was accused of mail fraud and was convicted and jailed. Deported to Jamaica, Garvey never regained his effectiveness as a leader, but his concept of racial pride persists.

WALKWAY MEDALLIONS, 1992. Bronze, five plaques, each diam. 28″.
Cedar Sq. Park, Cedar St., off Washington St.
Gregg LeFevre (*see* Fenway [Boston University]: *Untitled*), Theodore Green, Gevel Marrero, Sylvester Odoms, Stalin Valerio, and Lee Ware.

Commissioned to do a work reflecting the history of Fort Hill, LeFevre visited art teachers at all the schools in Roxbury and picked five teenagers to choose themes. Each student did a plaque of his own design: towers and slices of Roxbury buildings, the zoo at Franklin Park, an abstraction of the elevated railway torn down in the late 1980s, and historic figures who have lived nearby: artist Gilbert Stuart, colonial governor John Winthrop, patriot Joseph Warren, and Black Muslim leader Malcolm X. Commissioned by the Browne Fund.

MURAL, 1984. Exterior paint, h. 12½′ × 100′.
Beulah Pilgrim Holiness Church, 455 Blue Hill Ave.
Elizabeth Carter (*see* Cambridge [Central Square]: *Floating Down Mass. Avenue*).

Populating the mural are figures from the neighborhood and from Boston black history, including Judge George Ruffin, singer Roland Haynes, and sculptor Meta Fuller.

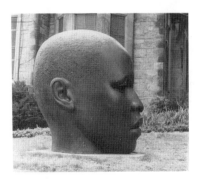

★ ETERNAL PRESENCE, 1987. Bronze, h. 8′.
In front of National Center for Afro-American Artists, 300 Walnut Ave.
John Wilson (1922–   ).

Professor emeritus of sculpture and drawing at Boston University, Wilson was born in Boston and studied art at the Boston Museum School. He worked under painter Fernand Léger in France and later worked in Mexico, where muralists had a profound influence on his work. There Wilson turned toward what he calls "democratic" forms of expression, public art and printmaking. He worked for a time in Chicago and New York before coming to B.U. in 1964. In 1986 he was commissioned to create the portrait bust of Martin Luther King, Jr. for the U.S. Capitol. This monumental head is, the artist says, "a symbolic black presence infused with a sense of universal humanity." It memorializes the 350-year history of black people in Massachusetts. Commissioned by Elma Lewis.

THE LAST MASK, 1988. Polychromed steel tubing, rubber, h. 11′ × 5′.
At NCAAA, 300 Walnut Ave.
Howard McCalebb (1947–   ).

McCalebb, a New York artist, was born in Indianola, Miss. He earned his B.A. at California State University at Haywood and his M.A. at Cornell; from 1973 to 1975 he taught sculpture at UMass/Amherst. His work has been shown at the Museum of Harlem and in galleries at Cornell, in San Jose, Cal., and in Charlotte, N.C. He is working on commissions for Hotos Community College in the Bronx and for the Louis Armstrong Cultural Center in New York City.

Functioning as linear drawing in space, the tubular pipes here outline abstracted, geometricized mask shapes. After this work was exhibited in Boston at the Artists' Foundation at City Place, the NCAAA arranged an extended loan from the artist.

ROSIE, 1984–85. Fiberglass and wood, h. 5′ × 8′ × 8′.
At NCAAA, 300 Walnut Ave.
Robert Tinch, Jr.

Born in Roxbury, Robert Tinch, Jr. studied at the University of Hawaii, Hunter College, the New York Studio School, and New York University. He has taught at Wesleyan University, Sacred Heart University, and the Silvermine School of Art.

FIRST BREATH, 1993. Latex paint, h. ten stories.
East wall of Summerfield Self-Storage, Traveler and Harrison Sts.
Wyland (1956–   ).

Described as a cross between Jacques Cousteau and P. T. Barnum, Wyland (he has dropped his first name for promotional purposes) dedicates himself to painting megamurals to raise public awareness of marine creatures. Born in Michigan, he learned airbrush painting technique through the art program at Lamphere High School in Madison Heights, Mich. A certified diver, he says he was inspired by marine researcher Cousteau. Thanks to publicity generated by the murals, Wyland's smaller paintings and sculptures are carried in galleries worldwide. Using automotive airbrush, he draws his fish and whales directly on the wall without preliminary sketching. This mural, featuring a female humpbacked whale raising its newborn to the surface for its first gulp of air, was the third of a series of seventeen created in East Coast cities in a period of seventeen weeks. Funded by in-kind donations and sales of books, T-shirts, and souvenirs.

At Boston City Hospital (818 Harrison Ave.):

YES AND NO, 1977. Two mobiles, bronze.
   Lobby.
   Artist unknown.
   Gift of Mrs. Benjamin Jeffries.

GEN. LEONARD WOOD, 1931. Bronze plaque, h. 4'.
   Entryway, Administration Bldg.
   Bruce Wilder Saville (*see* Quincy: *The Doughboy*).

ABRAHAM SHUMAN, 1920. Bronze plaque, h. 4'.
   Entryway, Administration Bldg.
   Fred K. W. Allen.

SOUTH BOSTON

CYBELE, 1889. Bronze, h. 64".
   In front of Boston Design Center, Marine Industrial Park, Summer St.
   ★ Auguste Rodin (*see* Wellesley [Wellesley College]: *Walking Man*).

   A contemporary casting (1986) from a plaster original by the great
   French master, this *Cybele* is one of three in the U.S. It is said to be a
   study for Rodin's *Gates of Hell* series, bas-relief doors based on
   Dante's *Divine Comedy*. In the religion of Phrygia (an ancient country
   occupying what is now northwest Turkey), Cybele, the Great Mother,
   was a principal deity. Her cult competed with those of Greek and Roman gods until the second or third century A.D. Casting commissioned
   by Lucy Billingsly and Trammell Crow Co.

THE DIALOGIA SERIES, 1988. Fabric and bamboo, seven fan-shaped
   elements, each h. 9' × 16'.
   Interior, overhead, Black Falcon Cruise Ship Terminal, Drydock Ave.
   Napoleon Jones-Henderson (*see* South End/Roxbury: *Nyame Biribi Wo
   Soro*).
   Commissioned by Massport.

ICESKATES, 1982.
   Warming room, Francis L. Murphy Rink, Day Blvd.
   Elizabeth Carter (*see* Cambridge [Central Square]: *Floating Down Mass.
   Avenue*).
   Funded by 1% for Art.

CERAMIC TILE PANELS, 1983. Two units, h. 30" × 18".
   Exterior walls, Marine Park sanitary.
   Joan Wye (*see* MBTA [Davis Station]: *Children's Tile Mural*).

   Wye's small murals echo the marine theme of this area: dolphins
   (outside the men's room) and four species of food fish (outside the
   women's room). Funded by 1% for Art.

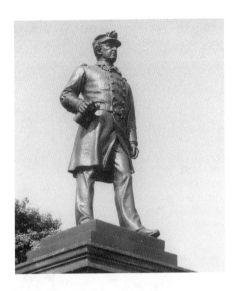

ADMIRAL DAVID GLASGOW FARRAGUT, 1893. Bronze, larger than life.
Marine Park, William J. Day Blvd. and Broadway.
Henry Hudson Kitson (*see* Lexington: *The Minuteman*).

Foremost naval hero of the Civil War, Tennesseean Farragut
(1801–1870) entered the U.S. Navy at the age of nine, and was competent enough to command a prize ship when he was twelve. His bold
seamanship enabled Federal ships to blockade the South, capture New
Orleans, cut off Vicksburg during Grant's siege, and control the Mississippi. It was while his fleet was penetrating the heavily mined and fortified Mobile Bay (mines were called torpedoes at the time) that the
admiral uttered his famed "Damn the torpedoes! Full speed ahead!"
Commissioned by the city on petition of South Boston Citizens Association.

JAMES BRENDAN CONNOLLY, 1987. Bronze, larger than life.
Columbus Park, Old Colony Ave.
Thomas Haxo.

An Artists Foundation fellowship winner in 1987, Haxo lives in western Massachusetts.
Long-jumper James Brendan Connolly, a South Boston boy, won the
first event in 1896 in Athens and thus became the first gold-medal winner of the modern Olympics. Underwritten by the Browne Fund.

WAVES, 1992. Forged, colored galvanized steel, h. 11′ × 60′ × 5.5′.
Gateway, Harbor Village, Mary Ellen McCormick Housing Development,
305 Old Colony Ave.
Dimitri Gerakaris (*see* Cambridge [Harvard Square]: *Longfellow Memorial*).

Mirroring the sea nearby, Gerakaris' wrought-iron waves gather force
and break into a frothing archway on granite "breakwater" gateposts.
Commissioned by the Browne Fund.

DORCHESTER

SCIENCE CONTROLLING THE FORCES OF STEAM AND ELECTRICITY
and LABOR, ART AND THE FAMILY, c. 1882. Marble, h. 30′.
Near Franklin Park Zoo.
Daniel Chester French (*see* Concord: *Minuteman*).

The Philadelphia centennial in 1876, celebrating the United States'
first hundred years, inspired imposing allegorical sculptures representing the virtues and ideals of the expanding nation. Among the first
American artists to sculpt such concepts, French designed these two
mammoth groups for the Boston post office. Brought here when it was
razed, they have been so severely eroded by weather it is hard to tell
whether they were once good or not. Grandiose, odd in scale, they
seem unlike the work of the sculptor whose hand a decade later produced the sensitive Milmore memorial (*see* Jamaica Plain [Forest Hills
Cemetery]: *Death Staying the Hand of the Sculptor*).

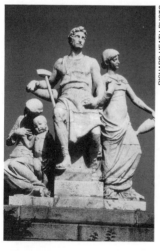

RICHARD HEATH PHOTO

EDWARD EVERETT, 1867. Bronze, larger than life.
Richardson Park (just east of Edward Everett Sq.), Columbia Rd. and
East Cottage.
William Wetmore Story (1819–1895).

Son of a jurist, W. W. Story took a law degree from Harvard, published both poetry and legal textbooks, and dabbled in art as a hobby.
When his father died in 1846, he was commissioned (although he had
never done anything remotely so ambitious) to create a memorial
statue, and promptly sailed to Italy to study sculpture. He and his wife
settled more or less permanently in Rome, center of an expatriate literary circle; Story was the model for the protagonist of Hawthorne's
novel *The Marble Faun*. Something of a dilettante, Story did achieve a
reputation as a sculptor and completed the marble statue of his father,

although it is not considered a strong work. The same may be said of this statue, with its trite declamatory gesture. So ill was it received that it has been moved three times before ending up on this spot.

A Unitarian minister before he was twenty, Everett (1794–1865) abandoned the pulpit to become a professor of Greek at Harvard and editor of *North American Review*. Elected to Congress at thirty and governor of Massachusetts at forty-one, Everett subsequently became ambassador to Great Britain, president of Harvard College, and Secretary of State. Capitalizing on his power as an orator, he toured the nation in an effort to avert the Civil War. He failed, of course, but he donated proceeds of the speaking tour toward the purchase for the nation of Mount Vernon, George Washington's home. Everett was the now-forgotten "other" orator who shared the platform when Lincoln delivered the Gettysburg Address. Funded by public subscription following Everett's death.

WE'RE ALL IN THE SAME GANG, 1992. Outdoor oil paint, 12′ × 52′.
Floyd St. at Blue Hill Ave.
Jameel Parker (1963–   ).

Art teacher Jameel Parker attended Prairie View (Tex.) A&M College before transferring to the Boston Museum School, where he earned a B.F.A. He teaches at Harriet Baldwin School in Brighton and at Cambridge Community Center, and has done temporary interactive works with teenagers for First Night, Boston's New Year's Eve celebration. Originally from Elizabeth, N.J., he now lives in Roxbury.

Looking for art-related summer employment, Parker was referred to the owner of Brooks & Brooks Catering, who wanted a mural that would discourage graffiti on the side of his building. Inspired by the rap record "We're All in the Same Gang," he had begun this mural as a statement against black-versus-black violence when Dominic Mount, 13, was shot nearby. Mount's friends urged Parker to paint the young victim into the mural. Instead Parker changed the right half of the painting, which was to have depicted black women, into a statistical statement about the tragedies of gang warfare.

CODMAN SQUARE MURALS, 1992. Acrylic, eight major murals and fifteen smaller ones, from approx. 12′ × 30′.
Codman Sq. area, primarily on Washington St. between Talbot and Stockton Sts.
Heidi Schork (1958–   ), Monecia Leonard, Sabrina Hargett, Shawn Saint, Narda Shakes, Tricia Thomas, and other members of Boston Youth Clean Up Corps.

Born in Elyria, Ohio, Schork studied communications at Tecnológico de Monterrey. She lived in Mexico for eight years, where her interest in wall painting was whetted by the Mexican mural tradition. Now a Spanish teacher for seventh and eighth grades at Graham and Parks School in Cambridge, she serves on a committee at the mayor's office to promote and continue mural-painting projects in the city.

These murals are intended to come and go with the changing face of the neighborhood. The Codman Square Business Initiative, which has funded some of them, has been successful enough that new businesses have painted signs over some murals. Other walls are provided, however, and mural creation is a continuing project.

Among the current (1992–3) murals are *What Africa Means to Me*, *Not All That Glitters Is Gold*, and a memorial mural to shooting victims of gang wars. The Rodney King mural, *History/Our Story* (done in Egyptian wall-painting style), generated objections from area police, who wanted to whitewash it. The community and the mayor's office opposed such censorship, but agreed to a mural showing the police doing "nice" things—thus the nearby paintings of youthful painters being watched by beat patrol officers and passersby, among whom can be found the figure of Malcolm X.

THE MATHER VILLAGE, 1990. Enamel on copper, h. 22″ × 16′.
Mather School, 1 Meeting House Hill.
Napoleon Jones-Henderson (*see* South End/Roxbury: *Nyame Biribi Wo Soro*).

Designs by students are incorporated by Jones-Henderson into this mural. Commissioned by the PTA of Mather School.

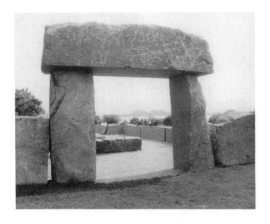

ARCHIVAL STONE, 1989. Granite, h. 11′ × 45′ × 35′.
Courtyard, State Archives Bldg., Columbia Point.
Carlos Dorrien (*see* Waltham [Bentley College]: *Portal*).
Funded by Massachusetts Art in Public Places Program and National Endowment for the Arts.

★ GAS TANK RAINBOWS, 1971. Painted graphic, h. 150′.
Victory Rd.; visible from Southeast Expressway.
Corita Kent (1919–1986).

This rainbow is the largest and perhaps now the best-known work of the printmaker who gained fame in the 1960s as Sister Corita. Born in Fort Dodge, Iowa, and reared in Los Angeles, Corita Kent became a Roman Catholic nun of the Sisters of the Immaculate Heart of Mary at the age of seventeen. She graduated from Immaculate Heart College in Los Angeles, became a grade school teacher in British Columbia, and in 1946 returned to her alma mater to teach art, later becoming head of the art department. In 1951 she earned a master's degree from the University of Southern California. Gaining fame as a print-maker, she exhibited for years at the Botolph Group Gallery (no longer extant) on Newbury Street. Her splashy silkscreened work, laced with humanistic quotations from poets, philosophers, and Scripture, gained such popularity that she was chosen to design the 1985 "LOVE" stamp. She resigned from her Catholic order in 1968, saying, "You should be true to your own conscience. That's a . . . way of saying you know what God's will is." She settled in Boston and contributed her commissions to those causes that support the downtrodden, world-wide.

The idea of having Kent invent a megadesign for the gas storage tanks originated with Eli Goldston (d. 1975), chief executive officer of Eastern Gas and Fuel Co. This design is the largest object ever copy-righted by the U.S. Copyright Office. Commissioned by Project '70 and Boston Gas Co.

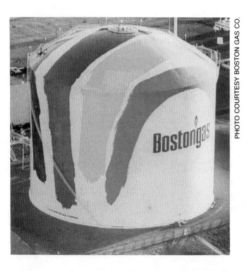

PHOTO COURTESY BOSTON GAS CO.

JAMAICA PLAIN

PARKMAN MEMORIAL, 1906. Marble, h. 20'.
On Parkman Dr., west side of Jamaica Pond.
★ Daniel Chester French (*see* Concord: *Minuteman*).

Francis Parkman (1823–1893), first great American historian, chroni-cled the English and French settlement of North America and the con-flicts of those two nations on this continent. He was the first historian to understand the character and motives of the Native American. Here a chieftain in Iroquois dress represents the five Indian nations about which Parkman wrote.

Victim of a neurological disorder that made him hypersensitive to light, Parkman spent much of his adult life in a darkened room. He had books read to him, and invented a mechanism that helped him take notes and write his manuscripts with his eyes shut. Although of delicate health as a boy, in his teens he undertook a wilderness trip to New Hampshire that fired his ambition to chronicle the French and Indian wars. He became a proficient woodsman; he had a gift for handling horses, both tame and wild—skills that aided him when he and a Harvard classmate spent some months among the Oglala Sioux. These rugged experiences failed to save him from decades as an invalid, through which he persisted with his life work, *France and England in the New World*, twenty-seven years in the writing. A horticulturist by avocation, developer of some new hybrid, he rallied enough to spend his fiftieth year teaching horticulture at Harvard. This monument is on the site of his house in Jamaica Plain.

FISH MURAL, no date. Paint on masonry.
Seaverns Ave. side of Hailer's Rexall Pharmacy, 674 Centre St.
Joseph Scanlon and Christine Cooper.

GALLERY: African American Master Artists in Residency, 76 Atherton St.

MURAL, 1987, installed 1990. Marine enamel on marine plywood, h. 17.5′ × 36′.
Exterior (rear), Hernandez School, 61 School St.
Roberto Chao and students.

As part of a project called Fresh Walls for Egleston, Chao designed this mural beside the playground and recruited students under fifteen to help him paint it. Funded by the Heritage Foundation.

In Forest Hills Cemetery:

Mount Auburn Cemetery in Cambridge pioneered the concept of the parklike "garden cemetery," with landscaping, sculpture, and architect-designed monuments. Forest Hills, consecrated in 1848, followed close behind. There is room here to list only the most prominent works. The cemetery offices will provide maps and a booklet for visitors interested in more detail.

★ DEATH STAYING THE HAND OF THE SCULPTOR, 1892. Bronze relief, larger than life.
Grave of Martin Milmore, just inside entrance.
Daniel Chester French (*see* Concord: *Minuteman*).

The sculptors French and Milmore had neighboring studios in the Studio Building in Boston; when Milmore died at the age of thirty-seven, his family approached French for a memorial. French's concept of the Angel of Death as a woman, dignified, tender, almost maternal, created a sensation; it was hailed as the noblest and most sublime conception ever produced by an American artist. People wrote poems and letters to French about it; clergymen preached sermons. In Paris, where it was cast, it won a gold medal in the spring salon, although the

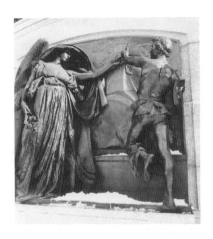

artist was unknown in Europe. French here indulges the popular concept of the sculptor attacking his stone directly with chisel, although
sculptors of the era, Milmore and French included, actually worked in
clay and hired skilled artisans to transfer the model to stone. Milmore is
depicted working on his *Sphinx*, now at Mount Auburn Cemetery, Cambridge.

SOLDIERS' MONUMENT, 1867. Bronze, larger than life.
  Martin Milmore (*see* Framingham: *Civil War Memorial*).

  Although it sometimes seems that a successful monument salesman
traveled New England selling Civil War soldiers leaning on their rifles,
the fact is that many of them are by the same artist, Martin Milmore.
This one was the first.

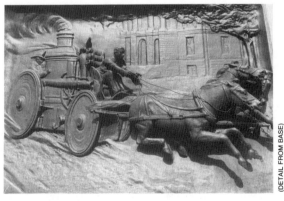

(DETAIL FROM BASE)

FIREMEN'S MONUMENT, 1906. Bronze, larger than life.
  John A. Wilson (b. 1878).

  Not to be confused with the contemporary John W. Wilson, this John
Wilson was born in Nova Scotia and was a student of H. H. Kitson and
Bela Pratt. Commissioned by the Boston Fire Department in memory of
fallen comrades.

ROSLINDALE

STAR POOL, 1987. Stone pavement, 16′ diam. circle.
  Adams Park, Washington St. and Cummins Hwy.
  Be Allen (*see* Somerville: *Flag*).

   Allen here translates her conceptual star patterns, done as a set of
mobile screens in the Somerville police department lobby, into granite,
bluestone, and puddingstone. Commissioned by Townscape Institute.

WEST ROXBURY

DR. JOSEPH WARREN, 1904. Bronze, larger than life.
  At Roxbury Latin School, Centre and St. Theresa Sts.
  ★ Paul Wayland Bartlett (1865–1925).

   A native of New Haven, Conn., son of sculptor Truman Howe Bartlett, Bartlett was sent to France as a schoolboy at the age of nine and
spent most of his life there. He studied at the Ecole des Beaux Arts
and became a skilled animal sculptor, often collaborating with other
sculptors who did not do animals well. His interest lay in historical and
symbolic figures; his Columbus and Michelangelo stand in the U.S.
Library of Congress, and his equestrian Lafayette is in Paris.
   Dr. Warren (1741–1775) was born in Roxbury and was a graduate
and at one time schoolmaster of this second oldest secondary school
in the country, dating from 1645. A graduate of Harvard and a respected physician, he drafted the Suffolk Resolves urging opposition,
by force if necessary, to British taxes. He was president of the third pro-
vincial congress. Commissioned a major general in the Colonial forces,
he was killed in the battle of Bunker Hill (a statue of him by Henry Dexter stands there).
   After sixty years on Warren Street in Roxbury, the statue was displaced by new traffic designs, moved to storage at Franklin Park, and
subsequently rescued by Warren's alma mater in 1969.

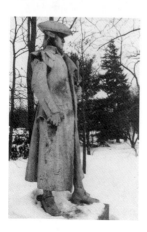

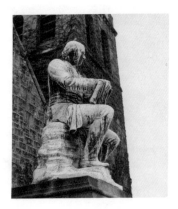

THEODORE PARKER, 1887. Bronze, larger than life.
At Theodore Parker Unitarian Church, Centre St.
Robert Kraus (*see* Boston Common: *Boston Massacre Monument*).

Born in Lexington, Parker (1810–1860) was a grandson of Capt. John Parker, who commanded the militiamen at the Battle of Lexington. A schoolmaster at seventeen, he enrolled in Harvard but pursued his studies while still working at his family's farm, traveling to Cambridge for exams. Entering the theology school, he found himself extremely antagonistic to the popular Calvinist religion of the day. Preacher and reformer rather than thinker/philosopher, Parker was a fearless advocate of emancipation, active in the Underground Railroad, and a friend and supporter of John Brown. Parker's admirers intended this likeness for Boston Common, but the Boston Art Commission refused it. It was stored until 1902, when it was retrieved by members of the First Church in West Roxbury, where Parker had held his first pulpit, 1837–1845. Funded by public subscription.

HYDE PARK

UNTITLED, 1987. Bronze, h. 4′ × 9′ × 4′.
Outside Bajko Rink.
Mark Cooper (*see* Brockton: *Political Trilogy*).
Funded by 1½% for Art.

CELEBRATION OF THE FIGURE EIGHT, 1988.
Stainless steel wall relief, h. 5′ × 20′ × 4′.
Interior, Bajko Rink, Turtle Pond Pkwy.
Peter Lipsitt (1940–   ).

After earning a B.A. from Brandeis, then a B.F.A. and an M.F.A. (1965) from Yale, Lipsitt spent two years in the Peace Corps teaching at Haile Selassie University Laboratory School. He has also taught at Brandeis, Wheaton, Concord Academy, and at the University of Wisconsin, and has held a fellowship from Triangle Artists' Workshop, New York, and a Brookline Arts Council grant. Funded by 1½% for Art.

MATTAPAN

TIME/SPAN, installation planned 1993–4. Brick, granite, steel, polycarbonate
panels, diffraction grating, h. 40′ × 120′.
Two sections: South span, Blue Hill Ave. at River St. and Cummings Hwy.;
north columns, Blue Hill Ave. at Babson St.
Robert Behrens (1939–   ).

   This site-specific sculptor is interested in edges between places—
transitions from rural to urban spaces, for instance. A resident of
Sonoma, Cal., Behrens was born in New Jersey. He studied architecture at Pratt Institute and subsequently earned a B.F.A. from Kansas
City Art Institute in 1965, a graduate degree in environmental design
from the University of Wisconsin in 1966, and an M.A. from the University of Denver graduate school of art in 1972. His grants and fellowships include an Art in Public Places grant from the National
Endowment for the Arts in 1975.
   Among Behrens' commissions are a gateway at the Fairbanks,
Alaska, airport, which he describes as "a gateway into the interior,"
and a mall design in New Orleans, "a gateway to the Mississippi
River." He envisions this gate at the southern perimeter of Boston as
the entrance to the city from the south and as a cultural bridge celebrating the multiethnic history of Mattapan Square. Generated by the community, photographic images silkscreened on the bridge on the south
will be drawn from history; the incomplete north towers, bearing images
of today's youth, represent the possibilities and challenges they face.
Funded by the Browne Fund.

MBTA (Massachusetts Bay Transportation Authority)

*The oldest subway system in the United States (1897), Boston's "T"
during the 1980s underwent a modernization program incorporating
art as each station is renovated.*

ON THE RED LINE: ⟶

*This section of the "T," dating to 1912, was extended in both direc-
tions between 1978 and 1985. Arts on the Line, a collaboration between Cambridge Arts Council and the MBTA, placed a rich set of
installations both under and above ground. Most of the artists live and
work in Massachusetts. Community participation encouraged art indicative of each place.*

Alewife Station:

*The architecture of this end-of-the-line parking garage is sculptural in
itself. It contains six works, all so thoroughly integrated they may not
be recognized as art.*

END OF THE RED LINE, 1985. Neon, $12' \times 300' \times 10'$.
    Above outbound subway platform.
    Alejandro and Moira Sina.

    Kinetic artists using light, neon, and motion as media, Alejandro and
Moira Sina have been collaborating since 1978. Alejandro was born in
Santiago, Chile; he received a master's degree and then taught at the
Universidad de Chile. On a Fulbright scholarship he traveled to M.I.T.
in 1973, becoming a fellow at the Center for Advanced Visual Studies
under Gyorgy Kepes and, subsequently, Otto Piene. Trained in interior
design, Moira began as his assistant. Having grown up in a career
Navy family, she has lived in Boston longer than any place else. They
maintain a studio in Brookline. The Sinas caution that most of their
pieces are more effectively viewed after dark.

    The Sinas' pun, a series of red neon tubes hanging at the terminus
of the northbound track, is typical of the whimsy found in a good deal
of "T" art.

TWO SCULPTURAL BENCHES, 1985. Wood.
    Park-and-ride waiting area.
    William Keyser, Jr.

    Keyser is a Rochester, N.Y., woodworker.

DECORATIVE BRONZE FLOOR TILES, 1985.
    Scattered throughout mezzanine.
    Nancy Webb (*see* Lechmere: *Untitled*).

    Fish and other aquatic creatures hint at the source for the name of
this station: Alewife Brook. (Alewives are a species of herring that,
swimming up freshwater streams to spawn, were once an important
food source on the New England coast.)

PORCELAIN TILE WALL MURAL, 1985. Ceramic panels.
    Rindge Ave. ramp.
    David Davison.

ALEWIFE COWS, 1985. Painted panels.
    Bus waiting area.
    Joel Janowitz.

    This fool-the-eye painting evokes the rural scene that once existed
here at Alewife Brook.

ABOVE GROUND at Alewife Station: *see* North Cambridge: *Environmental
Site Work*.

Davis Station:

POETRY, 1985. Incised brick. Eleven sections, varying sizes.
    Platform, underfoot.
    Richard C. Shaner.

These works may be the hardest of all to find and the most pleasing. Unexpected intellectual fodder beneath the feet of the waiting commuter, they materialize almost as if in answer to the idle thought, "I wish I had something to read." The poems, each about ten bricks long and five wide, quote Walt Whitman, Emily Dickinson, and lesser-knowns, including Shaner himself.

SCULPTURE WITH A 'D,' 1985. Painted aluminum.
Wall, outbound platform.
Sam Gilliam.

Variations on the letter "D" form the design for this wall sculpture.

CHILDREN'S TILE MURAL, 1985. Ceramic tiles.
Mezzanine wall.
Jack Gregory and Joan Wye.

Ceramicists Wye and Gregory are partners in the Belfast Bay Tile Works in Somerville, founded by Wye in 1974. Gregory studied graphic arts and has taught at the Boston Museum School. Wye focused on painting at the Art Students League, New York, and worked in bronze and wood sculpture in Provincetown.
Drawn by children in nearby schools and fired at the tile works, these signed tiles provide an amazing ethnic census.

ABOVE GROUND at Davis Station: *see* Somerville: *Untitled*.

Porter Station:

★ THE GLOVE CYCLE, 1985. Bronze, life-sized gloves.
Placed throughout the station.
Mags Harries (*see* Chelsea: *Bellingham Square*).

★ THE LIGHTS AT THE END OF THE TUNNEL, 1985. Aluminum and mylar mobile sculpture.
Above exit stairs.
William Wainwright (*see* East Boston, Logan Airport: *Windwheels*).

In Wainwright's current work, he uses diffraction gratings—tiny grooves that break up light and create rainbows in the same way a prism does. These forms, crafted to imply three-dimensionality, are in actuality single planes. This work was awarded a Massachusetts Council on the Arts Regional Governors' Design Award in 1986.

ABOVE GROUND at Porter Station: *see* Cambridge [Porter Square]: *Gift of the Wind, Ondas, Embroidered Bollards, Porter Square Megaliths*.

Harvard Station:

STAINED GLASS WALL, 1985, length 110'.
Bus station.
★ Gyorgy Kepes (1906–   ).

The "red line" pun runs through Kepes' glowing blue wall, whose colors evoke the stained glass of the great cathedrals of Europe. Kepes, Hungarian-born, was nurtured among the *wunderkind* in the academy at Budapest until he began to paint in the Cubist style. Expelled, he went to Berlin, London, and finally to Chicago to teach at the New Bauhaus (now the Institute of Design). He taught a course on light, which included photography and much more. He came to the department of architecture at M.I.T. in 1946. Kepes has had a long and distinguished career as a particularly lyrical Abstract Expressionist painter. In 1967 he founded the Center for Advanced Visual Studies at M.I.T., committed to closing the gap between art and technology by using technological media for aesthetic purposes.

NEW ENGLAND DECORATIVE ARTS, 1985. Ceramic tile.
Bus ramp.
Joyce Kozloff.

Designed to mimic quilt patterns, Kozloff's colorful wall mural refers to such regional folk art as weathervanes, ship figureheads, nautical etchings, stenciling, and gravestone carving.

ABOVE GROUND at Harvard Station; *see* Cambridge [Harvard Square]: *Omphalos* and [Brattle Square] *Gateway to Knowledge*.

Central Square Station:

MURAL, 1987. Ceramic, fused glass, and enamel tiles, seven sections, each 4′ × 12′.
Seating bay areas.
Elizabeth Mapelli (1949–   ).

Oregonian Liz Mapelli earned her B.F.A. and M.F.A. at the University of Colorado and followed with post-graduate study at U.C.L.A. and the University of Washington. She is a regular exhibitor at international exhibitions of art glass and has executed a dozen commissions like this in the West.

MEDALLIONS, 1986. Ceramic tile, 100 units, each 12″ sq.
At top of columns.
Dennis Cunningham and Anne Storrs (1953–   ).

Ceramicist Storrs attended the Art Institute of Chicago and the University of Oregon; she has held a fellowship from the Oregon Arts Commission. Cunningham, a printmaker, is a graduate (B.F.A.) of Pacific Northwest College of Art and has been recognized with three Art in Public Places awards.

Kendall/MIT Station:

★ THE KENDALL BAND, 1987. Audiokinetic sculptures, aluminum, stainless steel, teak, three parts: *Pythagoras*, h. 14′ × 48′; *Johann Kepler* and *Galileo*, each h. 11′ × 5′.
Paul Matisse.

Designed for riders to play as they wait, these three musical works are tuned to the same key so their sounds will be harmonious, however randomly they ring. The sixteen aluminum chimes, titled *Pythagoras*, may be played by pulling levers that activate teak hammers; the aluminum ring, *Johann Kepler*, will resonate for five minutes; the sheet steel, *Galileo*, provides what the artist calls "musical thunder." Matisse, grandson of French painter Henri Matisse, lives and works in Groton.

Park Street Station:

★ CELEBRATION OF THE UNDERGROUND (*see* Green Line: *Celebration of the Underground*).

BENEDICTIONS, 1989. Bronze, two units, h. 54″.
Ralph Helmick (*see* Charles River Esplanade: *Arthur Fiedler*).

These forms are constructed of seventy to eighty stacked layers (Helmick's characteristic work style) but, unlike the Fiedler portrait, are then cast in bronze. The artist says these hands "should imply 'safe passage' and 'peaceful welcome,' functioning as generic St. Christopher images." They also indicate "Boston" in American sign language.

Downtown Crossing Station:

GRANITE BENCHES, 1987. Forty units, h. 18″ or 25″.
Randomly placed on platform.
Lewis C. (Buster) Simpson.

Seattle artist Buster Simpson majored in sculpture at the University of Michigan (B.F.A.; M.F.A. 1969), has participated in many collaborative and sound-installation projects, and has worked as consultant and advisor to artistic and historic projects in Seattle.

South Station:

UNTITLED, installation planned 1994. Steel and bronze, 91′ × 91′.
Overhead, lobby, Dewey Sq. entrance.
Jeffrey Schiff (*see* Charlestown: *Untitled*).

Schiff's installation is a metaphor for journeys: near the door, twenty-five cables, like tracks leaving a terminal, leave spools, pass through a barrier, and spread across the ceiling, switching directions and crossing paths, arriving eventually at bronze castings which represent destinations. The artist says the work also represents "any kind of journey, past the threshold toward an object of desire." Commissioned by MBTA.

MUSCLEBOUND FOR MIAMI. Cast iron, h. 7′.
Mayer Spivack (1936–   ).

Dual interests in architectural design and psychiatry have led Spivack to become an expert consultant on the influence of architectural spaces and settings upon human behavior. Spivack attended Boston University and the Boston Museum School before taking a master's in city planning at M.I.T.; he has held grants from the Public Health Service and the National Institute of Mental Health to study the psychological and therapeutic aspects of art and architecture. His multifaceted career comprises kinetic light sculpture, objects such as this, photography, and inventions in the fields of optics, medical equipment, prosthetics, tools, papermaking, navigation, toys, and sporting equipment.

Components of this sculpture are railroad car couplings, two-and-a-half pairs, welded together in a muscular totemic vertical. This is a particularly successful example of what is sometimes termed "junk" sculpture, or assemblage—a work formed from found industrial objects (Spivack likes the term "foundiron"). The artist's eye has perceived the resemblance between these functional parts a human head; he has chosen the repetitions of a totem; he has also seen that three complete heads would be too much and has truncated the top one by using a single coupler. This work is both parody and an entity in itself, a statement at once strong and humorous. Commissioned by Federal Railway Administration.

NEON INSTALLATION. Red neon, 96' × 48'.
Suspended from ceiling, Red Line level.
Christopher Sproat (1945–   ).

Educated at Boston University, the Boston Museum School, and Skowhegan, Sproat has worked in a variety of media, from light to art-as-furniture. He has held grants from the National Endowment for the Arts and the Massachusetts Arts and Humanities Foundation.

MURAL, planned for 1994. Industrial enamel on metal panels, two sections, each h. 6.5' × 30'.
Second story, interior of rotunda, proposed Transportation Center.
Todd McKie (1944–   ).

McKie is a 1966 graduate of Rhode Island School of Design; he now lives in Boston, making ceramics and paintings in a distinctive style full of ethnographic connotations. This design, he says, is about "moving from place to place, whether physically or visually or in your imagination."

Broadway Station:

UNTITLED, 1984. Painted aluminum, sixty forms, h. each 2'–3' on 16' × 40' wall.
Stairway to platform level.
Jay Coogan.

Coogan's black-and-white forms are abstracted from the shapes of tools and functional objects.

CHILDREN'S TILES, 1992. Ceramic, approx. 200 units, each 8" square.
Broadway Station.
Ellen Barton Schorr (1942–   ) and children.

Overseen by Schorr, the tiles were handmade by fourth-, fifth- and sixth-graders at the neighboring Condon School and St. Augustine's

School. Founder of Mudflat Pottery School in Cambridge, Schorr now is owner/operator of Beluga Pottery in Newton. She was born in New York City and received her B.A. from Jacksonville (Fla.) University.

This project was cited by the Boston Society of Architects in its 1993 artist/architect collaboration competition. It also won the highest award in Spectrum '93 Ceramic Tile and Stone Competition sponsored by the Ceramic Tile Distribution Association. Commissioned by MBTA.

Andrew Station:

ANDREW STATION TIME CAPSULE PROJECT, 1993. Assorted boxes and
    containers in an area $10' \times 10' \times 10'$.
    Ross Miller (*see* Downtown: *Dancing Trellis*).

Miller has collected a trove of quotidian items relating to the surrounding neighborhood, such as grocery shopping lists and dirt from playing fields, and sealed some of them into a time capsule to be opened in seventy-five years. He has also asked residents about their relationship with the neighborhood and their hopes and fears for the future; some of those questions are replicated where they can be read. But the boxes stand for "imaginings, hidden and revealed," Miller says.

Ashmont Station:

TWO INTERSECTING SIXTEEN-CELLED POLYTOPES IN A HYPERCUBE,
    1982. Stainless steel wire, eight units, $4' \times 12' \times 20'$.
    Overhead.
    David Brisson (d. 1982).

PHOTOMURALS. Ten $4' \times 8'$ porcelain enamel panels.
    Eugene Richards, Ken Robert Buck, and John Heymann.

Quincy Adams Station:

CIRRUS CLOUDS, 1982. Stainless steel and diffraction mylar. Three sec-
    tions, each $6' \times 24' \times 10'$.
    Overhead.
    Elaine Calzolari.

Calzolari sought to enhance the airiness of the station with sculpture that would react to wind and light, offering different aspects to changes in the hour and the season.

FOSSIL, 1982. Aluminum, h. $7' \times 2'$.
    Red Line car no. 1506.
    Mags Harries (*see* Chelsea: *Bellingham Square*).

This work is a handprint sculpted into a standard aluminum standee pole in a subway car, as if a rider had stood and held onto it so long the metal softened. One critic has written that Harries is interested in forms "indicative of recurrent human situations." A playful (if frustrating) aspect of this work is, as the artist says, "You can never go to find it— it finds you."

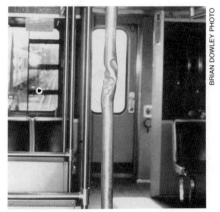

BRIAN DOWLEY PHOTO

HARRIES, FOSSIL

ON THE ORANGE LINE: ⟶

Most of the Orange Line follows the Southwest Corridor, a 4.7-mile strip cleared in 1966 for a massive highway. Thanks to public outcry and more enlightened urban planning, Governor Francis Sargent stalled the plan in 1970, and it was aborted in 1975. Instead, the underground Orange Line was built, and an ugly elevated railway over Washington Street was torn down. The cleared highway corridor has become a park. Poems and prose selections chiseled into granite stelae in or near each station are, along with visual artworks, part of the Arts in Transit program designed by UrbanArts, Inc. of Boston for the Orange Line and funded by the federal Department of Transportation.

A small map, Art, Architecture and Literature on the Orange Line, *is available free from UrbanArts, tel. (617) 864-2880.*

State Street Station:

ABOVE GROUND at State Street Station: *see* Downtown: *Courtyard Gate.*

Chinatown (formerly Essex Street) Station:

COLORS ON THE LINE, 1987. Painted sheet steel, 9′ × 360′.
Safety niches, wall, inbound side.
Toshihiro Katayama (1928–   ).

Printmaker, environmental artist, and graphic designer, Katayama has been a teacher of graphics and visual design at Harvard since 1966. He describes himself as self-taught. Born in Osaka, Japan, he became a free-lance designer, was recruited by Geigy AG to work as a designer for that company in Switzerland, and subsequently was invited to teach at Harvard. His work is included in the collection of the Museum of Modern Art, New York, which also published his collaboration with Octavio Paz, *Visual Poetry*. He is the designer of the Alewife Station "T" sign and the State Street "star" sign.

Reflecting the activities of the subway platform, Katayama's bars are clustered where crowds are dense, sparser where the population of riders thins out. His colors are chosen to set up a tension and dynamism which will appear different from the platform and from the moving train.

New England Medical Center Station:

CARAVANS, 1989. Painted aluminum, four units averaging 17' × 27'.
Stairway walls.
Richard Gubernick (1933–   ).

A graduate of the State University of New York at Buffalo, Gubernick is currently professor of fine arts there. He also holds degrees from the Yale University School of Music and Art and from the University of Massachusetts at Amherst (M.F.A.). Gubernick has constructed a similar wall relief for a transit station in Buffalo.

THE GREAT WORLD TRANSFORMED (Prose).
Gish Jen.

Jen holds degrees from Harvard and the University of Iowa Writer's Workshop. She has been a fellow of the Bunting Institute, the MacDowell Colony, and the Michener Foundation, and has taught writing at universities in Boston and the Midwest. Her short stories have been widely published; her first novel, *A Typical American*, was published by Houghton-Mifflin.

MR. YEE IS IN THE GARDEN (Poetry).
Marea Gordett.

Gordett's poems have been published in such journals as *The Nation* and the *Chicago Review*, and in her volume of poetry, *Freeze Tag*. She has been a resident artist in the Massachusetts Poetry in the Schools program.

Back Bay Station:

NEONS FOR THE BACK BAY/SOUTH END STATION, 1990. Neon, four units, varied sizes.
In arched windows over both entrances to station lobby.
Stephen Antonakos (*see* Waltham [Brandeis University]: *Neon for the Rose Art Museum*).

PHILIP RANDOLPH, 1989. Bronze, heroic size.
Rail terminal lobby.
Tina Allen.

Tina Allen has studied both painting and sculpture in New York and Venice. She lives and works in New York and Los Angeles.
Dean of the Civil Rights movement, A. Philip Randolph (1889–1979) was founder and president of the first recognized black union, the American Brotherhood of Sleeping Car Porters. Many of this union's members settled in Boston not far from Back Bay Station. The son of a clergyman, Randolph was born in Florida and attended City College of New York. In 1917 he launched *The Messenger*, a radical journal that

urged blacks to join labor unions. He planned a 1941 march on Washington that impelled President Roosevelt to issue a fair employment practices order, and after World War II Randolph led the movement to desegregate the armed forces. He became a vice-president of the AFL-CIO. In 1963 he was a director of the March on Washington for Jobs and Freedom.

FAREWELL TO STEAM, 1976–79. Welded steel, 9′4″ × 18′ × 18″.
Amtrak platform #2.
George Greenamyer (see Marshfield: *Webster, the Farmer of Marshfield*).

Formerly at Essex Street Station, this piece was moved to Back Bay in 1990. Funded by MBTA and 1% for Art.

COUNTERPOINT (Prose).
Jane Barnes.

Barnes' short stories and poems have appeared in more than thirty-five literary journals and anthologies; she is the author of three volumes of poetry.

IF MY BOUNDARY STOPS HERE (Poetry).
Ruth Whitman.

Author of seven books of poetry and three translations of contemporary Yiddish poetry, Whitman has been a Bunting Fellow and a Senior Fulbright Writer-in-Residence Fellow. She has been honored with a grant from the National Endowment for the Arts and the Alice Fay di Castagnola Award from the Poetry Society of America.

Massachusetts Avenue Station:

MASSACHUSETTS AVENUE INSTALLATION, 1989. Carbon steel, slotted and textured. Three units, each h. 12′ × 2′ diam.
Suspended over staircase.
Bruce Taylor (1950–   ).

Coloradoan Bruce Taylor has done works for corporate and public sites in Denver and northern Colorado. He holds a B.F.A. from the University of Denver.

I KNOW MY ROBE GONNA FIT ME WELL (Prose).
Peter Rodman.

Currently a technical writer for Lotus Development Corp., Rodman graduated from Hamilton College and Columbia University. He teaches writing at Massasoit Community College, Brockton. His free-lance work has appeared in *Boston Magazine*, *Fate Magazine*, and *The Real Paper*.

DRUM (Poetry).
Sharon Cox.

Cox has been writing for nineteen years. Her work has appeared in such publications as "Alternative House Brochure" and *Radical*

America, and in several anthologies, including *Hear My Soul's Voice*, *Open Windows*, and *Flowers in a Field of Thorns*.

Ruggles Station:

GEOME-A-TREE, 1991. Painted masonry, h. 18′ × 50′.
    Exterior staircase wall.
    Paul Goodnight (1946–   ).

   A former Artists Foundation Fellow, Paul Goodnight attended Vesper George School of Art, Roxbury Community College, and Massachusetts College of Art, taking a B.F.A. in 1975. He has exhibited in China and Africa and has done murals in Nicaragua and Russia, as well as in Boston. Among owners of his work are the Smithsonian Institution and Howard University. Goodnight lives in Roxbury.

STONY BROOK DANCE, 1990. Painted aluminum, thirty units suspended from three 36′ cables.
    Overhead, concourse.
    John T. Scott (1940–   ).

   An alumnus of Xavier University (B.F.A., 1962), John Scott is now professor of fine arts there. He holds a master's of fine arts from Michigan State University. His work is in the collections of the Dallas Museum of Art and Fisk University. He was a 1992 MacArthur Fellowship recipient.
   Scott's art reaches deep into his African cultural heritage. In this kinetic work the long forms are based on the shape of the diddle-bow, a one-stringed African musical instrument.

FOUR LETTERS HOME (Prose).
    Will Holton.

   Associate professor of sociology at Northeastern University, Holton is also a fellow of the McCormack Institute of Public Affairs at UMass/Boston. He founded Discovering Boston Walking Tours, has co-authored a Boston ethnic directory, and writes about Boston neighborhoods.

HARRIET TUBMAN A.K.A. MOSES (Poetry).
    Samuel Allen.

   Poems by Allen have been included in more than 200 anthologies, including *Poetry of the Negro* and *The Poetry of Black America*. He was recipient of an NEA fellowship in poetry, is author of four collections of poems, and is translator of Sartre's *Orphée Noir*. He has taught at Wesleyan University, Tuskegee University, and Boston University, where he is professor emeritus.

Roxbury Crossing Station:

NEIGHBORHOOD, 1990. Sailcloth, five units, one 8′ × 8′, four 8′ × 5′.
    Overhead, lobby.
    Susan Thompson.

   A resident of Dorchester, Susan Thompson attended Hunter College. She teaches at Paige Academy and at the Neighborhood Arts Center in Roxbury, and is a member of the African American Master Artists in Residency Program at Northeastern University.

These banners bear images, both historic and present-day, from the surrounding communities of Mission Hill and Highland Park.

HOMETOWN (Prose).
Luis Virgil Overbea.

Overbea is a reporter for the *Christian Science Monitor*.

AT ROXBURY CROSSING (Poetry).
Jeanette DeLello Winthrop.

Raised in Boston's Mission Hill neighborhood, Winthrop teaches elementary school in Canton.

Jackson Square Station:

FACES IN A CROWD, 1990. Reinforced resin, h. 4′ × 7′.
Wall above outbound track.
James C. Toatley, Jr. (1941–1986).

James Toatley earned both his B.F.A. and M.F.A. (1977) at Boston University; previously, he studied at the University of California at Los Angeles and at Pennsylvania Academy of the Fine Arts. He was awarded a Cresson fellowship for European study. Interspersed with his teaching career, Toatley was sculptor/designer for several toy companies, including Mattel and Hasbro. His teaching stints included Carney Academy in New Bedford, Boston University, Southeastern Massachusetts University, Brockton Art Center, and Philadelphia Art Institute.

Toatley based his design on the "glimpses and short impressions" subway riders get of one another. Following the artist's untimely death, this work was completed by UrbanArts in collaboration with Toatley's widow.

GRANDMOTHERS (Prose).
Christine Palamidessi Moore.

Moore has written reviews and feature articles for many film and video magazines; she is now working on a novel set in Boston's North End. After graduating from the University of Pittsburgh, she pursued graduate studies in writing at Johns Hopkins University.

ANY GOOD THROAT (Poetry).
Christopher Gilbert.

Author of a new book of poems, *Demos/Music of the Striving That Was There*, Gilbert has been repeatedly honored for his work: two NEA fellowships, the 1986 Robert Frost Award and residency at the Frost Center, and the 1983 Walt Whitman Award from the Academy of American Poets. He was editor of two anthologies of Black American and third world literature. He teaches psychology at Bristol Community College, Fall River.

Stony Brook Station:

LIFE AROUND HERE, 1990. Ceramic tile, h. 8'9" × 40'.
   Lobby.
   Malou Flato (1953–   ).

   Texan Malou Flato completed her bachelor's degree in theater arts at Middlebury College in 1975. She has executed public and corporate commissions in Texas, California, and Washington. This work depicts people and scenes from the surrounding neighborhood.

THE DINNER (Prose).
   Rosario Morales.

   Morales is author of "Getting Home Alive," written with her daughter. Her short stories and nonfiction articles have appeared in feminist journals and anthologies.

MRS. BAEZ SERVES COFFEE ON THE 3RD FLOOR (Poetry).
   Martin Espada.

   Lawyer and poet, Espada was recently awarded the first PEN/Reuson Foundation fellowship for his third book, *Rebellion Is the Circle of a Lover's Hands*. He has also held fellowships from NEA and Massachusetts Artists Foundation. His poems have been widely published, and were included in *Under 35: The New Generation of American Poets*.

Green Street Station:

COLOR PASSAGE, 1990. Stained glass, painted perforated metal. Twenty units, ranging from 3' × 5' to 3' × 10'.
   Temporarily removed; to be suspended in front of windows, station interior.
   Virginia Gunter (*see* Needham: *Color Sweep*).

   Much of Gunter's earlier art, based on her interest in fabric and sewing, exploited light and shadow on netting gathered into sculptural forms. Although her medium here is larger and coarser, her interest is again in light transmitted through translucencies.
   "T" engineers, ignoring the artist's recommendations, have had some difficulty hanging these pieces properly. Reinstallation is promised, although the date is vague.

REFLECTIONS (Prose).
   Daria MonDesire.

   Born in Roxbury, MonDesire received a B.A. in literature from Bennington College and an M.S. from Simmons College. Her writing has been published in *The American Literary Review*. She is author of *Screams*, a collection of poetry and short stories, and is now working on a novel.

DRIFT (Poetry).
   Mary Bonina.

   A graduate of the M.F.A. writing program at Warren Wilson College, Bonina has worked with the Massachusetts Poets in Schools program and has edited the magazine *The Little Apple*. In 1980 she received an award for achievement in poetry from the Educational Association of Worcester.

Forest Hills Station:

TRANSCENDENTAL GREENS, 1990. Aluminum, seventeen units approx. 14′ × 12′.
Lobby and exterior walkway.
Dan George (1949–   ).

A former artist-in-residence at Bennington College, Dan George has done site projects for Poughkeepsie and Lake George, N.Y. He was educated at Academie v. Shönekunsten in Antwerp, Belgium, and at the Art Students League in New York, and has been awarded grants from the New York Foundation for the Arts, New York State Council on the Arts Works in Public Places, and Collaborations in Art, Science and Technology.
George's leaf forms, attached to concrete columns, evoke the nearby open space of Franklin Park and Arnold Arboretum.

LIES (Prose excerpt).
Ethan Canin.

Short stories by Canin have twice been anthologized in *Best American Short Stories* (1985 and 1986). His work has appeared in *The Atlantic*, *Esquire*, and *Ploughshares*. He is author of two novels, *The Blue River* and *Emperor of the Air*.

THE SUBWAY COLLECTOR (Poetry).
Thomas Hurley.

Hurley teaches writing at UMass/Boston, runs tutorial writing programs at Simmons College, and reviews poetry and music for the *Cambridge Chronicle*. Born in Albany, N.Y., he holds a B.A. in English from Siena College and an M.A. from the University of Virginia. He lives in the South End.

ON THE GREEN LINE: ⟶

PHOTOMURALS, 1975.
North Station.
Col. H. S. Bingham Associates.
Funded by MBTA.

★ CELEBRATION OF THE UNDERGROUND, 1976–78. Ceramic and found objects, h. 10′ × 110′.
Park Street Station.
Lilli Ann Killen Rosenberg (*see* Newton: *Five Concrete Mosaic Sculptures*).

This mural is located at the site of the initial excavation for the oldest subway system in America, opened in 1897; the braces seen between the panels are the original supports for the first tunnel. Alongside the

turn-of-the-century trolley, the artist has incorporated antique trolley
parts, tools, gears, bones, horseshoes, shells, fossils, Italian glass, mar-
bles, and rail spikes into the work.

PHOTOMURALS, 1967.
  Arlington Station.
  Bill Goodwin.
  Funded by MBTA.

PHOTOMURALS, 1970.
  Copley Station.
  Beder & Alpers Inc.
  Funded by MBTA.

PHOTOMURALS, 1970.
  Kenmore Square Station.
  Alonzo Reid.
  Funded by MBTA.

ON THE BLUE LINE: ⟶

PHOTOMURALS, 1968.
  Bowdoin Station.
  Sert-Jackson and Associates.
  Funded by MBTA.

DIAGONAL STRIPES ON A SPECTRUM, 1971.
  State Street Station.
  Robert V. Kennedy.
  Funded by ICA and MBTA.

GEOMETRICS, 1968. Photomural.
  Aquarium Station.
  Funded by MBTA.

PHOTOMURALS, 1966.
  MBTA Airport and Maverick Stations.
  Arthur Hoener.
  Funded by MBTA.

Cambridge

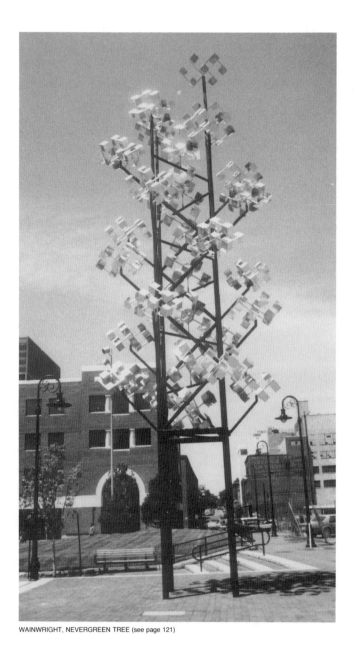

WAINWRIGHT, NEVERGREEN TREE (see page 121)

LECHMERE AREA

For photographs of new work and more detail, see the pamphlets "Mosaic: A Guide to Public Art in Cambridge" and "Red Line Northwest Extension," both available from Cambridge Arts Council, City Hall, Cambridge 02139. CAC has sponsored more than a hundred works in the city; the listing below is partial. (CDBG is the acronym of Community Development Block Grant.)

★ NEVERGREEN TREE, 1987. Windsculpture, diffraction grating on stainless steel, h. 35′.
Lechmere Canal Park.
William Wainwright (*see* East Boston, Logan Airport: *Windwheels*).

BUBBLE CHAMBER SERIES, 1987. Bronze, six splash pavers, five each 16″ sq., one 30″ sq.
Lechmere Canal Park.
David Phillips (*see* Porter Square: *Porter Square Megaliths*).

   Phillips has used the abstract graffiti drawn in a bubble chamber by subatomic particles as an overlay for actual castings of beach fragments. The work is a comment on this area's history, the marine detritus recalling the days when the Charles River Basin was the Back Bay, a tidal flat open to the sea.

THE FACES OF CAMBRIDGE, 1986. Bronze, life-size, h. 9′.
Lechmere Canal Park.
James Tyler (*see* Somerville: *Untitled*).

THE BRITISH ARE COMING, THE BRITISH ARE COMING, 1988. Enamel paint on steel panels, two sections each h. 8′ × 13′4″.
Bridge over Lechmere Canal.
David Judelson (*see* *Flag Fragments* below).

   When Gen. Gage's men rowed across from Boston to Cambridge to begin their ill-fated march to Lexington and Concord in April, 1775, they landed near this spot.

THE GRASS IS GREENER ON THE CAMBRIDGESIDE, 1990. Exterior mural, latex, h. 69′ × 300′.
Cambridgeside Galleria, First St.
Wade Zahares (1960–   ).

121

Maine-born, Zahares earned a B.F.A. from Maryland Institute College of Art in 1983. His specialty is interior murals for corporate offices. His studio is in South Boston.

GALLERIA VEILS and NEON SPROUTS, 1990. Neon, electronics, 6′ × 4′ × 6′ and 16.5′ × 10′ × 2′.
Cambridgeside Galleria, under both escalators and inside the elevator well, First St.
Alejandro and Moira Sina (*see* MBTA [Red Line]: Alewife Station).

FLAG FRAGMENTS, 1987. Ceramic, forty elements, varying sizes.
East Cambridge Parking Facility, First St. between Spring and Thorndike Sts.
David Judelson (1941–   ).

Artist/architect David Judelson holds degrees in architecture and city planning from M.I.T. He has received grants from the Massachusetts Council for the Arts and Humanities and in 1986 was among winners of the Governor's Design Award. In recent years Judelson has turned to three-dimensional architectural constructions.

The flags of the world are here, but largest are the major nationalities of East Cambridge: Italian, Irish, Polish, Portuguese, and Lithuanian.

EAST CAMBRIDGE—1852, 1988. Welded steel, h. 24′ × 24′ × 5′.
Outside wall of Lechmere Parking Facility, First St.
George Greenamyer (*see* Marshfield: *Webster, the Farmer of Marshfield*).

The glass and furniture industries of this area are recalled by Greenamyer's details: glass blowers and furniture-makers, brick kiln buildings of Boston Porcelain and Glassworks, the factory of Geldowdsy's Furniture Co., and the proud presidents of both companies. Funded by 1% for Art.

CENTANNI PARK GARDEN SCULPTURES, 1988. Color-galvanized forged steel, two pieces, h. 5′ × 10′ × 6′, and h. 5.5′ × 3′ × 3′.
Otis St., between Second and Third Sts.
Dimitri Gerakaris (*see* Harvard Square: *Longfellow Memorial*).

When these buildings were renovated, this block of Otis St. was closed and the park created. Gerakaris, who likes to take his ideas from the environs of every site, found a profusion of neighborhood gardens and chose to replicate in steel some of the flowers in them. The larger work contains poppies, day lilies, and lilies of the valley. The smaller sculpture incorporates sunflowers, iris, grapevines, and other familiar plants. Funded by Cambridge 1% for Art.

EAGLE, circa 1870. Bronze, h. approx. 15′.
Bulfinch Sq., Thorndike and Second Sts.
Artist unknown.

This bronze eagle was made for the facade of the old post office building in Boston and salvaged when it was demolished. From the collection of Graham Gund.

UNTITLED, 1926. Bronze, assorted sculpture and reliefs.
Charles Park, Commercial Ave. at Charles St.
Nancy Webb (1926–   ).

As a high-schooler, Nancy Webb studied painting at Abbot and Phillips Andover academies with Maude and Patrick Morgan. She continued painting at Smith College and California School of Art and later explored printmaking at Columbia. After designing book jackets as art director for Noonday Press, she authored and illustrated three children's books. In 1965 she began making sculpture. (*See* MBTA [Red Line]: Alewife Station.)

Scattered about the park, in addition to one sculpture, are eleven high reliefs, two to four inches in diameter, and twenty-eight low reliefs, five to fifteen inches across, depicting insects and flowers. They are all numbered, and a bronze plaque near Charles Street thoughtfully identifies each species. Funded by Cambridge 1% for Art.

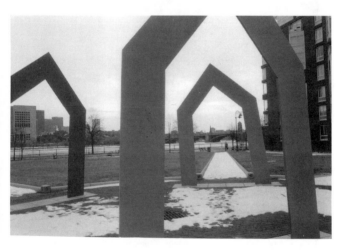

GATE HOUSE, 1987. Three painted steel arches.
Cambridge Pkwy. near Rogers St.
Lloyd Hamrol.

Hamrol is an artist from Venice, Cal. Funded by CAC.

LUPUS, 1985. Cor-ten steel, h. 41'.
55 Cambridge Pkwy., in front of Lotus Development Corp.
John Raimondi (1949–   ).

Raimondi grew up in East Boston and Winthrop, attended the Portland (Me.) School of Art and Massachusetts College of Art. After graduation he was artist-in-residence at Quincy Vocational Technical School, introducing sculptural concepts to welding classes. Purchased by Cabot, Cabot & Forbes, owners of the building.

ATHENA, 1988. Bronze, monumental size.
Atop Athenaeum House, 215 First St.
Adio di Biccari (*see* Boston [Boston Common]: *Parkman Plaza*).

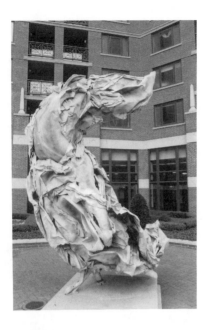

★ ATHENA, 1988. Welded scrap metal, h. 12'.
At River Court, Commercial Ave. between Rogers and Binney Sts.
Judith Brown (1931–1992).
Jeffrey Sass (1951–   ).

Brown, a native of New York City, was a student of Theodore Roszak at Sarah Lawrence College in the 1950s. Extensively collected, her
work is found in such major institutions as the Museum of Modern Art,
the Dallas Museum of Fine Arts, the Pepsico Sculpture Gardens, and
numerous others. Also a New Yorker, her assistant and collaborator
Sass is a graduate of Hiram College, Ohio, and a self-taught sculptor.
His own sculptures are inspired by his college major, children's literature.

Maintaining studios in New York and Vermont, Brown and Sass
would comb automobile graveyards and dumps for the used metal with
which she cloned and parodied classical sculpture. Part of the interest
in this work for the viewer is in identifying the spare parts that at first
appear to be limbs or draperies. Commissioned by H. J. Davis Development.

THALASSA, 1988. Bronze, h. 6'.
At River Court, First St. between Rogers and Binney Sts.
Ernest Montenegro (1949–   ).

Born in Albuquerque, N.M., Montenegro lived and worked for a time
in the Boston area but now is located in Claremont, N.H. He has studied at Boston Center for the Arts, but he says he learned most of his
art from his father, a professor of painting. In 1980 Montenegro won

the Grand Prix of Contemporary Art of Monte Carlo and more recently received a grant from New Hampshire Council on the Arts.

Entitled with the Greek word for ocean, *Thalassa* suggests the ebb and flow of tides. Commissioned by H. J. Davis Development.

At Royal Sonesta Hotel (5 Cambridge Pkwy.):

Sonesta International Hotels, under the guidance of chairman Roger Sonnabend and his wife Joan, an art dealer, has achieved some fame for its policy of placing original works of art, rather than reproductions and decor items, in its hotels. In this building, every guest room contains an original print, and the public spaces boast forty-six other works by both international and local artists. A partial listing follows.

BANNERS, 1992. Fabric, twelve units, 12′ × 3′.
Exterior, facing Land Blvd.
Aaron Fink (*see Cup* below), Peter Hutchinson, Todd McKie (*see* Boston [MBTA] South Station: *Mural*), Rob Moore, (1937–1993).

These four artists were commissioned by Royal Sonesta Hotel to design, each in his own style, permanent banners to enliven the neighborhood. Fond of magnifying ordinary objects, Fink enlarges blueberries for his banner. The triple ribbon design is by conceptual landscape artist Hutchinson, a native of London now living in Provincetown. McKie draws one of his typical capricious figures with folk and anthropological references. Sparse geometric abstractions were the metier of Rob Moore, an art history major at University of the South, Sewanee, Tenn., who taught at Massachusetts College of Art; the black and red flag is his.

UNTITLED, 1984. Painted metal sculpture, h. 13′4″.
Outside entrance.
Dennis Croteau (1948–1989).

Croteau was a Fitchburg, Mass., native who studied at a number of institutions including the Boston Museum School, Tufts University, Emerson College, the San Francisco Art Institute, and the New School for Social Research in New York.

I DREAMED I WAS HAVING MY PHOTO TAKEN, 1982. Silkscreen with unique painting, h. 78″ × 98″.
FLYING MAN WITH BRIEFCASE NO. 28169, 1983. Hanging sculpture, painted gatorfoam, h. 24″ × 94″ × 1″.
MOLECULE MAN, 1982. Lithograph, h. 96″ × 80″.
All in entrance lobby.
Jonathan Borofsky (1942–   ).

Born in Boston, Borofsky graduated from Carnegie Mellon University and took a master's degree from the School of Fine Arts at Yale University. Having taught at the School of Visual Arts in New York and at California Institute of the Arts, he now lives in Venice, Cal. His work has been widely exhibited in major museums both in this country and in Europe.

FLOWERS, 1970. Silkscreen, eight prints, h. 36″ × 36″.
Facing first-floor elevators.
★ Andy Warhol (1930–1987).

Andy Warhol is remembered for the statement that in the future "everyone will be world-famous for fifteen minutes." Jet-setter Warhol was the object of media attention for much longer than that, beginning with his Pop Art prints of huge Campbell's Soup cans in the early 1960s. Son of Czech immigrants, he was born Andrew Warhola in McKeesport, Pa., near Pittsburgh. He studied design at Carnegie Institute of Technology, moved to New York, and was a successful commercial artist for about a decade before his work began to receive international acclaim. His art is a commentary on the boredom and banality of mass-produced objects sold by slick packaging and promotion; his career has been said to be an example of same.

THE GLASS WISHES. Print from a series, h. 34″ × 27″.
Library.
★ James Rosenquist (1933–   ).

From Grand Forks, N.D., Rosenquist migrated east to the University of Minnesota and then to the Art Students League in New York. A leading Pop Art painter, he produced magnified realistic drawings and prints that sometimes reached billboard size. His work was included in the 1981 Whitney Biennial and frequently earns exhibition throughout America and Europe.

PAGODA WALL WITH ARROW, 1984. Mixed media on paper, 48″ × 40″.
Library.
Maggi Brown.

CASTING, 1989. Lithograph, 28″ × 60″.
Library.
Stuart Diamond.

New Yorker Diamond has been a Yaddo Fellow, has received a painting grant from the National Endowment for the Arts, and has taught and exhibited widely. His teaching posts include Parsons School of Design, Fordham University, Bennington College, and Cooper Union.

COLOSSAL SCREW IN LANDSCAPE—TYPE 1; SOFT SCREWS TUMBLING #2; ARCH IN THE FORM OF A SCREW FOR TIMES SQUARE, N.Y., 1976. Three lithographs, each 68″ × 41″.
In Charles Bar.
★ Claes Oldenberg (1929–   ).

Born in Stockholm, Oldenberg came to Yale to study art and literature, and later studied at the Art Institute of Chicago. For a time he was a reporter and illustrator for a Chicago newspaper; moving to New York, he took a job in the library of the Cooper Union and met a group of artists who were devising "happenings" instead of making objects. His first giant soft sculpture was exhibited in 1962, challenging the most basic concepts we have about commonplace objects. Turning the everyday into the monumental by vastly enlarging the scale occupied

Oldenberg for a number of years and brought him international fame. Some, like Philadelphia's clothespin, were built; others, like the Times Square arch, exist only in Oldenberg's drawings and prints.

INSIGHT, 1980. Steel, h. 76″ × 95″ × 36″.
　　Lobby, to right of reception desk.
　　★ Anthony Caro (1924–　　).

　　Caro was for two years an assistant to Sir Henry Moore, then went on to build an international career of his own. London-born, he was awarded the CBE (Commander of the British Empire) by the Queen in 1971. Caro has exhibited extensively in Europe and America; an example of his work is owned by most major museums. He now has a studio in New York state.

TWO REALMS WITNESS A CHANGE, 1984. Diptych, acrylic on canvas, 5′ × 7′.
　　Lobby, to right of reception desk.
　　Natalie Alper (1937–　　).

　　After earning a master's degree in history at Boston University, Alper attended the Boston Museum School. Her drawings and large-scale watercolors have been widely exhibited along the Eastern Seaboard.

CUP, 1983. Oil on canvas, h. 66″ × 72″.
　　Outside Somerset Room.
　　Aaron Fink (1955–　　).

　　Boston-born, Fink was educated at Skowhegan School of Painting and Sculpture, the Maryland Institute College of Art, and Yale University School of Art and Architecture. His works on paper have been exhibited in this country and in Europe and Australia.

NIGHT SUN, 1984. Ceramic tile, 11′ × 16′3″.
　　Outside ballroom.
　　★ Katherine Porter (1941–　　).

　　Considered a peripheral member of the Boston Expressionist School, Porter worked in a "gestural expressionism" characterized by calligraphic Xs, zigzags, and spirals. Such linear motifs may be seen in this ceramic work, commissioned specifically for this space. An Iowan by birth, Porter studied at Boston University and Colorado College, and now lives in Vinalhaven, Me.

UNTITLED, 1979. Welded steel sculpture, h. 52″ × 50″.
　　Outside ballroom, second floor.
　　Jacqueth Hutchinson (1942–　　).

　　Hutchinson, Boston-born, studied at Bennington College, Vt., and St. Martin's School of Art, London. She has exhibited throughout New England and New York, and in Holland.

THE HOUSE THAT FRONTS THE WATER, 1985. Acrylic on linen and burlap, 104″ × 145″.
　　Outside ballroom.
　　Frank Van Hemert.

UNTITLED (FROM FLOWER SERIES), 1981. Color photograph, 40″ × 80″.
Outside ballroom.
Chris Enos.

UNTITLED, 1984. Watercolor on paper, 60″ × 60″.
Outside ballroom.
Dennis Croteau (*see Untitled* above).

PICABIA I, II AND III, 1971. Lithograph with collage, 35″ × 53″.
Outside ballroom.
Jim Dine (*see* Boston [Government Center and Environs]: *Double Boston Venus*).

THE MALE FERN, 1987. Wall sculpture, painted wood, five elements
110″ × 95″ × 20″.
East Tower staircase.
Chris Hearn.

FOUR COURTS, DUBLIN. Lithograph with color photographs, diptych, each
29″ × 31.5″.
Second-floor staircase landing.
Jan Dibbets (1941–).

Dutch artist Dibbets was trained as an art teacher at Academie voor
Beeidende en Bouwende Kunsten, studied painting with Jan Gregoor,
then received awards enabling him to continue his studies in London
and Rome. Professor at the Kunstakademie, Dusseldorf, he lives and
works in Amsterdam. Exhibitions of his work have been held in the
Guggenheim and the Museum of Modern Art in New York, the Walker
Art Center in Minneapolis, the Detroit Institute, and many others.

TWELVE AROUND ONE, 1981. Portfolio of thirteen screen prints, each
30″ × 40″.
Outside second-floor conference rooms.
★ Buckminster Fuller (1895–1983).

Perhaps the twentieth century's foremost futurist and visionary designer, Buckminster Fuller was born in Milton, graduated from Milton
Academy, went on to Harvard but was expelled for cutting classes and
(Fuller said) ''general irresponsibility.'' After service in the Navy in
World War I Fuller attended the Naval Academy. This series of prints
displays some of his ideas, both those that have entered the main-
stream (the geodesic dome) and those that failed to gain acceptance
(the Dymaxion car). At his death, Fuller was professor emeritus at
Southern Illinois University and the University of Pennsylvania, and
world fellow-in-residence at University City Science Center in Philadelphia.

UNTITLED, ca. 1970. Set of four serigraphs, each h. 42″ × 40″.
Corridor to Lotus Development Corp.
Neil Welliver (1929–).

Welliver's lyrical sylvan paintings and prints are widely held in New
England. From Millville, Pa., Welliver went to the Philadelphia Museum

College of Art, took a graduate degree at Yale, and taught there for a decade. Since 1966 he has taught at the University of Pennsylvania in Philadelphia.

EAST CAMBRIDGE

GALAXY, 1990. Bronze, steel, chrome, water, steam, h. 5′, pool diam. 15′.
    Point Park, Main St. and Broadway.
    Otto Piene (1928–   ).
    Joe Davis (1951–   ).
    Joan Brigham (1935–   ).

Concept and design of this fountain were by Piene, director since 1974 of the Center for Advanced Visual Studies (CAVS) at M.I.T., a center dedicated to the melding of art and technology. German-born, Piene was among the first fellows of CAVS, in 1967. He developed the concept of Sky Art, producing huge inflatable sculptures and organizing international Sky Art conferences in the 1980s; his profession, he says, is designing celebrations.

A fellow of CAVS for ten years, Davis is now associated with the Alexander Rich Laboratory at M.I.T. He fabricated the pseudo planet, "Earth Sphere," at the center of the fountain. Mississippi-bred, Davis believes artists must use the technology of their time in order to "tell the truth." He has done laser research at laboratories in Ohio and Wisconsin and has been visiting artist at NASA Goddard Space Flight Center, Gilford College, N.C., New College in Sarasota, Fla., and the Hochschule fuer Technik in Bremen, Germany. A specialty of his is the internal carving of transparent materials with laser beams.

Environmental artist Brigham, an associate professor of fine arts at Emerson College, has also been a fellow of and is now a research affiliate at CAVS. Born in Oklahoma, she grew up in California, attended Pomona College and Harvard University, and settled in Cambridge. Interested in the dramatic possibilities of steam, she mastered the pipe-fitter's trade and began to experiment with steam and water mist as artistic mediums. Brigham has made small kinetic solar-powered steam sculptures, as well as collaborative performance art combining lasers, film and word projections on steam, audio, electronic music, and viewer interaction by means of photocells. (*See also* Harvard University: *Tanner Fountain*.)

Thought of as a gateway landmark for motorists and "T" commuters entering Cambridge from Boston, the fountain celebrates the four elements: earth, air, fire, and water. Twelve "Moon Lights" circling the basin resemble phases of the moon. Commissioned by Cambridge Redevelopment Authority.

FOUR FIGURES, 1987. Bronze, h. approx. 18″ on 6′ support pole.
    Sennot Park, Broadway at Tremont St.
    Gene Cauthen (1942–   ).

A teacher at Mount Wachusett Community College, Cauthen lives in Royalston. He graduated from the University of Texas in 1964 with a

B.F.A., spent a year studying at Cleveland Institute of Art, then earned an M.F.A. at Yale.

SUN ARC, 1981. Stainless steel, five units, h. 3′–6′.
   Sennot Park playground.
   Beth Galston (1948–   ).

   Environmental artist Galston makes sensitive installation art, simple yet stunning in effect, but little of it is permanent—this early piece is an exception. A 1970 graduate of Cornell, she took a B.F.A. from Kansas City Art Institute, a master's in visual studies from M.I.T., and has been a fellow of the Center for Advanced Visual Studies.
   Doing double duty as climbing structures and light sculptures, Galston's Sennot Park frameworks are designed to cast interesting shadows on the sand, their configurations changing as the sun moves.

PARK BENCH GROUP, 1987. Bronze, h. 18″ plus 5′ support pole.
POLE CLIMBERS, 1987. Bronze, h. approx. 7′.
   Columbia Park, Columbia and Washington Sts.
   Gene Cauthen (*see Four Figures* above).

   Pole Climbers depicts the *pola en ceval*, or greased-pole-climbing contest, a traditional competition of Hispanic festivals.

ARBOR, 1987. Bronze, h. approx. 5′.
   Park, Harvard St. between Clark and Moore Sts.
   Gene Cauthen (*see Four Figures* above).

GROUND MURAL, 1981. Ceramic, 18′ × 37′.
   Hurley St. playground.
   David Judelson (*see* Lechmere: *Flag Fragments*) and Elee Koplow.

   Koplow is a graduate of the Boston Museum School; she also studied at San Miguel School of Art, Mexico.

PLAY IS CHILD'S WORK, 1983. Ceramic tile, h. 7′ × 12′.
   Roberts School, Harvard and Windsor Sts.
   Judith Inglese (*see* Central Square: *I'd Hammer Out Love*).
   Funded by 1% for Art.

BUTTER IN THE BATTER, 1982. Acrylic on masonry, 13′ × 45′.
   Rosie's Bakery, Inman Sq.
   Heddi Siebel.
   Funded by CDBG.

TREES AND FLOWERS, 1979–80. Mosaic murals, various sizes.
   Interior and exterior, Miller's River Houses for elderly and handicapped, Cambridge and Lambert Sts.
   Lilli Ann Killen Rosenberg (*see* Newton: *Five Concrete Mosaic Sculptures*), with participation of tenants and neighborhood schoolchildren.

GLASS COLUMNS WITH PINK, 1988. Stained glass, h. 88″ × 57″.
   Miller's River Apartments, 15 Lambert St.

Linda Lichtman (*see* Central Square: *Untitled*).
Funded by Draper Laboratory Inc. and Cambridge Arts Council.

RAINBOW OF TROUT, 1990. Diffraction grating, h. 6′ × 40′.
201 Broadway.
William Wainwright (*see* East Boston, Logan Airport: *Windwheels*).
Commissioned by Jonathan Davis.

S&S Mural, 1990. Silicate paint, h. three stories.
1334 Cambridge St.
Joshua Winer (*see* Boston [Back Bay]: *Newbury Street Mural*).

Painting a false window to complement the real one, Winer has included fourteen members of four generations of the S&S deli's owners.

At M.I.T.:

For a complete listing and discussion of the 1000 or more works owned by Massachusetts Institute of Technology, consult the paperback Art and Architecture at MIT: A Walking Tour of the Campus, *available at the List Arts Center (Wiesner Bldg.) on Ames St. Only the most visible works will be listed here.*

FOR MARJORIE, 1961. Red-painted steel, h. 18′.
West end of campus, off Memorial Dr. between Audrey St. and Amherst St.
★ Tony Smith (1912–1980).

Minimalist sculptor Tony Smith is known for his "cubes," works ordered by telephone from steel fabricators, to exemplify the interrelationship between art and contemporary technology. Born in New Jersey, Smith studied architecture at the New Bauhaus in Chicago, was briefly an assistant to Frank Lloyd Wright, worked initially as a toolmaker and draftsman, spent twenty years as a practicing architect and then another twenty as a sculptor. He taught at New York University, Cooper Union, Pratt Institute, Bennington, and Hunter College. Many of his large works are sliced from geometric forms; *For Marjorie* would fit within a tetrahedron.

BELLTOWER FOR MIT CHAPEL, 1953–55. Aluminum, h. 45′.
★ Theodore Roszak (1907–   ).

M.I.T. also owns the drawings and models for this functional sculpture, developed in collaboration with the architect Eero Saarinen. Springing from richly encrusted arches, the three vertical elements symbolize the three major Western religions intended to be served by the interdenominational chapel.

ALTARPIECE SCREEN, 1955. Brass, h. 20′.
Inside chapel.
★ Harry Bertoia (1915–   ).

Italian-born, Bertoia came here as a teenager and studied at Cranbrook Academy of Art in Michigan. Like the narrow reflecting moat, the screen is designed to scatter light inside the chapel.

SPINNING BOX, 1991. Neon, motor, electronics, $4' \times 4' \times 1'$.
  M.I.T. Student Center/Toscannini's, Massachusetts Ave.
  Alejandro and Moira Sina (*see* MBTA [Red Line]: Alewife Station).

THREE PIECE RECLINING FIGURE, DRAPED, 1976. Bronze,
  h. $8'8'' \times 15'7'' \times 8'8''$.
  Killian Ct., main bldg., Memorial Dr.
  ★ Henry Moore (1898–1986).

   Widely acknowledged as the greatest sculptor of the twentieth century, Moore has worked with the figure throughout his career. His drawings of families sheltering in London subways during the German air
raids of World War II inspired many of the *Reclining Figure* pieces. An
earlier and smaller reclining figure is in the courtyard near M.I.T.'s
Wiesner Building on Ames Street, and another is at Harvard University.
   Moore's earliest figure drawings display a tendency toward bulk and
monumentality. His distinctive organic forms, with their references to
bones and beach pebbles, are universally familiar now. The negative
spaces—hollows and holes in the sculpture—are as important visually
as the positive forms. When Moore first pierced the figure, however, his
style became the subject of caricature on a par with Picasso's Cubist
faces.

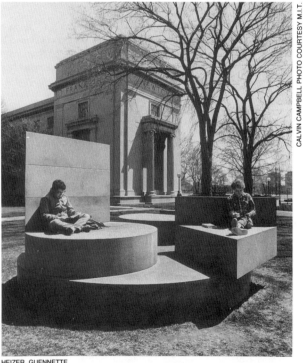

CALVIN CAMPBELL PHOTO COURTESY M.I.T.

HEIZER, GUENNETTE

GUENNETTE, 1977. Granite, eleven pieces.
Killian Ct.
★ Michael Heizer (1944–   ).

Heizer is an environmental artist best known for his *Double Negative*, a trench 1500 feet long by fifty feet deep cut across the flanks of a
gorge in the Nevada desert. *Guennette*, forty-six tons of pink Canadian
granite from the town of Guennette, is a set of variations on circles and
circle fragments. M.I.T. does not discourage tactile enjoyment of its public sculpture, and this work is a popular spot for readers, sunbathers,
and occasional musicians. On long-term loan from the Metropolitan
Museum of Art, New York.

ANGOLA, 1968. Cor-ten steel, $7' \times 8\frac{1}{2}' \times 6'$.
On Memorial Dr., in front of Hayden Memorial Library.
Isaac Witkin.

Born in South Africa, Witkin emigrated to England in the mid-1950s,
where he studied with Anthony Caro and became an assistant to Sir
Henry Moore. In 1965 he served as artist-in-residence at Bennington
College, Vt.

ELMO-MIT, 1963. Bronze, h. $65'' \times 56''$.
Outside Hayden Library.
Dimitri Hadzi (*see* Brookline: *Primavera*).

The first work commissioned for M.I.T.'s outdoor collection, *Elmo-MIT*
presages Hadzi's much larger *Thermopylae* in City Hall Plaza, Boston.
A Hadzi work in radically different style (*Omphalos*) stands in Harvard
Square.

THE BATHER, 1923–25. Bronze, h. $76'' \times 29'' \times 28''$.
Courtyard, Hayden Library.
★ Jacques Lipchitz (1891–1973).

Lipchitz was born in Lithuania, but before he was twenty went to
study sculpture in Paris, where he was intimate with such innovators as
Brancusi, Modigliani, Picasso, and Gris. He escaped to New York in
1941 and continued working there, his style becoming less abstract,
more emotional, and more dramatic. Many of his late works reflect Biblical texts.

Of the collection of familiar Lipchitz works in the Hayden courtyard,
only this one is permanent; the others are on long-term loan from the
sculptor's widow. This, Lipchitz' first life-size sculpture, reflects his
involvement in the Cubist movement in Paris. The other works here mirror important changes in the sculptor's style up to 1957. Gift of Yulla
Lipchitz.

★ THE BIG SAIL, 1965. Painted steel, h. 40'.
McDermott Ct., in front of Green Bldg., M.I.T.'s tallest.
Alexander Calder (1898–1977).

Third-generation of a family of Philadelphia sculptors, Calder is
famed as the inventor of the "mobile," free-hanging sculpture that is

moved by currents of air. By contrast, *The Big Sail* is one of a series of "stabiles," related in their planar construction to the mobiles but unmoving. Calder studied mechanical engineering at Stevens Institute of Technology before becoming an art student in New York and, later, in Paris. This work was fabricated under Calder's direction in an ironworks. A small preliminary version of the piece stands at the entrance of Building 9 on Massachusetts Ave.

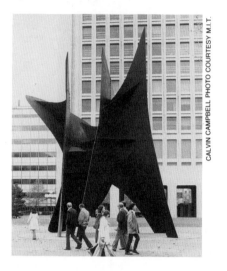

CALVIN CAMPBELL PHOTO COURTESY M.I.T.

TRANSPARENT HORIZON, 1975. Painted Cor-ten steel, h. 20′ × 21′ × 18′. Near Landau Bldg., Ames St.
★ Louise Nevelson (1899–1988).

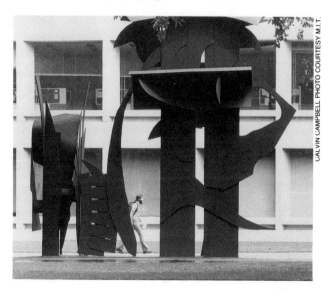

CALVIN CAMPBELL PHOTO COURTESY M.I.T.

Nevelson was well known for her all-black (or, later, all-white) assemblages of wooden "found objects" such as newel posts, lintels, and other architectural scraps, carefully placed in compartments of wall-sized cases. Although born in Russia, Nevelson was brought to Maine at an early age and lived and worked in New York from the 1920s until her death.

M.I.T. students have never liked this work, and one winter buried it completely in snow. It tends to be a natural "bulletin board" for posters, as well.

NIAGARA, 1973. Cor-ten steel, h. 9' × 22' × 18'.
Compton Ct., near Alumni Pool.
Michael Steiner (1945–   ).

Steiner's study in the interrelationships of steel slabs has puzzled M.I.T. students even more than the Nevelson. From time to time it contains a chair or two, as if it were a ramshackle kids' clubhouse; when the work was first installed, pranksters tried to equip it as an outhouse.

★ RECLINING FIGURE: WORKING MODEL FOR LINCOLN CENTER SCULPTURE, 1963. Bronze, h. 5'.
Upper courtyard, Wiesner Bldg.
Henry Moore (see *Three Piece Reclining Figure, Draped* above).

Gift of Albert and Vera List in memory of Mrs. List's brother, Samuel Glasner, a 1925 graduate of M.I.T.'s School of Architecture and Planning.

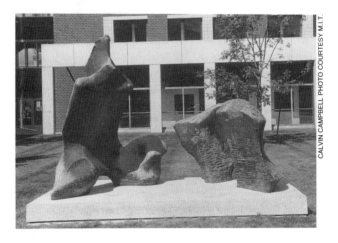

CALVIN CAMPBELL PHOTO COURTESY M.I.T.

UNTITLED COLLABORATION, 1985.
At the Wiesner Bldg. (List Arts Center).
BANQUETTES, BALCONY and RAILINGS: Scott Burton (1939–   ).
SCULPTURE GARDEN: Richard Fleischner (1944–   ).
EXTERIOR and ATRIUM WALL PATTERN.
★ Kenneth Noland (1924–   ).

Designs by these three artists, in collaboration with architect I. M. Pei (an M.I.T. graduate), were integrated into the planning and construction of the arts center and its surrounding plaza. Acknowledged as one of the most powerful practitioners of Minimalism, Noland is best known for his series of color studies in target and chevron patterns. He was born in Asheville, N.C., and attended Black Mountain College and the Institute of Contemporary Art in Washington, D.C. During World War II he served in the U.S. Air Force as a glider pilot and cryptographer. He has taught at the Institute of Contemporary Art in Boston, at Catholic University in Washington, and at Bennington College, Vt. Burton, a maker of sculptural furniture in stone and wood, studied literature and art history at Columbia and New York University (M.A., 1963), and then studied art with Hans Hoffman at Provincetown. Fleischner earned a master's degree in sculpture at Rhode Island School of Design in 1968 and has taught at Brown and at RISD. For a time he made large-scale earthworks; now Fleischner builds big sculptured forms using groups of blocks of uniform size as a common denominator (*see* North Cambridge [Alewife Station]: *Environmental Site Work*). He has designed environments at the Dallas Museum of Fine Arts and at the University of California, San Diego.

Whether in sarcasm or in genuine constructive criticism, college pranksters for the first year of this building's existence repeatedly altered colorist Noland's color scheme by painting one tile near the entrance a sickly green. The Institute gamely kept cleaning it off, and the critics now seem to have graduated.

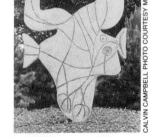

CALVIN CAMPBELL PHOTO COURTESY M.I.T.

FIGURE DÉCOUPÉE, 1958–63.
  Cast concrete, h. 11′6″.
  Wadsworth and Amherst Sts.
  ★   Pablo Picasso (1881–1973)
  and Carl Nesjar.

Less a sculpture than a drawing, this work was cast, using a process called "bétongravure" (concrete-engraving), by the Norwegian artist Nesjar from a wooden maquette by Picasso. *Figure Découpée* translates "Cut-Out Figure," one of a series of such planar cut-outs made by Picasso in the 1950s and 60s. This one represents a bird with wings outstretched above.

Picasso, probably the best-known painter of our century, worked in a number of styles as he addressed the formal problems of art in the modern day. What is less commonly known is that Picasso was a consummate draftsman. He learned his craft from his father, a Spanish painter specializing in realistic pictures of doves; when the boy was twelve, the father recognized that the son had surpassed him and turned his brushes and palette over to Pablo. Picasso's experiments with an expressionist form of Cubism have led to a popular cliché, the profile portrait with both eyes visible. Later in life Picasso experimented with ceramics and sculpture of vast creative verve and lack of inhibition.

Not part of the official M.I.T. collection (thus not listed in the catalog of Art and Architecture) are five wall hangings of C. Fayette Taylor, professor of engineering who logged a twenty-year career as a professional sculptor after his retirement from M.I.T. (see Government Center and Environs: Upward Bound). His works at M.I.T. are:

UNTITLED, 1966. Stainless steel, 34″ × 60″.
    Faculty Club.
PENDULAR, 1970. Brass and steel, 48″ × 66″.
    Chemistry Department.
RECTANGULAR, 1979. Brass and steel, 3′ × 5′.
    Mechanical Engineering Department.
WATER MILL, 1971. Brass, stainless steel, plastic, h. 2½′ × 5′.
    Hydraulic Laboratory.
AIR MILL, 1982. Brass, stainless steel, plastic, 2′ × 3′.
    Sloan Automotive Laboratory.

CENTRAL SQUARE

ANIMAL WEATHER VANES, 1981. Painted steel, four pieces.
    Main St. at Bishop Allen Dr.
    Joseph Barbieri.

Barbieri is known for his fanciful paintings of animals impeccably garbed. He studied at Pennsylvania Academy of Fine Arts and in Florence; he has taught at Harvard Graduate School of Design and at children's workshops at the Fogg Museum. Funded by CDBG and NEA.

ENGINE COMPANY 5, 1976. Exterior enamel paint on brick, h. 15′ × 25′.
    Inman Sq. firehouse, Hampshire and Cambridge Sts.
    Ellery Eddy.

Eddy, a young artist living near Inman Square, concluded that the most unifying element in her diverse neighborhood was the firehouse; her reasoning won her the commission for this work. To the portraits of the men in the engine company, Eddy whimsically added George Washington, once a volunteer fireman, and Benjamin Franklin, founder of America's first fire insurance company. Funded by CETA.

FLOATING DOWN MASS. AVENUE, 1978. Acrylic on masonry wall, 20′ × 28½′.
    Putnam Furniture Leasing Bldg., 614 Massachusetts Ave., Central Sq.
    Elizabeth Carter (1950–   ) and Michael Stanton.

Carter and Stanton both studied at Antioch College and began doing murals in Ohio. Carter later studied at Massachusetts College of Art and at Boston Museum School. She has received Artists Foundation grants for teaching, serving as artist-in-residence at elementary and high schools in Boston-area communities.

Carter's river murals are meant to comment on nostalgic uses of the Charles River, before pollution was a factor. Working at night, Carter and Stanton projected a pair of slides on the wall and traced the outlines, combining a "reflection" of the neighborhood with an old-fashioned boating scene. Funded by CAC and Art Army.

CROSSWINDS, 1992. Enamel on masonite, h. 24' × 41'.
Middle East Restaurant, 472 Massachusetts Ave.
Daniel Galvez (*see Crossroads* below).
Underwritten by private funding and Cambridge 1% for Art.

CENTRAL SQUARE WINDSCULPTURE, 1977. Gold-plated stainless steel and steel, h. 26' × 4' × 4'.
Central Sq.
Michio Ihara (*see Lowell: Pawtucket Prism*).
Funded by CDD, private donations, and by the artist.

COLUMNS, LINTELS, GLASS AND LEAD, 1987. Stained glass, h. 6' × 15'.
LBJ Apartments for the Elderly, 51 Erie St.
Linda Lichtman (see *Untitled* below).
Funded by Draper Laboratory, Inc. and Cambridge Arts Council.

INNER CITY TOTEM #1, 1981. Steel, landscape timbers, h. 15' × 4' × 15".
Cambridge Community Center, 5 Calender St.
Vusumuzi Maduna (*see Boston [South End/Roxbury]: The Judge*).
Funded by Cambridge Arts Council.

INNER CITY TOTEM #2, 1983. Steel, landscape timbers, h. 10' × 3' × 10".
Margaret Fuller House, 71 Cherry St.
Vusumuzi Maduna (*see Boston [South End/Roxbury]: The Judge*).
Funded by CDBG.

MARTIN LUTHER KING MEMORIAL, 1971. Sculptural mural, steel, h. 14' × 40'.
Martin Luther King Junior School, 100 Putnam Ave.
Vusumuzi Maduna (*see Boston [South End/Roxbury]: The Judge*).
Funded by City of Cambridge.

EDUCATION IS LIBERATION: THE ROSA PARKS MURAL, 1988. Acrylic, h. 10' × 25'.
Lobby, Graham and Parks School, 15 Upton St.
David Fichter (*see Lawrence: Bread and Roses Mural*).

This collaborative school mural is based on the life of Rosa Parks, whose refusal to move to the back of the bus initiated the Alabama bus boycott and the Civil Rights movement. Funded by 1% for Art.

I'D HAMMER OUT LOVE, 1984. Ceramic tile, 4'6" × 22'.
Saundra Graham and Rosa Parks Alternative School, Upton St.
Judith Inglese.

Inglese's many murals include a forty-foot-long work for the National
Zoo in Washington, D.C. Her style imitates in clay the techniques of
stained glass, cutting shapes that follow the patterns of color. She studied at Sarah Lawrence College, the Boston Museum School, and at the
Accademia di Belle Arti in Rome. The title here is taken from a folk
song, and some of the lyrics are stamped into the mural. Funded by
CDBG and 1% for Art.

BEAT THE BELT, 1980. Acrylic on masonry wall, 13' × 75'.
Back of Stop & Shop supermarket, Memorial Dr.
Bernard LaCasse.

This mural celebrates the triumph of people over bureaucracies: the
successful effort in the 1970s by residents to block the construction of
the Inner Belt, Interstate 95, through the city. Funded by CAC, neighborhood donations, and the artist.

MEMORIAL TO MARTIN LUTHER KING, JR., 1986. Ceramic, mosaic, h.
7' × 3'.
Martin Luther King Plaza, Franklin St. entrance to Central Sq. Library.
Lilli Ann Killen Rosenberg (*see* Newton: *Five Concrete Mosaic Sculp-
tures*).
Commissioned by CAC.

UNTITLED, 1980. Stained glass, 7' × 3'.
Central Sq. Library, Green St.
Linda Lichtman (1942–   ).

Now working full-time as a stained-glass specialist, Lichtman has
been on the staff at the Museum School and at Hayden Gallery, M.I.T.;
she has taught at Tufts University and at Middlesex and Bunker Hill
community colleges. After taking degrees in psychology and social
work at Simmons College, Lichtman returned to Massachusetts College
of Art for an M.F.A. She also attended the Boston Museum School,
and has traveled to England, Ontario, and Washington state for appren-
ticeships and workshops. Funded by CDBG.

FLOOR MURAL, 1979. Three parts, 3½' × 3½' and 2' × 4'.
Central Sq. Library, Green St.
David Judelson (*see* Lechmere: *Flag Fragments*).
Funded by CAC.

REMEMBRANCES, 1982. Mosaic, h. 5' × 7'.
Left side, Pearl St. entrance, Central Sq. Library.
Lilli Ann Killen Rosenberg (*see* Newton: *Five Concrete Mosaic Sculp-
tures*).

The aquatic motifs here remind that sections of Cambridge were
once marsh areas. Commissioned by CAC.

At Hyatt Regency Hotel (575 Memorial Dr.):

In guest rooms and suites here are fine-art prints by Vasarely, Josef Albers, Jergens Peters, and Mark Rothko, and original oils by Hector Leonardi. The following is a partial listing from the forty works placed in public spaces:

VENETIAN WALL. Trompe l'oeil mural, h. 21′ × 36′.
   Atrium.
   Richard Haas (*see* Boston [Back Bay]: *West Facade*).

ARGON CLUSTER, 1977. Argon, glass, electronics, 90′ × 25′ × 4′.
   Main atrium.
   Moira and Alejandro Sina (*see* MBTA [Red Line]: Alewife Station).

LOOKING FOR AN ISLAND, 1976. Fabric collage.
   Entry lobby.
   Clara Wainwright (*see* Boston [Fenway] [Children's Hospital]: *Folk Tales From the Four Corners of the Earth*).

EDGES #1, 1979. Textile relief collage, 49″ × 45″.
   Diana D. Filippi.

UNTITLED (CYCLAMEN), 1981. Pastel on paper, 95″ × 95″.
   At foot of escalator.
   Michael Mazur (1935–   ).

   New Yorker Michael Mazur has reversed the customary procedure for artists, leaving New York and establishing himself in Boston. After graduation from Amherst College in 1958, Mazur garnered a B.F.A. and an M.F.A. from Yale and almost immediately found recognition as a printmaker, his works gaining entry to exhibitions at the Museum of Modern Art and the Whitney. Turning to painting, Mazur has become a force on the Boston scene, his painterly realism incorporating increasing quantities of expressionism. Mazur's work is owned by nearly thirty museums, nationwide.

IOS. Watercolor on paper.
   Lobby at base of escalator.
   Susan Shatter.

SUDDEN, 1976. 52″ × 152″.
   At Pallysadoe Lounge.
   Friedel Dzubas (*see* Boston [Downtown]: *Crossing*).

CROSSROADS, 1987. Mural, h. 28′ × 46′.
   Pearl St. parking garage, between Green and Franklin Sts.
   Daniel Galvez.

   From Oakland, Cal., Galvez has organized community mural-painting in other New England localities. This one was painted in connection with the 1987 Cambridge River Festival, enlisting volunteer artists from the neighborhood. It is based on photos of local scenes and people. Funded by CAC.

LEVITATED STONE, 1987. Bronze and granite, h. 8'.
Dana Park, Magazine and Lawrence Sts.
David Phillips (*see* MBTA [Red Line] [Porter Square Station]: *Porter Square Megaliths*).

FIVE REVOLUTIONARY FIGURES, 1987. Steel.
Fort Washington Park, Waverly and Talbot Sts.
Madeline Lord.

Lord is an artist working in Bedford.

STONE WORK, 1980. Granite and bronze, h. approx. 4'.
Riverside Press Park, Memorial Dr. east of Western Ave.
David Phillips (*see* MBTA [Red Line]: Porter Square Station).
Funded by CDBG and NEA.

HARVARD SQUARE

IN CONSIDERATION OF HALF-LIVES AND ATTITUDES, 1979, 1981.
Cement, bronze, clay, stone, enamels, h. 7' × 7' × 7'.
Harris Communications, 80 Trowbridge St.
Mark Cooper (*see* Brockton: *Political Trilogy*).

★ OMPHALOS, 1985. Granite, h. 21'.
Harvard Sq.
Dimitri Hadzi (*see* Brookline: *Primavera*).

The title translates "navel," and refers to stones used in ancient cults (such as Delphi) to mark the center of the universe; Hadzi correlates

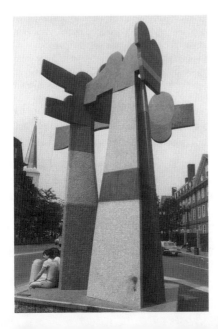

this site with the center of the educational universe. The artist chose his different-colored granites from quarries in Maine, New Hampshire, Rhode Island, Pennsylvania, South Dakota, Missouri, and India. Funded by MBTA and private donations.

UNTITLED, 1983. Stained glass, four panels, h. 48″ or 36″ × 18″.
Children's room, Cambridge Public Library, 449 Broadway.
Linda Lichtman (see Central Square: *Untitled*).
Funded by Cambridge Arts Council.

★ QUIET STONE, 1986. Marble, h. approx. 3′.
Winthrop Park, Harvard Sq., JFK Blvd. and Eliot St.
Carlos Dorrien (*see* Waltham [Bentley College]: *Portal*).

Dorrien likes to make "imaginary remnants" in stone, objects that look as if they have a history. His sculpture here summarizes contemporary thinking about public art: thoroughly melded into its site, full of arcane references to the place, witty, a little puzzling, inviting interaction. New Towne was the first name of Cambridge, and this spot was its marketplace. From Eliot Street the work looks like an authentic ruin, the lintel of the now-vanished market fallen to earth. Its opposite side would look like unworked stone, except that Dorrien has thoughtfully cut steps into it, inviting passers-by to do what they would do anyway—climb, sit, or lie on it.

THE LONGFELLOW MEMORIAL, 1989. Forged steel, forged bronze, h. 14′ × 24′ × 1.5′.
At Cambridge Center for Adult Education, 56 Brattle St.
Dimitri Gerakaris (1947–   ).

A native of Chicago, Gerakaris majored in philosophy and art at Dartmouth College. Graduated in 1970, he settled in New Canaan, N.H., dividing his time between sculpture and practical metalsmithing. (See also Boylston Place, South Boston and Centanni Park, Cambridge.)

This spot is the site of the "spreading chestnut tree" and the smithy of Dexter Pratt, a blacksmith in Harvard Square in the 1830s and inspiration for Longfellow's poem "The Village Blacksmith." Gerakaris has abstracted the poet's tree and placed under it an anvil and the hammer and tongs he, Gerakaris, made and then used in making the rest of the sculpture. The window grid commemorates the Window Shop, which aided Holocaust refugees by providing employment; the bronze pastries replicate those sold by the bakery here. Gerakaris designed the crown of the tree so ivy can fill it and make it change and "live" with the seasons. Commissioned by Cambridge Center for Adult Education.

HARVARD SQUARE THEATRE MURAL, 1983. Paint on masonry; 57′ × 20′.
Harvard Sq. Theatre, Church St. at Massachusetts Ave.
Joshua Winer (*see* Boston [Back Bay]: *Newbury Street Mural*) and Campari Knoepffler.

Members of the First Unitarian Church, an 1833 edifice, were uneasy when Harvard Square's movie house shifted its entrance from Massachusetts Avenue to Church Street, directly across from the church. Negotiations between the owner, the church, the city's Historical Commission, and Renata von Tscharner and Ronald Reed of the Townscape Institute resulted in this tromp l'oeil mural. Winer and Knoepffler, then graduate architecture students at Harvard, refined and executed Townscape Institute's design ideas (adding their own visages to the masks of Comedy and Tragedy). The muralists used a new color coating based on liquid silicate technology that is guaranteed not to fade for at least a decade.

GATEWAY TO KNOWLEDGE, 1979–83. Brick, 20'6″ × 5'6″ × 5'.
Brattle Sq., one block west of Harvard Sq.
Ann Norton.

Norton studied at the National Academy of Design, the Art Students League, and Cooper Union. In the 1940s she left New York to teach in West Palm Beach, Fla.; late in life she was rediscovered and her work exhibited to acclaim in New York. She died before this work was completed. This is the seventh in a series of gateways, some constructed in Florida. Funded by MBTA.

SUMNER, 1900. Bronze, larger than life.
Harvard Sq., Massachusetts Ave. and Garden St.
★ Anne Whitney (*see* Boston [Quincy Market]: *Samuel Adams*).

Anne Whitney, perhaps suspecting the bias of the commission which set out to memorialize Sumner in 1875, submitted her model anonymously. She was right; it was judged one of the three best, but when the commissioners learned it was by a woman it was disqualified. It was, they said, unthinkable for a female to model the male body, even a thoroughly clothed one. (The argument made little sense, because Whitney had already been chosen to sculpt Samuel Adams for Statuary Hall in Washington.) With financial help from her friends, Whitney stubbornly completed the work anyway, finishing it in 1900 when she was almost eighty. It was her last major work.

It is fitting that Senator Charles Sumner (1811–1874) sits here near Harvard Law School, from which he graduated at the age of twenty-three. Sumner was also a graduate of Harvard College, and lectured there until his election to the U.S. Senate in 1851 (*see* Boston [Boston Public Garden]: *Charles Sumner*).

FALL and SUMMER, 1992. Epoxy laminate, h. 7'9″.
Lobby, The Inn At Harvard.
Robert Shure (*see* Boston [Back Bay]: *Teddy Bear*).

These figures are reworkings of "Seasons" allegories by an eighteenth-century German sculptor, Johann Gunther (1717–1789). The originals may be seen at the Harvard Center for European Studies (formerly the Busch-Reisinger Museum) on Kirkland Street. Commissioned by Harvard University.

At Harvard University:

The following list is partial:

JOHN HARVARD, 1884.
   In front of University Hall, Harvard yard.
   ★ Daniel Chester French (*see* Concord: *Minuteman*).

   At the unveiling of *John Harvard*, a physician complained to French, "You've given John Harvard the legs of a consumptive." The sculptor gently informed his critic that John Harvard died of consumption when he was scarcely thirty. Little else is known of the benefactor of the college. Harvard probably lived 1608–1638; he took bachelor's and master's degrees from Emmanuel College at Cambridge University, came to Charlestown (it is thought) in 1637, died within the year, and is buried in Charlestown. He willed one-half his estate and his library of 302 books to the inhabitants of New Towne (now Cambridge), who had in 1636 founded a college, yet unnamed. In the absence of any record of Harvard's appearance, French's friend Sherman Hoar posed for the head.

DEATH AND VICTORY and THE COMING OF THE AMERICANS TO EUROPE.
   Widener Library, main staircase.
   ★ John Singer Sargent (*see* Boston [Back Bay] Boston Public Library: *Judaism and Christianity*).

   One critic has described these murals, which record the arrival of American forces in France in World War I, as "probably the very worst works of public art ever done by a major American painter."

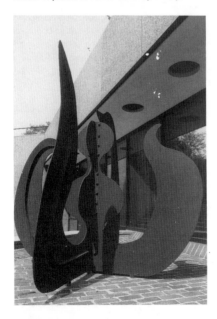

ONION, 1965. Steel, h. 6′.
   ★ Alexander Calder (*see* East Cambridge [M.I.T.]: *The Big Sail*).
   Gift of Susan Morse Hilles.

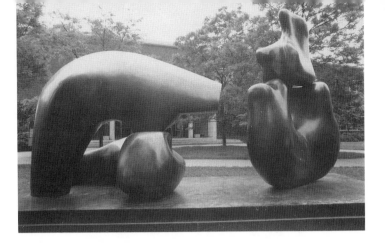

★ LARGE FOUR-PIECE RECLINING FIGURE, 1972–73. Bronze, h. 5′.
   Outside Lamont Library, near Quincy St.
   Henry Moore (*see* East Cambridge [M.I.T.]: *Three Piece Reclining Figure*).
   Gift of Sandra and David Bakalar.

CHINESE CH'ING DYNASTY STELE.
   Between Boylston Hall and Widener Library.
   From Yuan-ming garden.

   Harvard's alumni in China gave this stele to commemorate the college's tercentenary in 1936; at that time Yenching Institute, Harvard's center for Far Eastern research, occupied nearby Boylston Hall.

TANNER FOUNTAIN, 1984. Environmental work combining stone, steam, and water mist, diam. 60′.
   In front of Science Center, Cambridge St.
   Peter Walker and Joan Brigham (*see* East Cambridge: *Galaxy*).

   Peter Walker, designer of the fountain, is a member of SWA Group, a Boston landscape architecture firm.

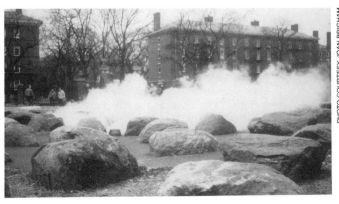

WALL SCULPTURE. Sand casting.
Science Center, first floor, west wing.
Constantino Nivola (*see* Boston [Downtown]: *Mural*).

DISCOBOLUS, ca. 5th century B.C. (copy). Bronze, life-size.
Outside Hemenway Gym.
★ Myron, Greek sculptor, 5th century B.C.

Although the original of this work was lost centuries ago, many copies exist from antiquity; this is a more recent version. The *Discobolus*
is considered transitional between the stylized, somewhat primitive Archaic period and the Classical sculpture usually associated with ancient
Greece; capturing the athlete's body in motion was a radical departure
from the usual static Archaic poses.

UNTITLED, 1973. Plexiglass and stainless steel, h. 18′ × 12′.
Courtyard, Perkins Astrophysical Library, Harvard College Observatory.
William Reimann (*see* Porter Square: *Embroidered Bollards*).

Commissioned by Ball Brothers Research Corp. to commemorate
the 500th anniversary of the birth of Copernicus.

SCULPTURE: RED BLUE, 1964. Painted stainless steel.
Peabody Terrace garage.
★ Ellsworth Kelly (1923–   ).

Initially a painter, Kelly has produced both two- and three-dimensional work of intriguing simplicity. Critics have placed him variously
with Minimalists, Constructivists, hard-edge, and color-field painters, yet
agree that he brings something of his own, an ability to "visualize es-
sences." Trained at Pratt Institute, the Boston Museum School, and the
Academie des Beaux Arts, Kelly served in World War II before continuing his art career. Among his teaching stints was one at the American
School in Paris, and another in Roxbury.

JUSTICE JOSEPH STORY, 1853. Marble, larger than life.
Law School.
★ William Wetmore Story (*see* Boston [Dorchester]: *Edward Everett*).

Hard as it is to believe when one sees the forest of memorials at
Mount Auburn Cemetery today, considerable controversy attended the
introduction of sculpture there. This statue was the first, proposed as a
memorial when Judge Story, Mount Auburn's first president, died in
1845. His successor, Dr. Jacob Bigelow (a respected physician sometimes described as a frustrated architect and stubborn admirer of sculpture) persuaded the board of trustees to commission statues of John
Adams, James Otis, and John Winthrop on the same scale. Money-
conscious proprietors—those who owned plots in Mount Auburn—objected to "lavish expenditures on unworthy objects," but Bigelow had
his way. The four statues initially stood in the Gothic chapel, then in
the rotunda of its adjoining office. When more office space was

needed, the four were offered to Harvard. The other three (see below) are in Harvard's Memorial Hall.

For thirty-six years an associate justice of the Supreme Court, Justice Story (1779–1845) is credited with important contributions toward Chief Justice Marshall's work in establishing the Court's powers. Story also established a body of opinion in admiralty law, patent law, and equity jurisprudence. He was a professor of law at Harvard. Funded by private subscription.

GOVERNOR JOHN WINTHROP, 1856. Marble, larger than life.
Refectory, Memorial Hall.
★ Richard Saltonstall Greenough (1819–1904).

Younger brother of Horatio Greenough, who is considered America's first professional sculptor, Richard Greenough was born into a well-to-do mercantile family. He chose to forgo the usual Harvard education and go into business with his family, but at the age of eighteen changed his mind and followed Horatio to Italy. Shuttling between Boston and Rome and between accounting and sculpture, he became established as a competent portrait sculptor. In 1853 he received the first commission awarded by the City of Boston in twenty-five years, this to sculpt a statue of Benjamin Franklin which now stands in front of Old City Hall. This work and the two below are the other three statues involved in the controversy described above under *Justice Joseph Story.* Commissioned by Mount Auburn Cemetery.

For Winthrop biography, *see* Boston [Back Bay]: *John Winthrop.*

JAMES OTIS, 1857.
Beside Sanders Theatre stage, Memorial Hall.
★ Thomas Crawford (ca. 1813–1857).

First American sculptor to settle permanently in Rome, Crawford was born in New York and apprenticed as a wood carver and gravestone cutter. After studying neoclassical sculpture (and mortuary anatomy) in Italy, Crawford brought to Boston in 1844 an exhibition which established his artistic reputation. He married New York heiress Louisa Ward, thus becoming the brother-in-law of Julia Ward Howe. The figure atop the U.S. Capitol, *Armed Liberty,* is Crawford's, as well as the pediment of the U.S. Senate, the bronze doors of the House and Senate, and colossal statues of History and Justice at the Senate.

Otis (1725–1783) was until 1769 recognized here and abroad as the leader of the rebellious spirit of the New England colonies. Trained in law at Harvard, he was advocate-general of Massachusetts in 1760 when George III decided to issue new writs of assistance, empowering customs officials to search any house for smuggled goods. Rather than represent the King in these matters, Otis resigned and became the principal voice in opposition. He was elected to the General Court (legislature) and served in 1775 as a volunteer at Bunker Hill. However, after 1769 except for brief periods he was harmlessly insane. He was killed by lightning, a death for which he had often expressed a wish. Commissioned by Mount Auburn Cemetery.

JOHN ADAMS, 1857.
Refectory, Memorial Hall.
★ Randolph Rogers (1825–1892).

Born in frontier Michigan, Rogers ended his schooling by the age of twelve and went to work as a baker and dry goods clerk. After designing several woodcut advertisements, he traveled to New York in 1847 in hopes of learning engraving. Unable to do so, he again took work as a retail clerk, but his enlightened employers discovered his talent for modeling busts, and underwrote a trip to Italy for him. After a year or two of study Rogers established a studio in Rome and remained there for the rest of his life. Among his major works were the bronze *Columbus Doors* of the U.S. Capitol; he also completed works left unfinished by Thomas Crawford's sudden death. This statue was Rogers' first public commission.

John Adams (1735–1826), second President of the United States, was born in Quincy, graduated from Harvard, and admitted to the bar in 1755. Inspired by James Otis' arguments for the rights of the Colonials, Adams espoused the crusade for legal rights of the Colonies. His influence was primarily as a constitutional lawyer; Adams lacked any qualities of popular leadership. He was courageous but impetuous, contentious, vain, and often vehement. In the Continental Congress, he was among the first and most persistent to advocate separation from Great Britain, and was instrumental in the acceptance of the Declaration of Independence. As President he suffered from the presence of an opposition Vice-President, Thomas Jefferson, and from intrigue by Alexander Hamilton, a leader of his own party. After a single term he was defeated by Jefferson and retired to the family estate in Quincy. Like Jefferson, he died on the 50th anniversary of the Declaration of Independence, July 4, 1826. Commissioned by Mount Auburn Cemetery.

FIGURE—UPRIGHT MOTIVE NO. 8, 1956. Bronze.
Lehman Hall.
★ Henry Moore (*see* East Cambridge [M.I.T.]: *Three Piece Reclining Figure, Draped*).

RHINOCEROSES, 1937.
Biology laboratories.
Katherine Ward Lane Weems (*see* Fenway: *Rhinoceros*).

The carved brick frieze (1932) and bronze doors (1933) were also designed by Weems.

FISH, 1972. Aluminum.
Gund Hall.
Alberto Collie.

ASPECT OF THE ORACLE: PORTENTOUS. Bronze, h. 6'.
Radcliffe Yard, near Radcliffe Institute.
Mariana Pineda (*see* East Boston: *Twirling*).

★ NIGHT WALL I, 1972. Steel, h. approx. 13′.
In front of Langdell Hall, Law School.
Louise Nevelson (*see* East Cambridge [M.I.T.]: *Transparent Horizon*).

MURAL.
Dining room, Harkness Commons.
★ Hans Arp (1887–1966).

Dadaist, then Surrealist painter, Arp is best remembered for relief
sculpture of whimsical simplicity.

PAINTING. h. approx. 5′ × 25′.
Mallory Smith room, Harkness Commons.
★ Joan Miró (1893–1984).

The Spaniard Miró claimed to paint in an "automatic writing" mode,
never planning, but simply letting his hand and brush go where they
might. The resultant Surrealist works are characterized by flat intersecting forms, often asterisks, moons, and protean animal and human
shapes.

TREE OF LIFE, ca. 1950. Steel.
Harkness Commons.
Richard Leopold.

MOUNT VERNON WALL PIECE, 1971. Cor-ten steel.
Currier House courtyard.
★ Beverly Pepper (*see* Boston [Government Center and Environs]: *Sud-
den Presence*).

EULOGY. Sculpture.
Currier House courtyard.
★ William Zorach (1887–1966).

An American, Zorach pioneered in carving directly in stone, rather
than making clay models to be translated by stonecutters.

ORPHEUS AND EURYDICE XIV½. Bronze.
Currier House courtyard.
Marie Zoe Mercier (b. 1912).

The artist is a 1933 graduate of Radcliffe.

DINING HALL GRAFITTO, 1959. Sand-cast concrete.
Dining hall, Quincy House.
STONE MURAL. Bas-relief carving.
Lobby, Quincy House.
Constantino Nivola (*see* Boston [Downtown]: *Mural*).

JAMES RUSSELL LOWELL, 1904. Bust.
Lowell House courtyard.
★ Daniel Chester French (*see* Concord: *Minuteman*).

I GIVE YOU A POND: MEDITATION 1 & 2. Pastel, 42″ × 84″.
 Kresge Hall, Harvard Business School (Allston).
 Judith Berman (1946–   ).

 Somerville artist Judith Berman draws on her fascination with natural
 history and on an intimate knowledge of biology. As a graduate student
 at the University of New Mexico she explored the desert and moun-
 tains around Albuquerque; she toured the Galapagos Islands to study
 the fauna there, canoed on the Amazon River, and became a certified
 scuba diver so she could study the undersea world of the Caribbean.

WALL SCULPTURE, 1986. Stainless steel, gold-plated brass, four elements,
 h. 9′ × 18′, 10′ × 12′, 11′ × 12′, 9′ × 20′.
 Burden Hall, Harvard Business School.
 Michio Ihara (*see* Lowell: *Pawtucket Prism*).

★ PRISMS, 1992. Acrylic filled with mineral oil, twenty large-scale prisms,
 l. approx. 8.5′ × 1′ × 1′ × 1′.
 Skylights, Class of 1959 Chapel, Harvard Business School (parking lot
 entry road), off North Harvard St., Brighton.
 Charles Ross (1938–   ).

 After taking a B.A. in mathematics (1960) and an M.A. in sculpture
 (1962) from the University of California at Berkeley, Ross began working with large-scale prisms. The job of art, he believes, is to create windows of awareness through which to view the natural order. His
 commissioned work for public spaces may be seen in San Francisco's
 international airport and in buildings in Lincoln, Neb.; Dallas, Tex.; Denver, Colo.; and fourteen other locations. His work is in major museum
 collections such as Los Angeles County, the Whitney (New York), the
 Walker (Minneapolis), Cornell, Berkeley, and Albuquerque. In Santa Fe
 recently he exhibited large-scale drawings made with dynamite. An on-
 going project is "Star Axis" in New Mexico, a natural observatory designed to make visible the "wobble" of the earth's axis, that is, the
 apparent changes in position of the North Star over a 26,000-year period.
 Architect Moshe Safdie wanted the richness of stained glass in this
 sanctuary, but felt traditional work would be inappropriate in a nonde-
 nominational chapel. His solution came in Ross' work. The prisms are
 mounted on a sun-tracking mechanism to prolong the effects on interior
 walls. This project, including the *Time-Piece Tower* below, was com-
 mended by the Boston Society of Architects in 1993 for artist/architect
 collaboration.

★ TIME-PIECE TOWER, 1992. Granite, glass, gold leaf, h. 24′.
 Outside Class of 1959 Chapel, Harvard Business School.
 Karl Schlamminger (1935–   ).

 German-born, Schlamminger was educated at Augsberg and the
 Academy of Fine Arts in Munich. In 1964 he was appointed a professor
 at the Academy of Fine Arts in Istanbul, beginning a life-long exploration of Islamic art and architecture. He spent eleven years teaching at
 the University of Tehran, returning to Munich with the fall of the Shah.

As a free-lance artist, he has executed public commissions in Athens, Tel Aviv, Riyadh, London, and Dusseldorf. In process is a mammoth earthwork for Munich International Airport, 1200 by 700 feet, to be seen during takeoff and landing.

Safdie at first proposed a gateway for this spot, then a column with an antique clock. Seeking a more contemporary statement, architect and artist evolved a tower that tells time, its golden globe traveling from nadir (midnight) to zenith (noon) and back during a twenty-four-hour period.

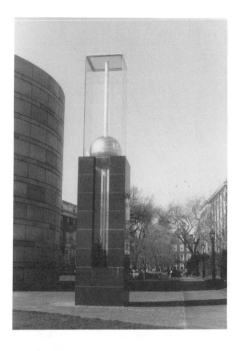

MUSEUM: Harvard Center for European Studies, formerly the Busch-Reisinger Museum, Kirkland St. and Divinity Ave. Founded in 1902 for the study of Germanic culture and bolstered by the addition of Netherlandish work, this collection provides a thorough survey of north-central European art. In addition to medieval treasures, it is strong in materials related to the Bauhaus movement.

MUSEUM: Arthur M. Sackler Museum, 45 Broadway.

MUSEUM: Fogg Art Museum, Quincy St. at Broadway. The epitome of the academic museum, the Fogg is said to have the most extensive collection of any university museum in the world, barring England. Particular strengths are drawings and prints, Far Eastern art, and European work around 1800. The Sackler, opened in 1985, has taken over the public exhibition functions of the Fogg.

JOHN BRIDGE, 1882. Bronze.
   Cambridge Common, Massachusetts Ave. and Waterhouse St.
   Thomas Gould (1818–1881) and M. S. Gould.

   A successful dry-goods merchant who practiced drawing and modeling as a hobby, Gould turned to portrait sculpture for a living when his
business went sour during the Civil War. He went to Florence in 1868
and was modeling this work at the time of his death; his son finished it.
   Bridge (1578–1665) came to Cambridge with the Rev. Thomas
Hooker and remained when Hooker and followers went off to settle
Hartford, Conn. Deacon Bridge is memorialized as founder of Cambridge's grammar school in 1635. Given to the City of Cambridge by
Samuel Bridge, sixth-generation descendent of John Bridge.

CIVIL WAR MEMORIAL, 1869–70. Granite and bronze.
   Cambridge Common.

   A Cambridge police officer wounded in the Civil War, Samuel E.
Chamberlain was the model for the heroic-size granite soldier atop the
monument. The eleven-foot bronze figure of Lincoln within is a casting
of Augustus Saint-Gaudens' Lincoln done for Chicago in 1887; it was
added here later. Erected by City of Cambridge.

THE HIKER. Bronze, larger than life.
   Garden and Concord Sts.
   Theo Alice Ruggles Kitson (*see* Malden: *The Hiker*).
   Erected by the City of Cambridge.

BUTTERCUP, 1984. Painted steel wall relief, h. 4½' × 9' × 2'.
   At University Pl., 124 Mt. Auburn St.
   Peter Lipsitt (*see* Boston [Hyde Park]: *Celebration of the Figure Eight*).

   The developer of this office complex asked a curator of the Boston
Museum of Fine Arts, Kenworth Moffett, to select for this space a collection of works by emerging artists, world-wide. Almost entirely abstract, the group of forty-one pieces is described by a brochure
available at the security desk. Hines plans to display the collection here
for five years, then replace it with newer work and offer this selection to
the MFA. Commissioned by Hines Industrial.

At Charles Hotel, Bennett and Eliot Sts.:

LOBBY GALLERY: rotating exhibitions from the collection of the Polaroid
   Corp. in Cambridge.

   *The permanent collection here focuses on views of Cambridge, Har-
   vard Square, and the Charles River by contemporary realists. Of more
   than fifty works, a partial listing follows:*

LONGFELLOW HOUSE, 1985. Oil on canvas, h. 6½' × 4'.
   Lobby.
   George Nick (1927–   ).

A resident of Concord, Nick was graduated from Yale and has long been a teacher of painting at Massachusetts College of Art. His paintings, usually not this meticulously realistic, are included in the collections of the Boston Museum of Fine Arts, the Metropolitan Museum of Art in New York, and many corporate collections.

Now maintained by the National Park Service, the historic Longfellow mansion, a few blocks from here at 105 Brattle Street, was for forty-five years the home of Henry Wadsworth Longfellow (1807–1882), Harvard professor and poet. Dating from 1759, the house was Washington's headquarters in 1775 when the fledgling Continental Army was encamped on Cambridge Common.

MASS. AVE., HARVARD SQUARE, 1985. h. 5′ × 20′.
  Lobby.
  Joel Babb.

A graduate of Princeton and the Boston Museum School, Babb is an instructor at Harvard University Extension School.

MURAL, 1987, h. 4′ × 23′.
  Bennett Street Cafe.
  Carol Acquiland.

MARTINI GLASS, 1985. Oil, h. 62″ × 42″.
  Second floor, outside Rarities Restaurant.
  Aaron Fink (*see* Lechmere [Royal Sonesta Hotel]: *Cup*).

SYCAMORES—CAMBRIDGE VIEW and SYCAMORES—CHARLES
  RIVER VIEW, 1985. Charcoal triptychs, h. 72″ × 45″.
  Third floor lobby.
  Michael Mazur (*see* Central Square [Hyatt Regency Hotel]: *Untitled*).

BIRCHES, 1982–3. Woodcut, h. 34½″ × 34″.
  Third floor corridor.
  Neil Welliver (*see* Lechmere [Royal Sonesta Hotel]: *Untitled*).

HARVARD STADIUM SERIES, 1986. Three units, each h. 26″ × 25″.
  Third floor corridor.
  Max Mason.

TWO VIEWS OF ANDERSON BRIDGE, 1985. Oil, h. 48″ × 62″; 40″ × 68″.
  Outside Regatta Jazz bar.
LONGFELLOW BRIDGE, 1985. Oil, h. 48″ × 62″.
  In Regatta Jazz bar.
  Emily Eveleth (1961–   ).

A native of Farmington, Conn., Eveleth began her studies at Smith College as a math major but took her degree in studio art. After graduation in 1983 she studied with George Nick. She has abandoned landscape painting for breakfast-table still lifes, which have evolved into critically acclaimed paintings of gigantic jelly doughnuts.

PORTER SQUARE

GIFT OF THE WIND, 1985. Red kinetic sculpture, painted steel, h. approx. 20′.
Susumu Shingu (*see* Boston [Waterfront]: *Echo of the Waves*).
Funded by MBTA.

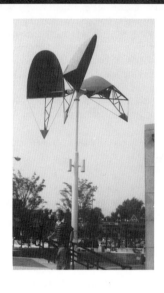

ONDAS, 1984. Carved granite wave (vertical ribbon), h. 24′.
On headhouse.
Carlos Dorrien (*see* Waltham [Bentley College]: *Portal*).
Funded by MBTA.

EMBROIDERED BOLLARDS, 1984. Six granite barriers, h. 27″ × 12″ × 12″.
Surrounding headhouse.
William Reimann (1935–   ).

A senior preceptor and head tutor in visual and environmental studies at Harvard, Cambridge sculptor William Reimann graduated from Yale, spent a fellowship year in England studying drawing and plastics technology, and took an M.F.A. from Yale in 1961. He has taught at Yale, Old Dominion University, and the University of Pennsylvania.

Interested in traditional textile patterns, Reimann has researched weaving and embroidery designs unique to various ethnic traditions. The patterns chosen here are based on cultures that have occupied the Porter Square area: Penobscot Indian, French-Canadian, Irish, Polish, Slav, Russian, Spanish, German, Italian, Scandinavian, Portuguese, African, Asian. These delicate motifs are created with a modern tombstone-cutting technique; a cutout rubber sheet is fixed to the stone, and sandblasting removes the exposed stone.

PORTER SQUARE MEGALITHS, 1980–84. Granite and bronze, 24′ × 24′.
MBTA Plaza at Porter Station.
David Phillips (1944–   ).

Phillips casts his own bronzes at his studio-foundry in Somerville. Born in Michigan, he took a B.F.A. in painting and an M.A. in sculpture at Cranbrook before coming to Boston in 1970. This work is typical of his style through the 1970s, granite boulders sliced with a stonecutter's saw, duplicated in bronze, and re-assembled mix-and-match style, a commentary on the beauty and mass of unworked stone. Funded by MBTA.

LANDSCAPE FRIEZE, 1990. Stained glass, h. 2′ × 21′.
North Cambridge Senior Center, 2050 Massachusetts Ave.
Linda Lichtman (*see* Central Square: *Untitled*).
Funded by Cambridge Arts Council and North Cambridge Stabilization Committee.

NORTH CAMBRIDGE SENIOR CENTER MURAL, 1988. Acrylic, two panels, each h. 9′ × 10′.
North Cambridge Senior Center, 205 Massachusetts Ave.
David Fichter (*see* Lawrence: *Bread and Roses Mural*).
Funded by Lotus Development Corp. and Cambridge Arts Council.

INTERFACE, 1986. Limestone, h. 6′, wt. 11 tons.
11 Linnaean St., at Nityanananda Institute.
David Rogers.

Rogers is an Indiana sculptor who has other public work at the Chicago Zoo and at the Dia Foundation at New Harmony, Ind. This sculpture is based on a mathematical concept, the Mobius strip, a loop with a twist in it that produces a geometric plane infinite in two directions. Commissioned by The Nityanananda Institute.

NORTH CAMBRIDGE

FRONT DESK, 1988. Birch, cherry, maple wood, 10′ × 10′.
Alma Boudreau Observatory Hill Branch Library, 245 Concord Ave.
Mitch Ryerson (1955–   ).

At the forefront of Boston's one-of-a-kind furniture artisans, Ryerson studied furniture design at the Boston University Program in Artisanry (B.A.A., 1982). Earlier, he learned boatbuilding in Lubec, Me. He has taught at Swain School of Design and Penland (N.C.) School of Crafts. Ryerson has held National Endowment for the Arts and Cambridge Arts Council fellowships; he exhibits his work widely.

Though a functional librarian's desk, this one is fitted with playful columns and fronted with a carved and painted low-relief of books framing the Observatory Hill skyline. Funded by Massachusetts Arts Lottery as administered by Cambridge Arts Council.

PAINTED PAINTER, 1981. Acrylic on masonry, 12′ × 50′.
57 Walden St.
Elizabeth Carter (*see* Central Square: *Floating Down Mass. Avenue*).

Photorealist Carter does a little fool-the-eye with her mural of the neighborhood, including the building on which the work is painted and life-sized figures painting the mural. Funded by CDBG.

UNTITLED, 1992. Granite, screens, pavers, plantings.
  Margaret Roethlisberger Park, between Garden and Sherman Sts.
  Edward Levine (1935–   ).

  Levine has been director of the Visual Arts Program of M.I.T.'s department of architecture since 1989; he has also taught art at East Carolina, Wright State, Drake, and Miami (Fla.) universities, and at Minneapolis, California State, and Temple Buell colleges. His degrees include a B.A. from Yale (1957) and an M.A. (1964) and Ph.D. (1975) from New York University. He has held fellowships from the National Endowment for the Arts, North Carolina Artists, Bush Foundation, and others. Collaborating in this project was John Kissida of Camp Dresser and McKee, Inc. Funded by Cambridge 1% for Art.

BRICKWORKER and BALLPLAYER, 1983. Handmade bricks, two figures, $7' \times 12' \times 6'$.
  Rindge Field, Pemberton St.
  David Judelson (*see* Lechmere: *Flag Fragments*).

  The committee overseeing this project decided that the work should be constructed of brick to commemorate the now-defunct brickworking industry of North Cambridge. Judelson made his own bricks and inscribed them with family names of Cambridge brickmakers and brick companies that once operated here. Funded by Vingo Trust and CAC.

THE SEASONS OF CHANGE, 1993. Acrylic, h. $4' \times 75'$.
  Cambridge Friends School, 5 Cadbury Rd.
  David Fichter (*see* Lawrence: *Bread and Roses Mural*), Laurie Tennant-Gadd, and Leslie Shelman.

  Art teachers Tennant-Gadd and Shelman aided students in the design of this, another of Fichter's collaborative school murals (*see* Wayland); it was painted by the entire school community. Commissioned by Cambridge Friends School.

UNTITLED, 1982. Stained glass, h. $1' \times 24'$.
  North Cambridge Public Library, 70 Rindge Ave.
  Linda Lichtman (*see* Central Square: *Untitled*).
  Commissioned by Cambridge Arts Council.

SAGINAW AVENUE MURAL, 1977 and 1984. Acrylic on masonry.
  Davenport St. at Saginaw Ave.
  Jeff Oberdorfer and Elizabeth Carter (*see* Central Square: *Floating Down Mass. Avenue*).

  Painted by a Cambridge architect and his neighbors, this work is intended to integrate the blank wall of a shopping center into the neighborhood. Restored, with addition of figures, by Carter in 1984. Funded by CETA and CDBG.

ENVIRONMENTAL SITE WORK, 1985. Granite.
  East of Alewife Station garage, at Alewife Brook Pkwy. and Rindge Ave.
  Richard Fleischner (*see* East Cambridge [M.I.T.]: *Untitled Collaboration*).

This work is an example of Fleischner's penchant for constructing sculpture with basic-common-denominator blocks, all of the same dimension.

CAMBRIDGE AND ITS WATERSHED, 1983. Acrylic on masonite, 8' × 16'.
At Cambridge Water Dept., 250 Fresh Pond Pkwy.
Michele Turre (1953–   ).

Aerial landscapes have been a motif for Michele Turre, a California native who studied at Sonoma State University and at the University of Iowa. She came East to paint at Cummington Community of the Arts, stayed on as assistant director, and now lives in the small Hampshire Hills town of Goshen. This painting is an aerial view highlighting the city of Cambridge and its reservoirs in the western suburbs. Turre says her work is not usually this literal; this one contains every street and almost every house within a thirty-mile radius. Funded by 1% for Art.

MOUNT AUBURN CEMETERY

A map showing the more interesting graves and memorials may be obtained at the cemetery offices just inside the entrance. Mount Auburn's records list more than forty carvers and sculptors; hundreds of monuments are not attributed. Only a small sampling can be listed here.

SPHINX, 1872. Granite, h. 10'.
South of Chapel.
Martin Milmore (*see* Framingham: *Civil War Memorial*).

Called the strangest of all Civil War memorials, this work was likely designed to please the cemetery's founder, Dr. Jacob Bigelow, who declared the "timeless" Egyptian style appropriate to cemeteries. Here the sphinx is Americanized, its uraeus snake replaced by an eagle. Commissioned by Dr. Jacob Bigelow.

NATHANIEL BOWDITCH, 1846. Bronze, life-size.
Central and Cypress Aves.
★ Robert Ball Hughes (1806–1868).

English-born, the precocious Hughes entered the school of the Royal Academy in London at the age of twelve; one of his works was shown at the Academy's exhibition of 1822. He emigrated to New York in 1829 and came to Boston in 1840.
Bowditch (1773–1838), mathematician and navigator, was born in Salem. A cooper and apprentice ship-chandler as a boy, he developed a taste for mathematics and learned Latin in order to study Newton. He made four long sea voyages in his twenties as a clerk and supercargo, proving such an excellent navigator that he commanded his own ship at the age of twenty-nine. He published *New American Practical Navigator*, a work of value to American sailing masters, and translated Laplace's treatise on celestial mechanics. Hughes depicts him with some of the instruments of navigation.

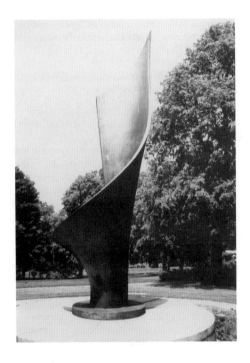

KNOLL GARDEN SCULPTURE, 1981. Cast iron, h. 21′.
Willow Pond knoll.
Richard Duca (1955–   ).

Richard Duca describes himself as largely self-taught, learning his
casting techniques as apprentice to his father, Alfred Duca (*see* Boston
[Back Bay]: *Boston Tapestry*). With few exceptions (this is one), he
casts and finishes his work personally. To make this piece, Duca produced a full-scale version in styrofoam, which was cast by a Pennsylvania industrial foundry using the foam vaporization technique pioneered
by Duca senior. The work is a single solid cast in ductile iron; it weighs
23,000 pounds. A departure from the cemetery's traditional stone carvings, Duca's sculpture is at once organic, in its references to plant
forms, and mathematical in its logarithmic curve, and, the artist says,
"spiritual, with its unfurling, uplifting shape." Duca lives and works on
Cape Ann. Commissioned through invitational competition by Mount
Auburn Cemetery.

HYGEIA.
Poplar Ave. at Lily Path.
★ Edmonia Mary Lewis (ca. 1843–ca. 1909).

The date and place of Lewis' birth and death are unknown. Daughter
of a black father and a Chippewa mother, she was raised by her
mother's family and admitted in 1859 to Oberlin College, the first co-ed-
ucational college to accept women and blacks. In 1862 she was ac-

cused of poisoning two fellow students and sent to trial. She was acquitted, but left Ohio for Boston, where abolitionist William Lloyd Garrison arranged for her to study sculpture with Edward Brackett. With proceeds from her first sale she went to Rome, was befriended by Harriet Hosmer, and became a member of the group of women sculptors working there. Departing from classical themes, Lewis often chose Amerindian and African subjects. Some of her work is owned by the National Museum of American Art in Washington.

Hygeia, goddess of health, is in Greek mythology daughter of Aesculapius, god of medicine.

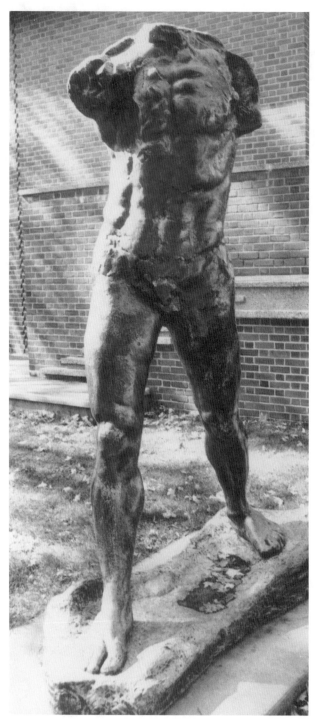

RODIN, WALKING MAN (see page 235)

Other Cities
and Towns

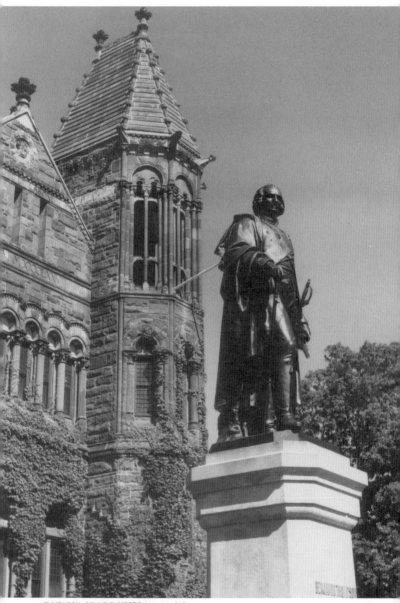
ZUMBUSCH, COUNT RUMFORD (see page 242)

ACTON

SLAP-A-PHONE, 1993. Four-inch PVC pipe, h. 8'.
At The Discovery Museums, 117 Main St.
Arthur Ganson (1955–   ).

Ganson has been described as "a gentle art-world mixture of the
Wright Brothers, Thomas Edison, and Dr. Frankenstein." A Hartford,
Conn., native, he earned his B.F.A. at the University of New Hampshire
in 1978. Although he has had no training in mechanics or engineering,
his art career has been dedicated to making whimsical machines—
some small, some large enough to be entered in the art community's favorite competitive sport, sculpture road races. He lives and works in
Somerville.

Designed to be played by youngsters using their bare hands, Ganson's sculptural instrument spans two octaves in half steps. To encourage experimentation, the keyboard is arranged differently from that of a
piano. The sculpture is dedicated to the memory of Andy Appleton, a
young Acton man who served as an Explainer, or docent, on the museum staff. Though legally blind, Appleton could see well enough to
ride a bicycle; he was on the last leg of a 3,600-mile fund-raiser trip
when he and another rider were killed by a truck. Funded by family and
friends of Andy Appleton.

ANDOVER

ARMILLARY SPHERE. Bronze.
At Phillips Academy, in front of library, on Rte. 28.
★ Paul Manship (1885–1966).

The *Prometheus Fountain* at Rockefeller Center in New York is likely
Manship's best-known work. In 1909 he won a Prix de Rome; his studies in that city left him a master of archaic Classicism. Returning to
New York, he garnered many commissions, awards, and honors, culmi-
nating in twenty-two years as chairman of the Smithsonian Art Commission. Commissioned by the John Hancock Mutual Life Insurance Co.

GALLERY: Addison Gallery at Phillips Academy, Rte. 28. Adjudged one of
the leading museums of American art in this region, the Addison
contains outstanding examples of American painting and (to some
extent) of sculpture from the eighteenth century to the present.

163

ANDOVER WINDSCULPTURES, 1988. Stainless steel, two units, h. 20′.
New England Business Center, off Old River Rd.
Michio Ihara (*see* Lowell: *Pawtucket Prism*).
Commissioned by Theodore R. Tye, National Development of New England.

ARLINGTON

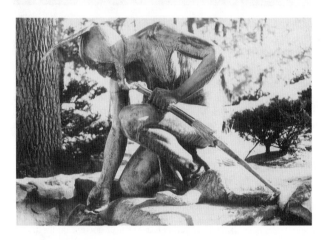

★ INDIAN HUNTER, 1911. Bronze, larger than life.
Park east of Town Hall, Massachusetts Ave.
Cyrus E. Dallin (1861–1944).

   Born in Utah, Dallin as a youngster made friends with Ute Indians living nearby; from this background came his portrayals of the dignity of native Americans. At age nineteen he came to Boston to study with Truman Howe Bartlett and opened a studio here. In Paris for two years of study, he saw Buffalo Bill's Wild West Show and was inspired to create his first equestrian Indian, *Signal of Peace*. After returning to Boston, then Utah, he taught briefly in Philadelphia before settling in Arlington for forty years of teaching, 1900–1940, at Massachusetts State Normal Art School (now Massachusetts College of Art). Other well-known works in Greater Boston include *Paul Revere* in the North End and *Appeal to the Great Spirit* in front of the Boston Museum of Fine Arts.

UNCLE SAM, 1976. Bronze, larger than life.
Massachusetts Ave. and Mystic St.
Theodore C. Barbarossa (1906–1992).

   Born in Vermont, Ted Barbarossa earned a B.F.A. from the School of Art and Architecture at Yale. After assisting a New York sculptor for eight years, he came to Boston to launch his own studio. His career was interrupted by a five-year stint in the army in World War II. His carvings in stone decorate the National Cathedral in Washington, D.C., St. Thomas' Cathedral in New York, and the Baltimore Cathedral.

Samuel Wilson (1766–1854), a native son of Arlington, is thought to be the prototype for the national symbol, Uncle Sam. Gift of Frederick A. Hauck of Cincinnati, Ohio.

On the Minuteman Trail, Rails to Trails bicycle pathway from Arlington to Bedford:

★ MILE MARKERS, 1992. Stone, 10 units, h. 4', one per mile.
   Marty Cain (1941–   ).

Now living in Newport, N.H., Cain has taught at the Boston Museum School, Pine Manor College, the University of Iowa, Thayer Academy, and Darrow School. After undergraduate work at University of New Hampshire, she earned an M.A. and an M.F.A. at the University of Iowa. An active member of the Boston art community for fifteen years, she has exhibited widely both in galleries and in ephemeral outdoor events: with Reclamation Artists (*see* Boston [Charlestown]), at Bradley Palmer State Park in Topsfield, and at Chesterwood in Stockbridge. She is currently associated with Boston Sculptors at Chapel Gallery (*see* Newton). Before forming her outdoor works, which utilize in a sensitive way materials she finds on the site, Cain says she customarily uses a dowsing stick to locate veins and loci of electromagnetic energy. In her travels to the British Isles, she has studied esoteric sites such as ancient cathedrals, holy wells, stone circles, and labyrinths, trying to understand what makes a site sacred. She has twice been a Millay Colony resident. Her work is owned by the Addison Gallery, AT&T, Price Waterhouse, several colleges, and by private collectors across the nation.

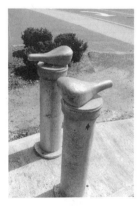

BIKE BOLLARDS, 1992. Cast iron
   and steel, h. 3', 63 units.
   At low-traffic crossings,
   from Lake St., Arlington,
   to Revere St., Lexington.
   John E. Ryther (1951–   ).

Landscape designer for this newly developed bikeway, Ryther is a principal of CityDesign Collaborative, Inc. of Boston. Born in Auburn, N.Y., he received bachelor's degrees in environmental sciences and in landscape architecture awarded jointly by State University of New York and Syracuse University. His work includes extensive park and streetscape design throughout New England.

GATES, 1992. Steel.
Bikeway intersections with Bedford Ave. and Hartwell Ave., Lexington.
Carlos Dorrien (*see* Waltham [Bentley College]: *Portal*).

BEDFORD

★ MILE MARKERS, BIKE BOLLARDS and GATES, 1992.
Minuteman Trail (*see* Arlington, Minuteman Trail).

BEVERLY

ARK, 1988. Ash, cherry, ash plywood, h. $14' \times 7' \times 5'$.
Temple B'nai Abraham, 220 Lothrop St.
Ruth Slavet (1938–   ).

Slavet earned a B.A. in sculpture in 1970 and an M.A. in 1980 from
Boston University. Her work is in the collections of the Boston Museum
of Fine Arts, the Boston Public Library, the Rose Art Museum, and others. She has taught at DeCordova Museum School, Radcliffe pottery
studio, and at B.U. She has a studio in the Fort Point artists' community. Commissioned by Temple B'nai Abraham.

BRAINTREE

ATRIUM SCULPTURES. h. 35'.
200 and 203 Union St.
William Wainwright (*see* East Boston/Logan Airport: *Windwheels*).
Commissioned by Morton Grossman.

BRIDGEWATER

At Bridgewater Massachusetts Correctional Institution SDP
Treatment Center:

The following were all commissioned by the Massachusetts Art in
Public Places Program:

A SCENE THROUGH THE TREES, 1986. Fabric on brackets.
Main lobby.
Sanghye H. Chang.

Chang is a South Korean artist.

FIVE CHAIRS, 1987. Acrylic on board, $4' \times 8'$.
HEDGE, 1987. Acrylic on board, $4' \times 8'$.

FLORIDA PALMS, 1987. Oil on canvas, 40″ × 46″.
BOAT AND ISLAND, 1987. Pastel on paper, 34″ × 26″.
    Janet Fredericks (1949–   ).

    A Burlington, Vt., painter, Fredericks attended Green Mountain Col-
lege in Poultney, Vt., took a B.F.A. from Barry University in Miami, Fla.,
in 1979, and in 1989–90 held the Bertek Fellowship from Vermont
Council on the Arts. She has exhibited both locally and in Europe; her
paintings are in a number of corporate collections.

BANNERS, 1987. Polyester, fifty-two units.
    Catherine Hall.

    Fabric artist Hall lives in Burlington, Vt.

BEYOND THE HORIZON, 1988. Mural, acrylic on canvas, 20′ × 60′.
    David Moore (1954–   ).

    An instructor at Bunker Hill Community College, Moore attended the
Boston Museum School, Skowhegan, and Massachusetts College of
Art (B.F.A.). His interdisciplinary studies at Bard College (M.F.A.) included music composition, poetry, film, and video, as well as visual art;
in his performance work he plays the musical saw. A Newton resident,
Moore has been a fellow at McDowell Colony, Yaddo, and Blue Mountain Center.
    As a condition of painting this mural, Moore asked to institute an art
program with patients of the center. A number of murals were completed, including the large *Predatory/Non-Predatory* in a corridor of the
treatment center.

BROCKTON

POLITICAL TRILOGY, 1978. Bronze, h. 12″.
    Outside City Hall.
    Mark Cooper (1950–   ).

    Cooper graduated from Indiana University and the Boston Museum
School; he teaches at Boston College and the Boston Museum School.
His first public commission, this bronze predates his later work in cement (*see* Burlington: *Catalyst I and II*). Heads Cooper modeled during
this early period were distinctively flattened profiles, set at right angles
to shoulders or bodies. Vandals have wrenched off and stolen two
parts of this three-part work.

ASSAULT ON BATTERY WAGNER and other Civil War scenes, 1895. Oil
    on canvas.
    City Hall west lobby.
    F. Mortimer Lamb (1861–1936).

    Son of a carriage-painter, Lamb was born in Middleborough and
lived much of his life in Stoughton. He attended Massachusetts Normal
Art School, the Boston Museum School, and Academie Julian in Paris.

Lamb both taught and exhibited widely; he liked to take pupils, many of whom were Brockton shoe factory workers, into the fields to sketch. He taught art in Brockton schools and at New England Conservatory of Music, was principal for twenty years of the Evening Drawing School in Taunton and later director of Medfield School of Art. The spandrels *War* and *Peace* in City Hall are also his work.

This work depicts the moment that Col. Robert Gould Shaw was killed leading his black troops against Fort Wagner, S.C. (*see* Boston Common: *Robert Gould Shaw and the 54th Massachusetts Regiment*).

GREAT BLUE HERON, 1990. Bronze, h. 5'.
D. W. Field Park, off Oak St.
Elliott Offner (1931–   ).

Andrew W. Mellon Professor of Humanities at Smith College (he teaches graphic arts), Offner possesses B.A., B.F.A., and M.F.A. degrees from Yale, the latter in sculpture. He maintains a sculpture studio in Northampton. His work is owned by many museums including the Hirschhorn, Brooklyn, and British museums; he recently completed a major public commission for Minneapolis. He has been visiting lecturer at Yale, Boston University, and the Royal College of Art, and artist-in-residence at Cambridge University, England. Among his numerous awards are the gold medal of the National Sculpture Society, and grants from the National Council on the Arts and Humanities, the National Institute of Arts and Letters, and from the Ford, Tiffany, and Merrill foundations.

This 200-pound bird was stolen by vandals in 1991. Found abandoned on a nearby roadside, it was repaired by the artist. Commissioned by the City of Brockton.

At Brockton Art Museum (Oak St. on Upper Porter's Pond):

Although some of Brockton Museum's outdoor art is visible without entering the museum, most of it is located in courtyards and on a terrace bordering Upper Porter's Pond.

GLACE BAY, 1975. Painted steel, h. 6½' × 20'.
Parking lot.
George Greenamyer (*see* Marshfield: *Webster, The Farmer of Marshfield*).

Brockton Art Museum can be identified by this whimsical steam-engine-like work, typical of Greenamyer's style.

REDTUBESING, 1989. Steel, wood, lead, h. 9' × 12' × 80'.
Entryway.
David Judelson (*see* Cambridge [Lechmere]: *Flag Fragments*).

Site-specifically designed for the 1989 Brockton Triennial, these overhead red tubes follow the visitor across the entry bridge to the doors. Counterweights activate noisemaking devices when the doors are opened, as a doorbell of sorts. Gift of the artist.

BROOKLINE

THE SOLDIERS MONUMENT, 1915. Equestrian bronze, heroic size.
    At Brookline Public Library, Washington and School Sts.
    ★ Edward Clark Potter (1857–1923).

    Potter collaborated frequently with Daniel Chester French on eques-
trian monuments, Potter sculpting the horse and French the rider.
Whereas French seldom portrayed animals, Potter could and did do
people; this mounted bugler is entirely his. Potter's first professional
training came in French's studio, 1883–85, followed by work in marble
quarries in Vermont and study in Paris. Among many other works, Potter created the mounts for French's *General Hooker* at the State House
and for *General Devens* in Worcester; he is responsible for the famous
lions in front of the New York Public Library and for a portrait statue of
Robert Fulton in the Library of Congress. This Civil War memorial was
commissioned by the City of Brookline.

TREE OF KNOWLEDGE, TREE OF LIGHT, 1991. Stained-glass window, h.
    12′ × 3.5′.
    Coolidge Corner Library, 31 Pleasant St.
    Linda Lichtman (*see* Cambridge [Central Square]: *Untitled*).
    Funded by Brookline Arts Lottery Council.

SIERRA SLICE, 1975. Cast cement play sculpture, h. 3½′ × 14′.
    Amory Park, Amory St. off Beacon.
    Gregg LeFevre (*see* Boston [Fenway]: *Untitled*).

NEON FOUNTAIN, 1984. Neon, brass, electronics, 18′ × 18′ × 5′.
    Main lobby, 1501 Beacon St.
    Alejandro and Moira Sina (*see* MBTA [Red Line]: Alewife Station).

THREE WOMEN, 1975. Bronze, h. 8′.
    In Hearthstone Plaza.
    Lu Stubbs (1925–   ).

    A native of New York City, Lu Stubbs graduated from the Boston Mu-
seum School and studied at L'Accademia di Belle Arti in Perugia, Italy.
She has taught at the Boston Museum School, Boston University, and
Milton Academy. She maintains a studio in Sharon.

HUSKY, replicated 1990. Bronze, h. 3′.
    Parsons Field, Northeastern University, Paquette St.
    Adio di Biccari (*see* Boston [Boston Common]: *Parkman Plaza*).

    Northeastern's mascot, originally sculpted for Alumni Auditorium, has
been duplicated for the football field.

WAVES OF TIME, 1971. Stainless steel, h. 30′ × 50′.
    Lobby, The Park School, 171 Goddard Ave.
    Alfred M. Duca (*see* Boston [Back Bay]: *Boston Tapestry*).

PULPIT, 1985. Carved cherry, h. 5'.
In St. Paul's Church, 15 St. Paul St.
Murray Dewart (1947–   ).

Born in Vermont, Dewart earned a B.A. at Harvard and an M.F.A. at Massachusetts College of Art. He has taught in Brookline Schools since 1979, and at Mass/Art for a year. His works in wood have evolved from liturgical carvings like this to massive bell frames and gates inspired by Japanese torii gates. A founder of Boston Sculptors at Chapel Gallery (*see* Newton), Dewart participates frequently in temporary outdoor installations; his work is owned by institutions ranging from the Boston Museum of Fine Arts to the Perchersky Monastery in Pskovo, Russia. (*See also* Milton [Milton Academy].) The work comprises five panels depicting scenes from the life of St. Paul.

★   PRIMAVERA, 1987. Granite, h. 15'.
Pine Manor College, in front of Annenberg Library and Communications Center.
Dimitri Hadzi (1921–   ).

Studio professor at Harvard, Hadzi was born in New York City of Greek immigrant parents. He was interested in art from childhood, but he at first thought it an avocation and became a chemist. After serving in the South Pacific in the Air Force during World War II, Hadzi began to study art part-time, then full-time. He graduated from Cooper Union with honors and won a Fulbright fellowship to Greece, where his aesthetic vision began to coalesce with his cultural heritage. Hadzi remained in Europe for fifteen years, garnering a Guggenheim fellowship and serving as an artist-in-residence at the American Academy in Rome, where he designed bronze doors for St. Paul's Church. His work is held by more than twenty-five museums, including the Museum of Modern Art in New York, the Whitney, the Hirschhorn, and the Guggenheim. *Primavera* is one of five Hadzi works in the Greater Boston area.

Stylistically, this work is related to Hadzi's *Omphalos* in Harvard Square. Dedicated in conjunction with Pine Manor's 75th anniversary, it was funded by Carolyn Mann Caswell and Ruth Barstow Dixon, alumnae of the college.

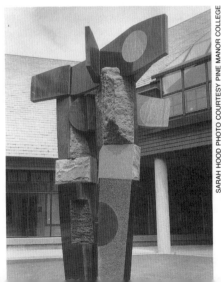

SARAH HOOD PHOTO COURTESY PINE MANOR COLLEGE

BURLINGTON

CATALYST I AND II, 1987. Two
pieces: outside, granite and
aluminum h. 18′ × 20′ × 20′;
hanging in lobby, cast and
fabricated aluminum, h.
75′ × 20′ × 20′.
American Landmark Corp.,
Bedford Rd.
Mark Cooper (*see* Brockton:
Political Trilogy).
Commissioned by Bruce
Silverman.

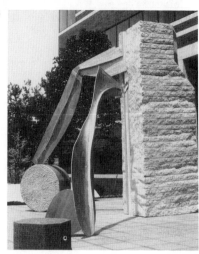

STELE XLVI, 1988. Steel, concrete, and fiber optics, h. 15′.
Exterior, Hewlett-Packard sales office, 29 Burlington Mall Rd.
Clyde Lynds.

A Wallington, N.J., artist, Lynds comments on art over time, juxtapos-
ing primitive geometries incised on rough concrete aggregate with
sleek, modern stainless steel, then lighting the work from within via a
computer-programmed fiber-optic network that continually changes the
light patterns. The cycle takes several days to complete.

AERIAL, 1988. Polymerized cast paper, length 100′.
Lobby, Hewlett-Packard sales office, 29 Burlington Mall Rd.
Gregg LeFevre (*see* Boston [Fenway], Boston University: *Untitled*).

Castings from actual rock faces in the road cuts of nearby Route 128
(touted as "America's Technology Highway") are combined with aerial-
view sculptings of highways, power lines, and agricultural patterns.
LeFevre sees the work as commentary on interactions between hu-
mankind and nature.

LAHEY CLINIC COLLECTION, begun 1978. More than 1000 works on paper.
Hung in all waiting rooms, some hospital rooms.
High school art students.

The idea of acquiring student work to fill the blank walls of this medical center originated with Terry Giggey (d. 1983), a resident of Burlington, who suggested it to a friend on the Lahey staff. Work only by
Burlington High School art students was chosen the first year; the
scope has now expanded to thirty schools in communities near Route
128. The artists donate their work and the clinic pays for framing; the
collection is permanent. About one hundred new works, on the aver-
age, are now selected each year.

CONTROL, installed 1987. Bronze, larger than life.
   In front of Bldg. 8, New England Executive Park, Mall Rd., off Middlesex Turnpike and Rte. 128.
   Victor Salmones, figure; Ed Monti (*see* Quincy: *Constitution Common Sculpture*), granite base.

   Salmones, a Mexican sculptor, often does figures in athletic poses that imply physical control. The work is located outside the physical fitness center of the complex.

WINDHOVER, 1972. Kinetic sculpture, painted aluminum, h. 12′ × 18′.
   New England Executive Park.
   Robert Amory (1942–   ).

   A native of Watertown, N.Y., now living in Watertown, Mass., Robert Amory is a graduate of Harvard. He has turned from kinetic sculpture (*see* Boston [Downtown]: *Helion*) to painting and drawing.

CHELMSFORD

ON EARTH AS IT IS IN HEAVEN, 1987. Appliquéd tapestry, h. 15′ × 5′.
   Entry lobby, North Building at Drum Hill, Rtes. 3 and 4.
   Linda DeHart (*see* Lexington: *Aerial Sculptures*).
   Commissioned by Drum Hill Realty Trust.

CHELSEA

CHELSEA CONVERSATION, 1977–78. Bronze, life-size.
   Chelsea Sq., Broadway and Park St.
   Penelope Jencks (1936–   ).

   Newton resident Penelope Jencks was born in Baltimore, attended Swarthmore College, and studied painting with Hans Hoffmann at Provincetown before taking a fine arts degree at Boston University in 1958. She also studied at the Kunstacademie in Stuttgart, Germany, and has taught at Brandeis, Boston College, and the Art Institute of Boston. She has been a MacDowell fellow and a Massachusetts Artists Foundation recipient. Her realistic and informal sculpted groups are located in London, Pittsburgh, and Toledo, Ohio, as well as in the Boston area.
   Described one hundred years ago as the most desirable location in the metropolitan area, Chelsea more recently was called the "junk capital" of New England because of its paper, cloth, and rubber recycling centers. A disastrous fire in 1973 destroyed all that and opened up the possibility of new uses for 300 acres of commercial district. The landscaping and art in this square is one result. Two of this group are based on real citizens of Chelsea, a high school track star and a retired science teacher (who originally was adjusting his eyeglasses before vandals made off with them). Jencks' daughter posed for the young girl. Funded by City of Chelsea.

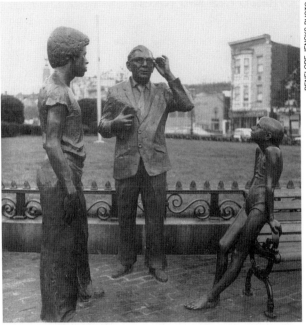

JENCKS, CHELSEA CONVERSATION

★ BELLINGHAM SQUARE, 1978–79. Bronze, life-size.
Bellingham Sq., Broadway and Washington St.
Mags Harries (1945–   ).

Welsh-born Mags Harries possesses one of public art's most fertile
imaginations. Harries took a diploma at Leicester College of Art and Design, England, in 1967, and followed it with a scholarship for graduate
study in the U.S., which led to a master's degree from the University of
Southern Illinois. After completing this commission she was a Bunting
Fellow in 1977–78; she has won a design excellence award from the
U.S. Department of Transportation (*see* MBTA [Porter Station]: *The
Glove Cycle*) and a Grand Bostonian Award. She is a member of the
faculty of the Boston Museum School.

Life-size bronze objects—a pocketbook, a pair of gloves—sit on
benches as if forgotten. Would-be scavengers find they are firmly
bolted down. Funded by City of Chelsea.

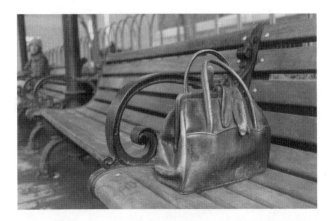

THE HIKER, 1934. Bronze, larger than life.
Broadway, at City Hall.
Theo Alice Ruggles Kitson (*see* Malden: *The Hiker*).

Chelsea's version of *The Hiker* has a time capsule sealed in the base.

SOLDIERS AND SAILORS MONUMENT, 1868. Granite, h. approx. 40'.
Basset Sq., Broadway, across from City Hall.

First erected in Union Park, this monument was moved in 1911 to its present location.

CRAB BRICKS, 1977–78. Bronze, sixty-five units each 8" sq.
Bellingham Sq., Broadway and Bellingham St.
David Phillips (*see* Cambridge [Porter Square]: *Porter Square Megaliths*).

Bronze insets into sidewalk and crosswalk remind passersby that this spot was once a fresh seafood market. Funded by City of Chelsea.

CHELSEA WALK, 1977–79. Silkscreened enameled panels.
In City Hall.
Collaboration: Ronald Lee Fleming, Peter Johnson, Thomas Kirvan, Susan Roberts.

Also called the Memory Wall, this installation depicts Chelsea-connected celebrities—actress Barbara Stanwyck, jazz musician Chick Corea, and songwriter George M. Cohan—as well as local personalities, such as street photographer Harry Siegel. Originally installed in a cut-through alleyway off Broadway and suffering from graffiti, this work was cleaned and reinstalled in the corridors of City Hall in 1989.

SCHOOL OF ALEWIFE, 1984. Aluminum, h. 15'.
Chelsea Naval Hospital Park, on the Mystic River under Tobin Bridge.
William Wainwright (*see* East Boston, Logan Airport: *Windwheels*).
Commissioned by MDC.

CONCORD

THE MINUTEMAN OF CONCORD, 1874. Bronze, larger than life.
At Old North Bridge (Minuteman National Park).
★ Daniel Chester French (1850–1931).

With the approach of the United States Centennial in 1876, contention heightened as to where the American Revolution really began. At Lexington, where rebel militia first confronted Redcoats (and were massacred)? Or at Concord, where the Colonials massed, turned back the King's troops, and inflicted the first casualties? Concord decided to press its claim by erecting a statue dedicated to its 1775 militiamen.
Son of a prominent Concord judge, the twenty-three-year-old French had never made a statue when he applied for the commission. He had

not even thought of sculpture as a career until, at seventeen, he had astounded his family by whittling a frog from a turnip. He studied drawing briefly with fellow Concordian May Alcott, anatomy with Dr. Rimmer in Boston, and sculpture for a month in the studio of J. Q. A. Ward in New York. He had cast a few small works by trial and error.

Nevertheless, the Concord committee accepted his model, agreeing to pay the costs of the work if the young sculptor would donate his services. French accepted those terms. Concord citizens searched barns and attics for authentic costume, plow, musket, and powder horn; the French family's farm hand, Patrick, posed for the minuteman's arms. One Concord citizen with influence in Washington arranged for the government to contribute bronze cannon for casting material and to pay for the casting process. After the dedication of the statue the satisfied town reconsidered and voted French a $1,000 fee. (On the base are the first lines of the commemorative poem written by Emerson for the dedication ceremony.) Funded by bequest of Ebenezer Hubbard, public subscription, the town of Concord, and the United States government.

MOURNING VICTORY, 1909. Granite, life-size.
Sleepy Hollow Cemetery.
★ Daniel Chester French (*see Minuteman* above).

A Concord schoolmate of French's, James Melvin, had watched his three older brothers enlist as privates in the Union Army. One died in battle, one in hospital, one in prison. James, sixteen in the last year of the war, also enlisted, but survived and vowed to become wealthy enough to commission a memorial to his brothers. The grieving figure is French's statement on the price of war, even victorious war.

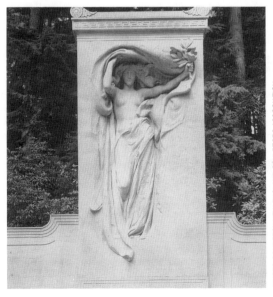

PHOTO COURTESY NEW ENGLAND SCULPTORS ASSOCIATION

CONNECTING THREADS: THE ART OF CHILDREN'S LITERATURE, 1989.
Fabric, h. 109″ × 70″.
Children's room, Concord Library.
Fifty volunteer quilters.

To celebrate the opening of the new children's wing, librarians Karen Ahearn and Fayth Chambland sent panels of cloth to thirty-four authors and illustrators of favorite children's books. Every one returned an autographed square, which was then quilted by volunteers with an illustration from the book. Included are works by Michael Bond, Eric Carle, Robert McCloskey, Tomie de Paola, William Steig, Dr. Seuss, Peter Spier, and Garth Williams.

A. BRONSON ALCOTT, 1882. Bust, life-size.
At Concord Library.
★ Daniel Chester French (*see Minuteman* above).

Known today, if at all, as the father of Louisa May Alcott, or as a dreamer and ne'er-do-well Utopian who couldn't provide for his own family, Bronson Alcott (1799–1888) was in his day one of the most famous men in America. A self-educated country boy, he became an iconoclastic educator, pioneering the idea that gentleness and thoughtful conversation were more conducive to learning than the birch rod. The Alcotts lived at Orchard House (now a Concord museum) on Lexington Road. Here Bronson founded his School of Philosophy, an early Chatauqua; the building still stands and is used for lectures in summer.

RALPH WALDO EMERSON, 1879. Bust.
At Concord Library.
★ Daniel Chester French (*see Minuteman* above).

Emerson (1803–1882), poet, essayist, Unitarian minister, and Transcendentalist philosopher, was the most renowned of the Concord intellectuals who were the nucleus of American thinking in the nineteenth century.

In a sense French was a protégé of Emerson, who served on the committee that commissioned the *Minuteman* and was probably instrumental in seeing that the young sculptor was paid at last. After a year of study in Italy, the diffident artist approached Concord's greatest man, then in his seventy-seventh year, to sit for a portrait bust. Always gracious, he did, and is said to have joked, "You know, Dan, the more it resembles me, the worse it looks." The philosopher and his family pronounced it the best likeness ever done of him. A copy of the bust is at Harvard's Memorial Hall.

RALPH WALDO EMERSON, 1914. Seated statue, marble, life-size.
Concord Library.
★ Daniel Chester French (*see Minuteman* above).

French's daughter Margaret relates that her father knew and loved Emerson so well he was almost afraid to embark on this commission so long after Emerson's death. The philosopher's family sent him Emerson's favorite heavy dressing gown (which the family called his "Gaberlunzey''), a garment he wore in his study on cold mornings. Drawing on his own memories, French portrayed Emerson leaning forward in a characteristic questioning attitude.

GALLERIES: Concord Art Association, 37 Lexington Rd.
Blanchard Trust Gallery, Emerson Umbrella Center for the Arts, 40 Stow St.

At Middlesex School (Lowell Rd.):

ABRAXAS, 1972. Cor-ten steel, h. 12'.
VASQUEZ, 1975. Cor-ten steel, h. 16'.
ASPECT #1, 1969. Mild steel painted, h. 12'.
ASPECT #3, 1970. Cor-ten steel, h. 7' (shown below).
David Lang (1941–   ).

Manhattan native David Lang studied at Paier School of Art in New Haven, earned a B.S. in biology at Fairfield University, then undertook a three-year graduate program at Massachusetts General Hospital in medical illustration. He has taught art at Middlesex since 1972 and been chairman of the art department since 1975. Known also as a watercolorist, Lang lives in Wayland.

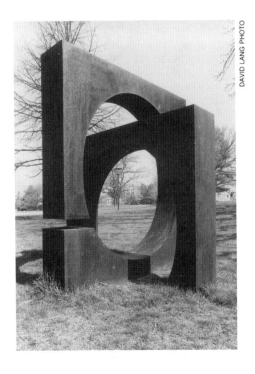

DAVID LANG PHOTO

DANVERS

WILLIAM PENN HUSSEY, 1916. Bronze, equestrian, larger than life.
    Water St., across from New England Home for the Deaf.
    George T. Brewster (1862–1943).

    A native of Kingston, Mass., Brewster studied at Massachusetts State Normal School, Cooper Union in New York, and L'Ecole des Beaux Arts in Paris. He sculpted the figure atop the state capitol in Providence, R.I., another in Indianapolis, and numerous other public monuments. He lived in Greenwich, Conn., teaching at both Cooper Union and Rhode Island School of Design.
    William Penn Hussey (1846–1910), born in North Berwick, Me., is described as an entrepreneur who had a checkered career and married a millionaire's daughter. To celebrate Danvers' 150th anniversary in 1902, he organized and underwrote the celebratory parade, naming himself Grand Marshal thereof. After his death his family decided to perpetuate the memory of that day by having him portrayed in bronze in his Grand Marshal's uniform (he had no military career). The work was erected on the Hussey estate, which in 1925 was sold to the New England Home for the Deaf.

DUXBURY

At Duxbury Art Complex Museum, 189 Alden St.:

WIND SCULPTURE, 1989. Stainless steel, h. 22′, kinetic element h. 5′ × 16′.
    Michio Ihara (*see* Lowell: *Pawtucket Prism*).

FIVE SHAKER HOUSES, 1976. Welded steel, painted, h. 7½′ × 20′ × 2′ .
    In front of Duxbury Art Complex Museum, 189 Alden St.
    George Greenamyer (*see* Marshfield: *Webster, the Farmer of Marshfield*).

TRILITH, 1982. Granite and bronze, h. 3′.
    David Phillips (*see* Cambridge [Porter Square]: *Porter Square Megaliths*).

NORDKAPP, 1984. Bolted aluminum, h. 17″.
    Rear courtyard.
    Miriam Knapp (*see* Boston [South End/Roxbury]: *Cityscape III*).
    Gift of David and Sandra Bakalar.

MILES STANDISH, 1926. Granite, h. 14′, atop 116′ tower.
    Miles Standish State Park, Crescent St., South Duxbury.
    John Horrigan (*see* Holbrook: *Soldiers Monument*).

    On a promontory of Goose Point, the obelisk formed by the Standish tower and statue provides a landmark up and down the coast. Its cornerstone was laid in 1872, but the monument was not completed until

1898. Originally bronze, the figure proved attractive to lightning; old clippings recount that the head and arms were knocked off in a thunderstorm in 1903, the head again in 1923. At that point Horrigan proposed to redo Standish in Quincy granite, producing the version that stands atop the tower now. The tower affords magnificent views of Duxbury, Kingston Bay, and Plymouth Harbor.

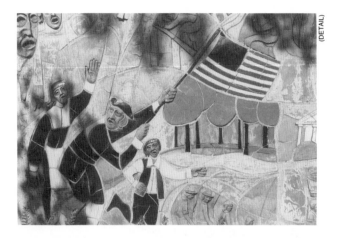

(DETAIL)

EAST BRIDGEWATER

MURAL, 1973. Ceramic, h. 6½′ × 68′ long.
  Grounds of East Bridgewater Unitarian Church, Central and Church Sts.
  John C. Moakley (1931–   ).

A graduate of the Boston Museum School and former teacher there, ceramicist John Moakley studied for two years in Florence on a Museum of Fine Arts traveling fellowship. Born in Lexington, he now lives and works in Dennis. For this wall Moakley researched town, church, and area history to create the 600 panels meant to be "a series of chapters" in that history. In 1991 the artist discovered the mural had been damaged and the present owners of the church, a fundamentalist sect objecting to panels referring to drugs and antiwar protests, planned to tear the wall down. Moakley sued under state artists' rights legislation that protects legitimate works of art. He lost; the judge opined that forcing the church to keep the wall would interfere with its freedom of worship. An appeal was planned, and an injunction protects the wall until there is a judgment on the appeal. Commissioned by the Rev. John Paul Rich, pastor of the church in 1973.

PARKER MEMORIAL FOUNTAIN, 1940. Stone, h. 5½′.
In front of Washburn Library, Bedford St.
Hildegarde Snow.

Snow was a Framingham artist. Bequest of Mary Folson Parker, who died ca. 1910.

EASTON

OLIVER AMES MEMORIAL, 1889. Bronze, larger than life.
Cemetery behind Unity Church of North Easton, Elm St.
Robert Kraus (*see* Boston [Boston Common]: *Boston Massacre Monument*).

Oakes Ames was a Congressman, his brother Oliver president of the Union Pacific Railroad, and both were tainted during the Credit Mobiliér scandals of the first Grant administration. Their children, believing them innocent, turned Easton into a showcase of art and architecture in their memory. In addition to this piece and other funerary monuments, the brothers are immortalized by a set of buildings designed by H. H. Richardson, Boston's famed builder of Romanesque brownstones: Oakes Ames Memorial Hall (1881), Oliver Ames Free Library (1871), the railroad station (now headquarters of the Historical Society), and assorted private mansions. Oliver became governor of Massachusetts, 1886–8.

EVERETT

THE HIKER, 1927. Bronze, heroic size.
At Parlin Library, Broadway and School St.
Theo Alice Ruggles Kitson (*see* Malden: *The Hiker*).

FOXBOROUGH

CIVIL WAR MEMORIAL. h. 10′.
Atop Foxboro library, South and Central Sts.
Charles H. Pizzano (1893–1987).

Born in Italy, Pizzano emigrated at age twelve to Boston, where he attended Bennet Street Industrial School and the Boston Museum School. Primarily a sculptor in wood, he carved works for many churches, including the National Cathedral in Washington.

FRAMINGHAM

LEADING EDGE, 1990. Stainless steel, cast bronze, gold plate, granite, h. 7′.
Lobby, New England Telephone Network Operations Center, 350 Cochituate Rd.
Richard Duca (*see* Cambridge [Mount Auburn Cemetery]: *Knoll Garden Sculpture*).

An interpretation of the Communications Center's logo, this work, like the one that follows, was commissioned by New England Telephone Co. after open competition.

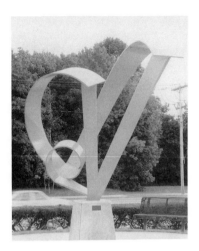

LEADING EDGE, 1990. Welded steel, painted, h. 9.5′.
  At New England Telephone Network Operations Center, 350 Cochituate
  Rd.
  Frances G. Pratt (1938–   ).

  A graduate of Connecticut College in 1960 (B.A., fine art), Pratt re-
turned to the Boston Museum School in 1984–85 to study sculpture.
She has exhibited widely on the East Coast; she lives in Cambridge.
Commissioned by New England Telephone Co.

CIVIL WAR MEMORIAL, 1872. Bronze, larger than life.
  Framingham Center, Oak St.
  Martin Milmore (1844–1881).

  Brought to Boston from Ireland as a child, Martin Milmore was educated at Latin School and then given art lessons at Lowell Institute. His
brother, who had become a cabinetmaker and stonecutter, taught him
stone carving; when he was fourteen, Martin persuaded a reluctant
Thomas Ball to take him as an apprentice, and he worked under Ball
during the years Ball created the equestrian Washington for the Public
Garden. Upon returning to Italy, Ball directed some commissions toward Milmore, whose career progressed from the success of the *Soldiers Monument* now in Forest Hills Cemetery to the large and
complex Civil War memorial on Boston Common. Milmore is described
as the consciously picturesque artistic figure, with dark hair and eyes,
affecting a cloak and a broad-brimmed soft hat. His premature death resulted in the famed memorial work by Daniel Chester French, *Death
Staying the Hand of the Sculptor* (*see* Boston [Jamaica Plain], Forest
Hills Cemetery).
  The sameness of Civil War monuments on New England town
greens leads one to think that they are factory reproductions. Such is
not the case; the ubiquitous statues are based on an original work by
Milmore, his *Soldiers Monument* in Forest Hills Cemetery. Leaning on

his rifle, heroic but pensive, perhaps grieving, Milmore's soldier best expressed the sentiment of the day. A few of the variations are by Milmore himself; this one, later and more mature, is one of his best. Commissioned by George Phipps.

THE MINUTEMAN, 1905. Bronze, larger than life.
Union and Main Sts.
Theo Alice Ruggles Kitson (*see* Malden: *The Hiker*).

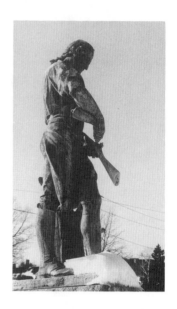

The popular theme of Colonial militiamen leaving their daily work to fight the English troops gets yet another variation here. This Kitson *Minuteman* is a blacksmith, complete with apron, forge, hammer, and tongs; he loads his rifle from his powder horn. The statue stands on what was once the drill field of the town's militia. Commissioned by the Town of Framingham and Framingham Chapter, Daughters of the American Revolution.

At Framingham State College:

DELTA 1-2-3, date unknown. Stainless steel, h. 30″.
Between Hemenway Annex and May Hall.
Arthur Mazmurian (d. 1979).

Seldom do the deceased create their own memorials, but such is the case here. Arthur B. Mazmurian, an assistant professor of art, had

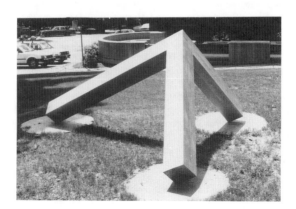

been teaching at Framingham State for eight years at the time of his unexpected death in 1979. The college dedicated this work of Mazmurian's as a memorial to him.

MUSEUM: Danforth Museum, 123 Union St. Founded in 1975, the Danforth owns a collection of nineteenth- and twentieth-century art; hosts bi-monthly contemporary exhibitions.

THE QUESTION IS THE ANSWER, 1977. Cor-ten, stainless steel, h. 14'.
In front of Danforth Museum, 123 Union St.
David Lang (*see* Concord: *Abraxas*, etc.).

GLOUCESTER

JOAN OF ARC, 1910. Bronze, larger than life.
Main and Washington Sts.
★ Anna Vaughn Hyatt Huntington (1876–1973).

As a child, Cambridge native Anna Hyatt summered on a Maryland horse farm and there acquired her love of animals. She studied with Henry Hudson Kitson in Boston and at the Art Students League in New York before going to France to pursue her career. At the age of forty-seven she married poet/philanthropist Archer M. Huntington; together they founded Brookgreen Garden in South Carolina, generally acknowledged to be the first outdoor sculpture garden.

The model for this sculpture won an honorable mention at the Paris Salon of 1910; a heroic-scale version was commissioned for New York City and in 1915 won a Purple Rosette from the French government. Because the sculptor lived in Gloucester for a time, the town commissioned this full-scale copy for its World War I memorial.

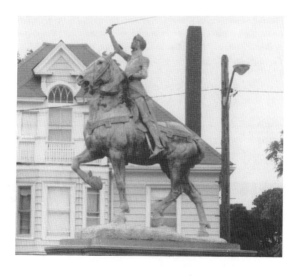

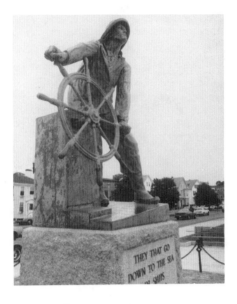

★ THE FISHERMAN, 1925. Bronze, larger than life.
Western Ave., on Pavilion Beach.
Leonard Craske (1877–1950).

A product of London and London University, Leonard Craske studied anatomy at St. Thomas' hospital and served as a demonstrator in anatomy and pathology. He learned etching, was an actor for a time, and later in life became a color photographer. After studying sculpture in England, he came to the U.S. in 1910, taking studios in Boston but summering in Gloucester. An enthusiastic sailor, he was engaged in a study of the characteristics of Gloucester fishermen when the town decided, as part of its 1923 tricentennial, to commission a permanent memorial. Craske was chosen. Asked later who his model was, he said that he went out on the *Elizabeth Nunan* one time and was aided by watching Capt. Herbert Thompson in action during a blow.

Twenty years later Craske designed a companion monument: a fisherman's wife, babe in arms, standing on the shore, with the inscription, "They also serve who only stand and wait." He was not able to raise funds to execute it.

WALL RELIEF.
Exterior, Coast Guard station.
Adio di Biccari (*see* Boston [Boston Common]: *Parkman Plaza*).

HINGHAM

VICTORY, 1922. Equestrian bronze, larger than life.
Rte. 3A at Hingham harbor.
Theo Alice Ruggles Kitson (*see* Malden: *The Hiker*).

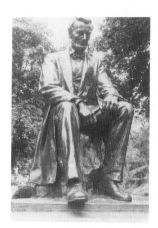

LINCOLN, 1922. Bronze, larger than life.
Lincoln and North Sts.
Charles E. Keck (1875–1951).

The seated Lincoln is a 1939 casting of a work originally done for Wabash, Ind., by Keck, a New York sculptor. Donor Everett E. Whitney conceived the idea of a Lincoln statue here to recognize the family's roots in Hingham: in 1637, six generations before the sixteenth President was born, a weaver named Samuel Lincoln came to Hingham, Mass., from Hingham, England. Whitney traced the lineage and researched statues done of Lincoln, settling on Keck's as most suitable for this location.

HOLBROOK

SOLDIERS MONUMENT, 1917. Bronze, life-size.
In Mary Wales Park, jct. Rtes. 37 and 139.
John Horrigan (1864–1939).

Largely self-taught, Horrigan grew up in Vermont and from boyhood worked in the Cornish quarries. His only formal education came in Vermont village schools and Quincy night school. Picking up tips in modeling clay from artists for whom he cut stone, Horrigan carved out a career as a sculptor of religious and military works.

HOPKINTON

THE DOUGHBOY, 1931. Bronze, larger than life.
Junction Rte. 135 and Ash St.
Theo Alice Ruggles Kitson (*see* Malden: *The Hiker*).

THE TORTOISE AND THE HARE, installation planned April, 1994. Bronze, tortoise h. 18″ × 4.5′ × 2.5′; hare h. 3′.
Somewhere on the Boston Marathon race course, between Hopkinton and Back Bay, Boston.
Nancy Schön (*see* Boston [Boston Common]: *Make Way for Ducklings*).

To celebrate the 100th anniversary of the Boston Marathon in 1996, the Boston Athletic Association plans to place art along the race course. This fabled racing pair was originally intended for a site near the starting line. The BAA says it might be placed near the finish line instead. (*See also* Newton: *Johnny Kelley*.)

HULL

WORLD WAR I MEMORIAL. Stone, h. approx. 15′.
Nantasket and Samoset Aves.
Gerald T. Horrigan (*see* Quincy: *Robert Burns*).

LAWRENCE

BREAD AND ROSES MURAL, 1986. h. 17′ × 50′.
Exterior, Greater Lawrence Family Health Center, 150 Park St.
David Fichter (1951–   ).

A graduate of Harvard College, Fichter has done half-a-dozen murals in this area as a grant recipient from the Massachusetts Council on the Arts and Humanities and arts lottery councils. He also does theater and poster design and paintings. This mural depicts Lawrence's history, including the historic Bread and Roses strike in 1912, which gave lasting impetus to the labor movement. Funded by WBZ Fund for the Arts and the Stevens Foundation.

CIVIL WAR MONUMENT, 1881. Bronze and stone, figures larger than life.
On the common, Lawrence and Common Sts.
W. R. O'Donovan.

WORLD WAR II MONUMENT, 1948. Bronze, larger than life.
On the common, Lawrence and Common Sts.
Leonard Craske (*see* Gloucester: *The Fisherman*).

SYMBOLIC WATER WHEELS, 1976. Steel, diam. 8′.
Massachusetts Commemorative Industrial Park.
William Wainwright (*see* East Boston, Logan Airport: *Windwheels*).

WORLD OF THE FUTURE—SPACE, 1973. Steel, h. 23′.
Haverhill St. side of library.
Sam Facella.

When this building was designed, the architect left a space facing the common for an object to beautify the grounds, without specifying

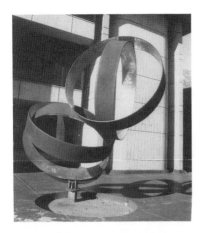

what it would be. Facella, president of an iron and steel company and a sculptor by avocation, designed a small model in his studio, and municipal and private sources provided the funds to build it full-scale.

LEXINGTON

★ THE MINUTEMAN, 1899. Bronze, larger than life.
Lexington Green, Massachusetts and Bedford Rds.
Henry Hudson Kitson (1863–1947).

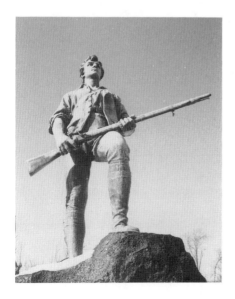

One of New England's more prolific makers of portrait statues and monuments, H. H. Kitson was English-born and trained in Paris. Shortly after coming to this country to work he took an interest in the career of a young Brookline woman, Theo Alice Ruggles (*see* Malden: *The Hiker*). He encouraged her to go to Paris to study, followed her, and married her in 1893. The Kitsons collaborated on a few works, but later separated and pursued independent careers.

At its inaugural, the press of the day, with considerable disregard for historical accuracy, dubbed this statue "Captain Parker," for the commander of the Lexington Minutemen. In 1775 Parker was forty-five years old, described as "a great tall man with a large head and a high, wide brow." Kitson's idealized young militiaman stands on the green where a tiny band of seventy-seven gathered in response to Revere's alarm in the early hours of April 19. Sent from Boston to search for arms and powder and, if possible, to capture Sam Adams and John Hancock, Gen. Gage's men marched through the night and arrived here about sunrise, arrogant and short of patience. Witnesses said that their captain shouted, "Disperse, ye damned rebels!"; no one agrees what happened next. A shot was fired—it is uncertain by whom—and both sides exchanged fire. As the smoke cleared eight Colonials lay dying; the Redcoats, without casualties, marched on toward Concord. Bequest of Francis Brown Hayes.

GEORGE WASHINGTON, 1979. Bronze, h. 4'6".
At Museum of Our National Heritage, 33 Marrett Rd.
Donald De Lue (1897–1988).

A major producer of commemorative and allegorical sculpture, Donald De Lue created *Quest Eternal* at the Prudential Center and the bronze doors at the Federal Reserve Bank in Boston. Among his dozens of large-scale commissions was *The Rocket Thrower*, a gigantic forty-five-foot bronze figure at the 1964–65 World's Fair in New York. He was also responsible for the Boy Scout memorial on the mall in Washington, D.C., and for bronzes at Valley Forge, Gettysburg, the Alamo, and Omaha Beach in Normandy, France.

This depiction of the nation's first President in full Masonic regalia was cast from the original half-scale model for a ten-foot statue for New Orleans. It is dedicated to the museum's first vice-president, the late Wayne E. Stichter (d. 1977), a thirty-third-degree Mason instrumental in the founding of the museum. Gift of the Stichter family.

SAMUEL ADAMS (*see* Boston [Quincy Market]: *Samuel Adams*), 1874. Marble, larger than life.
In Cary Hall, 1625 Massachusetts Ave.
Martin Milmore (*see* Framingham: *Civil War Memorial*).

JOHN HANCOCK (*see* Quincy: *John Hancock*), 1874. Marble, larger than life.
In Cary Hall, 1625 Massachusetts Ave.
Thomas R. Gould (*see* Cambridge [Harvard Square]: *John Bridge*).

LEXINGTON: A SENSE OF PLACE, 1987. Photomontage, 54″ × 70″.
  Lobby, Town Hall.
  Roy Crystal.

   Compiled by Lexington photographer Roy Crystal, this work consists
of fifty-two rear-illuminated transparencies, four large and forty-eight
small. Commissioned by Lexington Council for the Arts.

ART IN THE TOWN OFFICE BUILDING, purchased 1990, 1992. Sculpture,
  photographs, paintings, prints, fourteen pieces.
  Hallways, all three floors, Town Offices, 1625 Massachusetts Ave.

   All by Lexington artists, these works were purchased for a permanent collection by donations from patrons and by a grant from Lexington Council for the Arts.

ATLANTIC II, 1989. Bronze, h. 4′ × 4.5′.
  Courtyard off children's room, Cary Memorial Library, 1874 Massachu-
  setts Ave.
  Richard Filipowski (1923–   ).

   Born in Poland, Filipowski was brought to Canada at the age of four
and grew up in the Toronto area. He studied art and architecture at the
Institute of Design in Chicago. In 1950 he was invited by Walter
Gropius to teach design at Harvard; after two years he moved to
M.I.T., where he was on the faculty for thirty-six years. Although he has
many works in corporate settings, this is his only public work. Purchase
of Lexington Council for the Arts and Trustees of Public Trusts.

NEWS OF LEXINGTON, 1852. Oil on canvas.
  Oval room, Cary Memorial Library, 1874 Massachusetts Ave.
  Emanuel Lutze (1816–1868).

   A German painter, Lutze twice traveled to America to try his luck
with historical paintings; his most famed is *Washington Crossing the
Delaware*. He painted this one on his first trip here.

   *Cary Memorial Library distributes a ten-page booklet describing and
summarizing the history of two dozen art works displayed here and at
its East Branch, 735 Massachusetts Ave.*

AERIAL SCULPTURES, 1983. Two units, fabric, plexiglass, each h. 36′.
  Atriums, Lexington Office Park, 420 and 430 Bedford St.
  Linda DeHart (1939–   ).

   Connecticut-born Linda DeHart studied at Rhode Island School of Design, moved to Cambridge, and worked as a fashion designer for a
dozen years before turning full-time to sculpture. She has taught at Boston Architectural Center, and has been recipient of a 1% for Art grant.
Although these two works are in separate buildings and one employs
aluminum fabric, the other colored fabric, they are considered a related
pair. Commissioned by Boston Properties Inc.

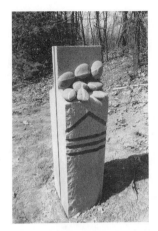

★ MILE MARKERS, BICYCLE
BOLLARDS, and GATES, 1992.
Minuteman Trail (*see* Arlington,
Minuteman Trail).

LINCOLN

At DeCordova Museum and Sculpture Park:

*Dream house of an eccentric Europhile, the "castle" and its grounds
were given to the town of Lincoln by its owner, Julian DeCordova. Since
1950 the museum has been a force in the recognition and collection of
art by New Englanders. The park, almost thirty-five acres surrounding
the castle and sloping down to Flint's Pond (also called Sandy Pond), is
operated by the museum as an outdoor gallery. Of the twenty or so
sculptures on site at any given time, about a dozen are actually owned
by the museum or are here on extended loan. Those are listed, with the
caveat that there will be others and that the museum rearranges the
display from time to time.*

X NOTION LIKE AN H, 1978. Steel, h. 12′ × 8′ × 4′.
Lila Katzen (1932–   ).

   Katzen is a New York sculptor.

★ 3 GARDENS, 1981. Shrubs and other media.
Mags Harries (*see* Chelsea: *Bellingham Square*).

   Although technically here on loan, Harries' three tiny gardens are lit-
erally rooted in place and likely to remain for a while. So small as to
seem parodies of the formal English garden, the three areas are meant
to contrast with the natural landscape of the museum's acreage. They
incorporate on a small scale many horticultural clichés: a sinuous
bricked walkway, one wrought-iron chair, an archway with yews trained
over it, a mergatroid (silver ball on a pedestal). Funded by Massachusetts Council on the the Arts and Humanities.

SKIMMER, 1989. Copper, h. 10′.
Jonathan Bonner (1950–   ).

Bonner graduated from Philadelphia College of Art in 1971 and was awarded a master's degree by Rhode Island School of Design in 1973. He lives in Providence.

A few years ago Bonner's father needed a weather vane for his house in Cape Breton, so his sculptor son made him one. The job inspired Bonner to try more fanciful shapes—fish, hot dogs complete with wavy rods for steam—that would still function as wind direction indicators. *Skimmer* is one of that series.

MASS. ART VEHICLE, 1970. Welded steel, h. 8'3" × 10' × 2'.
George Greenamyer (*see* Marshfield: *Webster, the Farmer of Marshfield*).

MIGRATION—SERIES NO. 7, 1976. Steel, h. 7½' × 5½' × 6'.
Dennis Kowal (*see* Wellesley [Babson College]: *Ominous Icon #6* and *Yaddo Study*).

ACADIAN GYRO, 1987. Bronze, h. 10'8".
Ed Shay (1947–).

Shay says that subconscious realizations unfolded as he developed this piece, begun as a primitive boat shape. The figurehead developed into a fishhead, and fins/oars/wings began to give a sense of ascending. In Shay's mind the piece evokes his Nova Scotia/New Brunswick heritage, providing direction and stability for him as a gyroscope does for a ship. Boston-born, Shay works in Carbondale, Ill.

BITTERSWEET STEPS, 1993. Steel and local vegetation, l. 23' × w. 9'.
From castle to Flint's Pond.
Ross Miller (*see* Boston [Downtown]: *Dancing Trellis*).

Miller intends for bittersweet, a rampant local vine that bears handsome berries in fall, to twine in and around his steel mesh staircase. The work deals, he says, with the exploratory edges of public art, with issues of culture, landscape, art, and change. Commissioned by DeCordova Museum.

CARDINAL POINTS, 1965. Welded steel, h. 9' × 9½' × 8'.
★ Alexander Liberman (*see* Waltham [Brandeis University]: *End Free Series XV*).

Unlike most sculptors, Liberman seldom draws or makes a model before he starts a work: "I like to go straight into scale," he says. He often cuts up discarded oil barrels as his medium for rough working concepts.

GROUP OF THREE, 1969. Concrete, h. 9' × 8' × 7'.
Hugh Townley (1923–).

Another version of this work stands in Providence, where Townley teaches at Brown University. The three abstract components can be read as letters which spell "ART."

LEANING TORSO, 1969. Forged steel, black marble, concrete, h. 5'2" × 3'2" × 2'8'.
Lawrence Fane (1933–).

The contrast of steel and concrete, the sculptor says, suggests the opposition of rigid and soft forms, bone and tissue, in the human figure.

COLLEONI, 1965. Bronze, h. 30″ × 28″ × 14″.
Richard Fishman (1941–   ).

The title refers to Verrochio's monumental equestrian statue in Venice, a prize of Renaissance art. Fishman's work attempts to deal with animal–human, physical–spiritual metamorphoses, "cohering into a new and powerful presence," the artist says. Temporarily removed for reconstruction of base.

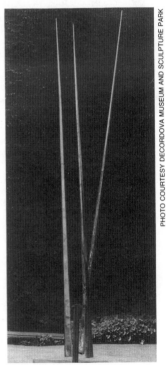

PHOTO COURTESY DECORDOVA MUSEUM AND SCULPTURE PARK

THREE LINES, 1964. Stainless steel, h. 18′.
★ George Rickey (1907–   ).

Minimalist studies in line and balance, Rickey's lines may be seen at such museums as the Hirshhorn in Washington, D.C. Done with calculated engineering skills, the blades are counterbalanced at the base, slender at top to allow a little wind resistance, but not too much. Critics liken their motion to ballet, and to the swaying of grasses and trees in the wind. Rickey says that his works attempt to concentrate movement itself; he thinks of his kinetic wands as "a limited but indeterminate drawing in space."

CAMPFIRE GIRLS, 1976. Cor-ten steel, h. 7′ × 8′ × 7½′.
David Stromeyer (1946–   ).

Stromeyer fabricates his steel works himself, developing, he says, "a dialogue with my material," and refining his ideas in the process. The intent of his abstraction is to challenge all the viewer's perceptions and concepts of space.

WAR MEMORIAL, 1929. Bronze, larger than life.
Bedford and Trapelo Rds., in front of Lincoln Library.
Anonymous.

Cast by T. F. McGann & Sons Co., Boston, this eagle by an unknown maker has become a town landmark.

LOWELL

The following acronyms may be encountered: LHPC (Lowell Historic Preservation Commission), LOCA (Lowell Office of Cultural Affairs), NEA (National Endowment for the Arts).

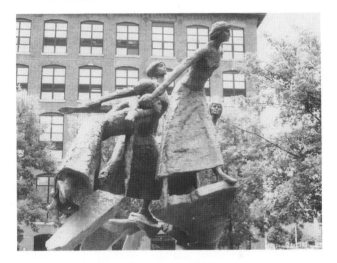

★ HOMAGE TO WOMEN, 1984. Bronze, larger than life.
Market Mills Park, Market and Palmer Sts.
Mico Kaufman (1924–).

A resident of Tewksbury, Kaufman studied at the Academy of Fine Arts in Rome and Florence, 1947–51. Much of his work is in the design of commemorative medals and miniatures issued in sets by commercial mints; he designed the official inaugural medals for Presidents Ford and Reagan. He was named sculptor of the year in 1978 by the American Numismatic Association, and in 1992 was awarded its highest honor, the Saltus Award. Kaufman's work is owned by its museum in Colorado Springs and by the Smithsonian Museum in Washington.

This work recognizes the role of women, such as the mill girls of Lowell, in the industrial revolution, and the changed role of women as a result. Funded by LHPC, federal, municipal, and private sources.

THE WORKER, 1985. Bronze, life-size.
Market and Shattuck Sts.
Ivan and Elliot Schwartz.

New Yorkers Ivan and Elliot Schwartz specialize in creating historically accurate figures for interpretative displays in museums, props for dance and theater companies, and promotional settings for retail stores. Among their clients is the National Air and Space Museum in Washington, D.C.

Lowell's 5.6 miles of canals, diverting the water which powered the mills, were dug by hand early in the nineteenth century. This work honors those laborers.

JACK KEROUAC COMMEMORATIVE PARK, 1988. Granite and stainless steel.
Eastern Canal Park, Bridge and French Sts.
Ben Woitena (1942–   ).

Texan Ben Woitena's sculpture occupies at least a dozen public sites in Texas, including the Houston and San Antonio Museums of Fine Arts. Born in San Antonio, he is a graduate of the University of Texas and a member of the faculty of the Glassell School.

Controversy surrounded the proposal of this memorial to Lowell native Jack Kerouac (1922–1969), an iconoclast whose *On the Road* rejected the conformism of the 1950s, spawned the Beat Generation, and paved the way for the social ferment of the 1960s. Some citizens felt that Kerouac's life style, particularly the alcoholism that caused his early death, was not a cause for civic pride. Others argued that the achievements of this native son far outweighed his personal shortcomings: author of twenty books, he is considered a major influence in literature and, like Hemingway thirty years before, chronicler of a generation. Kerouac attended Lowell High School, worked for a time at the *Lowell Sun*, and is buried in Edson Cemetery. Commissioned by LHPC.

NORTHERN CANAL ISLAND, in progress, 1993. Natural elements.
Northern Canal Island, School St. bridge.
Michael Singer (*see* Wellesley [Wellesley College]: *Untitled Sitework*).

Singer works his environmental magic to form a woodland garden of ferns, mosses, and native flowers bounded by stone, wood, and bittersweet. Sponsored by NEA, LOCA, and LHPC.

HUMAN CONSTRUCTION, 1987. Granite, two units, h. 16′, l. 40′–45′.
At Central St., in the Pawtucket Canal.
Carlos Dorrien (*see* Waltham [Bentley College]: *Portal*).

Placed atop old canal piers, Dorrien's post-and-lintel archways and stoneworks evoke ancient ways of building. Dorrien's style leaves large chunks of stone rough-hewn in homage to the material itself; he then works portions of each stone in ways that define its form.

Funded by Courrier Citizen Corp., Raytheon Corp., MA/Com Corp., and LHPC.

AGAPETIME, 1990. Bronze, h. 10′.
Lower locks, Pawtucket and Eastern canals.
Dmitri Hadzi (*see* Brookline: *Primavera*, and Boston [Government Center]: *Thermopylae*).

The artist writes the title lower case, *agapetime* (all the vowels are pronounced), and translates it as "love" or "esteem." Gift of Paul and Niki Tsongas.

THE LOWELL SCULPTURES: #1, #2, #3, 1990. Granite, brick, steel, three elements, h. 6'.
Boarding House Park, John and French Sts.
Robert Cumming (1943–   ).

Worcester native Cumming, now a resident of West Suffield, Conn., is also an inventor—a dual-purpose easel/chair is one of his designs. Here he evokes mill city forms: in #1, a profile of founder Francis Cabot Lowell; #2, a tipped thread spool; #3, a vertical shape derived from the spindle. Sponsored by Shawmut Arlington Trust, NHPC, LOCA, and NEA.

DR. PATRICK J. MOGAN, 1988. Bronze bust, larger than life.
Dr. Patrick J. Mogan Cultural Center, 40 French St.
Mico Kaufman (*see Homage to Women* above).

A visionary who worked for the designation of the abandoned Lowell mills as a national park, Mogan is considered "the father of Lowell National Park."

THE ROUSES MONUMENT, 1979. Bronze, life-size.
Kennedy Plaza, 50 Arcano Dr., adj. to City Hall.
Mico Kaufman (*see Homage to Women* above).

After policeman Christos Rouses was killed in a drug raid, his comrades on the Lowell police force raised funds to erect a memorial to him. Their initial concept was simply a statue of a police officer. Kaufman advocated enlarging the concept, telling the force, "A cop is a cop, but if you put a child next to him he becomes a policeman."

ITALIA, 1987. Bronze, h. 6'.
Kennedy Plaza.
Mico Kaufman (see *Homage to Women* above).

Commissioned by the Italo-American Cultural Committee of Lowell, this work is meant to commemorate the Italian heritage in Lowell. It incorporates a sample of Italian architecture (the communal palace in Siena) in the "boot" shape of southern Italy; verso are the mills of Lowell and a pair of immigrants.

PAWTUCKET PRISM, 1987. Gold-plated stainless steel, h. 20' × 19' × 13'.
Junction of the Pawtucket Canal and Concord River, at Lowell Hilton Hotel.
Michio Ihara (1928–   ).

Because of the structure, repetition, and controlled climatic elements in his work, Ihara has been called "the Vivaldi of metal." A former fellow of the Center for Advanced Visual Studies at M.I.T., Ihara has produced more than fifty commissioned works in this country, Japan,

Australia, New Zealand, Hong Kong, and Singapore. Born in Paris, Ihara grew up in Tokyo. After he earned a degree from the University of Fine Arts, a Fulbright grant allowed him to study art in architecture and to become a research associate at M.I.T. He has taught at Musashino Fine Arts University and has been an artist-in-residence at Newcastle College in Australia. He now lives in Concord.

A number of Ihara's works are kinetically engineered to move in the wind. To illustrate the theme "the power of water" here, Ihara has adapted his design so the fountain's flow will move his kinetic cubes. The Indian word "Pawtucket" is said to mean "falling water." Funded by Arthur Robbins, the Lowell Hilton Hotel, LHPC, and the City of Lowell.

CLAUDE DEBUSSY, MUSICIEN FRANCAIS, 1987. Bronze, h. 6′ × 8′ × 6′.
University of Lowell South Campus.
Mico Kaufman (*see Homage to Women* above).

Debussy (1862–1918), impressionist composer, was born in Paris, trained at the Paris Conservatoire, and won the Prix de Rome at the age of twenty-two. The compositions he submitted while in Rome were judged so formless and unacademic that they were denied the customary public performance. Debussy's originality began to be recognized with *Afternoon of a Faun* in 1894 and with his only opera, *Pelléas and Mélisande*, in 1902. Debussy rejected melody, writing, "Melody is powerless to express the constant change of emotion and life." Developing musical impressionism to a peak of exquisite sensitivity, he was credited with introducing a new system of color into music, and with revealing novel possibilities for the piano. His best-known work today is probably *La Mer* (*"The Sea"*). Cut into the base are scenes from *Afternoon of a Faun* (on the front) and *Pelléas and Mélisande* (on the back). Privately funded by the Claude Debussy Trust Fund, Inc.

LYNN

LYNN WORKS, 1987. Forged and welded steel, h. 22′ × 60′ × 4′.
At North Shore Community College, Lynnway and Broad St.
George Greenamyer (*see* Marshfield: *Webster, the Farmer of Marshfield*).

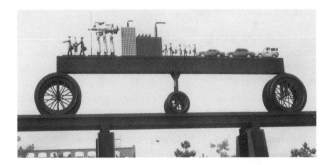

Greenamyer's delight in antique toys and Americana is well suited to this commemoration of Lynn's industrial history, from shoemaking to aircraft engine manufacture. Funded by 1% for Art.

UNTITLED, 1986. Acrylic on cotton duck, three panels.
Main lobby, North Shore Community College.
Natalie Alper (*see* Cambridge [Lechmere] [Royal Sonesta Hotel]: *Two Realms Witness a Change*).

UNTITLED, 1987. Thirteen terrazzo panels, 2' × 3'2".
Stairwell, North Shore Community College.
Andrea Blum.

Blum is a New York–based artist.

LYNN HERITAGE MURAL, 1987. Ceramic, mosaic, found objects, h. 6' × 120'.
Lynn State Heritage Park, 154 Lynnway, exterior of Seaport Landing.
Lilli Ann Killen Rosenberg (*see* Newton: *Five Concrete Mosaic Sculptures*).

As part of the package in developing condominiums here, Seaport Landing, Inc. gave this exterior wall to the city of Lynn. The mural celebrates Lynn's heritage and its waterfront. Clay pieces which became components of the mural were made by an assortment of groups in Lynn, from children on a playground through senior citizens. Commissioned by Seaport Landing, Inc. and the Massachusetts Department of Environmental Management.

EVERT, 1992. Bronze, h. 7'.
Central Sq., Broad and Union Sts.
Ralph Helmick (*see* Boston [Charles River Esplanade]: *Arthur Fiedler*).

"Evert" means to turn inside out; the sculptor says the figure is "on the cusp of internalizing, reflecting, and acting on knowledge." Partly realistic and partly in Helmick's layered style, this figure was commissioned by the MBTA to accompany its new commuter rail station nearby.

MURALS, 1984. Ceramic and mosaic, various sizes.
Interior and exterior, St. Mary's Houses for Elderly and Handicapped, 30 Pleasant St.
Lilli Ann Killen Rosenberg (*see* Newton: *Five Concrete Mosaic Sculptures*).

CIVIL WAR MEMORIAL, 1873. Bronze, three figures, larger than life.
Common and Commercial Sts.
John Adams Jackson (1825–1879).

Born in Bath, Me., Jackson went to Paris to study in the late 1840s, one of the first American sculptors to choose that city rather than Italy. He later settled in Florence and spent the last twenty years of his life there. Jackson is known primarily as a portraitist. The three figures represent War, Peace, and the City of Lynn extending the laurel wreath of victory and honor to her sons.

MALDEN

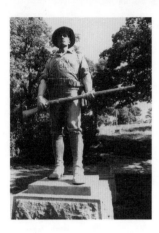

THE HIKER, erected 1938. Bronze, larger than life.
Pleasant and Elm Sts.
Theo Alice Ruggles Kitson (1871–1932).

    Daughter of the postmaster of Brookline, Theo Alice Ruggles
showed an early aptitude for sculpture and in her teens became a protégé of the sculptor Henry Hudson Kitson (*see* Lexington: *The Minuteman*). She studied in Paris, receiving at the age of eighteen an
honorable mention at the Paris Exposition of 1889 and another in 1890
at the Paris Salon, first American woman to receive such a distinction.
She and Kitson were married in 1893 and collaborated on several memorials (*see* Boston [Commonwealth Avenue]: *Collins Memorial*), but
are said to have separated about 1909. About 1915 Theo Alice moved
to Sherborn and then to Framingham, where she maintained a studio
until her death. Creator of a veritable army of military monuments, she
had a hand in at least fifty memorial sculptures around the country. In
1893 she was the first woman admitted to the National Sculpture Society.

    Some confusion exists as to whether Mrs. Kitson or her husband,
H. H. Kitson, sculpted the original of this statue; but it was she. Part of
the difficulty lies in the fact that Gorham Foundry continued to cast reproductions after Theo Alice Kitson's death; the work was so popular
that towns wanting to memorialize the Spanish-American War began to
specify a "Kitson-type memorial." As late as 1965, a *Hiker* monument
was erected—that one at Arlington National Cemetery. Erected by the
City of Malden.

THE FLAG DEFENDERS, 1910.
At Bell Rock Park, Main St. and Wilson Ave.
Bela Pratt (1867–1917).

    For many years a teacher at Boston Museum School, Pratt is best
known locally for his seated bronze figures of *Science* and *Art* in front

of Boston Public Library. He was born in Norwich, Conn., studied at Yale School of Fine Arts, and at age twenty went to New York to work under the great sculptors of the day, including Augustus Saint-Gaudens. He later studied in Paris. Among his more important commissions are allegorical figures for the Library of Congress in Washington, D.C.

Malden engaged the renowned landscape designer Frederick Law Olmsted to advise on the location of this memorial and to design the park. Funded by the City of Malden with contributions from Malden Chapter of the Sons of the Revolution, Malden Historical Society, and Deliverance Monroe Chapter of the Daughters of the Revolution.

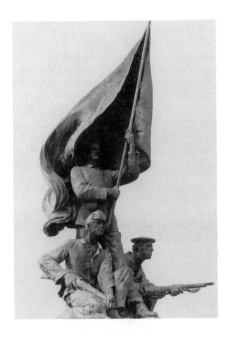

GALLERY: Malden Public Library, 36 Salem St.: Thanks to bequests in 1903 and '04 from Mr. and Mrs. Elisha Slade Converse (of Converse Shoes), Malden Public Library has steadily amassed a small but fine collection of paintings. Copley, Homer, Inness, Turner, Constable, and Millet are among the artists represented; the collection extends from seventeenth-century Dutch and Flemish schools into this century.

MARBLEHEAD

THE SPIRIT OF '76. Oil on canvas, h. $18' \times 12'$.
 Selectmen's Office, Abbot Hall, Washington St.
 Archibald M. Willard (1836–1918).

Possibly the most-reproduced American painting of the nineteenth century, this canvas is the original version of *The Spirit of '76*. It was purchased and presented to the town by Col. John Henry Devereux, a native of Marblehead, whose son Henry K. Devereux posed for the drummer boy.

After serving in the Civil War, A. M. Willard returned to his native Ohio and took a job with a wheelwright, painting wagons. He began decorating the wagon boxes more and more elaborately, even painting scenes on them, and in his spare time tried to study painting. Willard achieved financial success with homespun, humorous paintings that could be reproduced by chromolithography and sold in quantity. This work, at first titled *Yankee Doodle*, was conceived as a money-maker to be reproduced and marketed in connection with the Centennial of 1876; early versions portrayed three lighthearted figures at a rural patriotic celebration. When Willard's father, who was posing as the central figure, became ill (he died before the painting was finished), the painter's concept sobered. This final version proved an overwhelmingly popular expression of American sentiment of the day. The model for the fifer was Willard's friend and war comrade Hugh Mosher, said to be the best fifer in Northern Ohio; Willard chose young Devereux from among cadets at a military prep school in Cleveland. The painter had not dreamed that his work would be exhibited at the Philadelphia Centennial, but the public insisted. The painting then toured the country for an empathetic populace before being bought for Marblehead.

GALLERY: Marblehead Art Association, 8 Hooper St.

MARSHFIELD

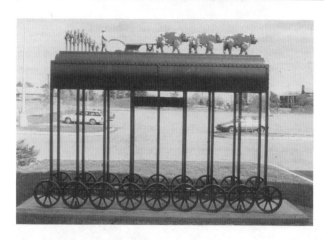

WEBSTER, THE FARMER OF MARSHFIELD, 1986. Forged and welded steel, painted, h. 7'6" × 12' × 20".
In front of Ventress Library, Library Mall, Ocean St. (Rte. 139).
George Greenamyer (1939–   ).

Almost all of Greenamyer's sculptures have wheels, as if they were wacky machines; he has, indeed, "raced" them in the occasional Great Sculpture Race in Cambridge, usually competing to turn in the slowest time. These humorous welded vehicles refer in multiple ways to old-time Americana, Yankee ingenuity, industrial methodology in fabrication and forging, strength, and implied kineticism. Greenamyer was educated at the University of Kansas and at the Philadelphia Museum College of Art; he has been a fellow of the Center for Advanced Visual Studies at M.I.T. His twenty-plus public works are sited from Maine to Alaska. He lives in Marshfield and teaches sculpture at Massachusetts College of Art.

Statesman Daniel Webster, great orator of the mid-nineteenth century, owned a 1500-acre estate in Marshfield, about a mile from this site. Despite his fame, Webster most liked to think of himself as a farmer, according to town historians. Born in New Hampshire of rugged farming stock, Webster early in life showed such a passion for books that his family educated him, at great sacrifice, at Phillips Exeter Academy and Dartmouth College. He became a lawyer and an orator of clear, massive, gorgeous, overwhelming eloquence. Twice a congressman, he was elected to the Senate in 1827. His presidential aspirations were never fulfilled; he was twice Secretary of State, and the most concrete achievement of his career was negotiating the treaty with England that fixed this country's northeastern boundary in 1842. Funded by Marshfield Arts Lottery Council and gift of the artist.

MEDFORD

ORIENTAL LANTERN. Stone, h. 8½'.
In front of City Hall, Salem St. and I-93.

This Japanese lantern was a gift to the city in the mid-1970s from its sister city, Nobeka, Japan. The inscription reads, "Given by Asahi-Japan to the citizens of Medford." Asahi-Japan is a corporation with a branch, Asahi-America, in Medford.

WORLD WAR I MEMORIAL. Granite, h. 8'.
At entrance to Oak Grove Cemetery, Playstead Rd.
Emilius R. Ciampa (*see* Boston [Charles River Esplanade]: *Maurice J. Tobin*).

WORLD WAR II MEMORIAL. Bronze angel, h. 11'.
In Oak Grove Cemetery.
Emilius R. Ciampa (*see* Boston [Charles River Esplanade]: *Maurice J. Tobin*).

At Tufts University:

AZTEC FIGURE, ca. 15th C. Volcanic stone, h. 29".
Lobby, Campus Center.
Mexican, artist unknown.
Gift of Seth Merrin, 1983.

ELEPHANT FOUNTAIN. Bronze, h. 4'.
  Outside Wessell Library.
  Carl Wilhelm Emil Milles (1875–1955).

MAN AND PEGASUS. Bronze, h. 24".
  Inside Wessell Library.
  C. W. E. Milles.

COMMON GROUND, 1984. Wool, 6' × 9'.
  Cohen Auditorium.
  Rhoda Cohen (*see* Natick: *Fiber Revival*).

LONG WHITE CLOUD, 1986. Fabric, 3' × 7'.
  Wessell Library.
  Rhoda Cohen (*see* Natick: *Fiber Revival*).

GALLERY: in Cohen Arts Center, Talbot Ave. Exhibits thesis shows of
  graduate students of the Boston Museum School, which is affiliated
  with Tufts for the awarding of academic degrees.

MILFORD

GENERAL DRAPER, 1912. Equestrian bronze, larger than life.
  In Draper Park, Main and Congress Sts.
  Daniel Chester French (*see* Concord: *Minuteman*).

   This park was purchased by the widow of Gen. William F. Draper in
1910 in order to create a memorial to her husband, veteran of the Civil
War, congressman, and ambassador to Italy. Draper (1842–1910) enlisted in the 25th Massachusetts Regiment, was elected lieutenant,
transferred to the 36th Massachusetts Regiment and was commissioned captain, served on Burnside's staff, saw action at Antietam and
Fredericksburg, was sent West and participated in the capture of Vicksburg and the siege of Knoxville, was promoted to lieutenant colonel,
was wounded in the Battle of the Wilderness, and left the army—all before his twenty-third birthday. Draper was later awarded the brevet
ranks of colonel and brigadier general in recognition of gallantry.

WAR MEMORIAL, 1992. Milford granite, h. 18", oval wall encircling walkways.
  Draper Park.
  Robert Desmond (1962–   ).

   A competition for a design to honor those who served in World War
II, Korea, and Vietnam resulted in this solution by Desmond. A Cambridge landscape architect, Desmond has a master's degree from Harvard. Funds raised by the Milford War Memorial Committee included a
donation from Texas millionaire and would-be politician Ross Perot.

MILTON

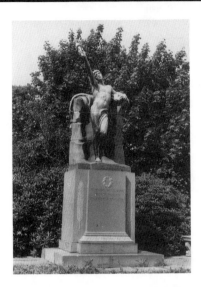

IN FLANDERS FIELDS, 1925. Bronze, larger than life.
In front of Town Hall, Canton Ave.
★ Daniel Chester French (*see* Concord: *Minuteman*).

Every New England town formed a committee to erect a memorial to
the dead of World War I, and French's services by this time were in
great demand. For this commission in Milton he needed a new idea.
The sculptor's daughter relates that a family friend, the sculptor
Malvina Hoffman, suggested the John McCrea poem which ends, "To
you from failing hands we throw/ The torch; be yours to hold it high./ If
ye break faith with us who die/ We shall not sleep, though poppies
grow/ In Flanders fields." She mounted the model stand and struck a
pose with a whiskbroom for a torch, and the sculptor made a quick
sketch in clay which became the prototype for this work.

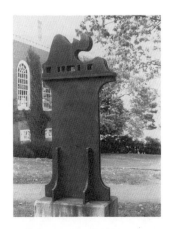

At Milton Academy:

WAVES OF ANOTHER
DIMENSION, 1978. Cor-ten
  steel, h. 8'.
  On Centre St., between Wigg
  Hall and Strauss Bldg.
  Dennis Kowal (*see* Wellesley
  [Babson College]: *Ominous
  Icon #6* and *Yaddo Study*).

BLADE OF LIFE, 1990. Oak, 7'.
   Outside Cox Library.
   Murray Dewart (*see* Brookline: *Pulpit*).

MURAL, 1983. Acrylic on homosote, h. 8' × 116'.
   Attached to front of Science Bldg., south side of Centre St.
   This student project depicts "windows" on Boston.

FAMILY ALBUM IN BRONZE. Collection of small bronzes.
   Inside Science Bldg.
   Robert Cook (1921–   ).

   An alumnus of Milton, Cook studied in Paris. His works are at the
Whitney Museum in New York and the Hirschhorn in Washington.

GALLERY: Nesto Gallery, basement of Science Bldg. Rotating exhibitions.

NATICK

FIBER REVIVAL, 1986. Quilt, 36" × 54".
   Interior, Leonard Morse Hospital.
   Rhoda Cohen (1934–   ).

   Painter turned quiltmaker, Cohen begins with the quilt form but segues into collage, departing from formal patterning to create imagery.
Cohen studied various artistic disciplines at the schools of the DeCordova Museum and the Boston Museum of Fine Arts before turning to
fabric. She has been artist-in-residence at Point Bonita, Cal., and has
taught and lectured in the U.S., Europe, Australia, and New Zealand.
Her quilts have been exhibited in those countries as well as in Africa,
Holland, and Japan. In this work Cohen used as raw material scraps
and castoffs given her by batik artist Sharon Engler, who works in Wayland.

NEEDHAM

COLOR SWEEP, 1983. Painted wood, sixty-five posts, h. 5½',
   in two lines, 50' each.
   Cooks Bridge, Needham Housing Authority, Evergreen Rd.,
   off St. Mary's St.
   Virginia Gunter.

   A graduate of Massachusetts College of Art, Gunter has had a dual
career as creative artist and museum administrator, having been direc-

tor of exhibitions at Mass/Art. She is a fellow of the Center for Advanced Visual Studies at M.I.T. and has held grants from Massachusetts Council on the Arts and Humanities. Gunter has exhibited widely, often working in fiber, often creating short-lived environmental works for festivals such as First Night. "Light," she says, "is a primary factor" in her sculpture; "reflections, shadows, and captured color are . . . integral to the sculpture . . . and allow the work to activate the passage of time."

Here Gunter's lines of painted posts function in two ways: they emphasize the contours of the landscape, drawing an arc up each hill, and they record the passage of sunlight, changing aspect with the angle of light and shadow.

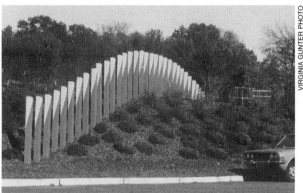

VIRGINIA GUNTER PHOTO

WYETH PAINTINGS, various dates. Oil on canvas.
At Needham Library, 1139 Highland Ave.
N. C. Wyeth (1882–1945).

Wyeth, founder of what has become a famous American painting family (son Andrew, grandson Jamie), was a native of Needham. At the age of twenty he traveled to Wilmington, Del., to study at the Howard Pyle School of Art, Pyle being a famous illustrator of children's books and fairy tales at that time. He married in Delaware and established himself in Chadds Ford, Pa. In 1921 he and his family returned to Needham, but within two years resettled in Chadds Ford. At about this time he received the commission to paint the outsized ship paintings that grace the lobby of Bank of Boston.

AN ECUMENICAL QUILT, 1992. Fabric, 81″ × 81″.
Needham Public Library, or Town Hall, 1471 Highland Ave.
Thirty-five volunteer quilters.

The concept of Mary Donovan, a member of St. Joseph's Church, this quilt is intended as a permanent reminder of the church's seventy-fifth anniversary year. Eleven Needham churches and two synagogues, plus a Newton church that serves some Needham parishioners, are depicted by members of their own congregations. Donated to the town by St. Joseph's Church.

NEWBURYPORT

★ THE VOLUNTEER, 1903. Bronze, larger than life.
Atkinson Common, High St. and Moseley Ave.
Theo Alice Ruggles Kitson (*see* Malden: *The Hiker*).

This sensitive portrait has more to say than most about the sacrifice of youth to the exigencies of war; it was reproduced as a Civil War memorial in six other cities. It is unfortunate that vandals have bent the rifle barrel.

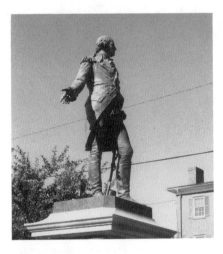

GEORGE WASHINGTON, 1878. Bronze, larger than life.
High and Pond Sts.
★ John Quincy Adams Ward (1830–1910).

The initials of J. Q. A. Ward are to be found on a surprising number of late-nineteenth-century sculptures. Along with the younger but better-known Saint-Gaudens, Ward is credited with infusing American sculpture with the vitality of naturalism. Born on a farm near Urbana, Ohio, Ward was offered the best schooling available there, but often played hookey to visit the local potter's workshop. To please his father, he studied medicine for a bit, improving his understanding of anatomy. An older sister who lived in New York introduced him to the sculptor Henry Kirke Brown, who accepted him as an assistant and generously included him in both his work and his friendship. Brown's instruction was at the time the best in this country; Ward made the most of it and rejected the idea of joining the colony of expatriate artists working in Italy. In Washington he modeled portrait busts of a number of notable politicians; then he set up shop in New York. His first really ambitious work, *Indian Hunter*, was done after a journey among the Indians of the West. It was widely acclaimed; its admirers raised funds to erect it in Central Park, and Ward's career was launched. This work was presented to the town by Daniel I. Tenney.

WILLIAM LLOYD GARRISON. Bronze, larger than life.
Pleasant St., across from City Hall.
David French (1827–1910).

David French is apparently no relation to the more famous and more prolific Daniel Chester French. A resident of Newburyport, he studied under Stevenson in Boston; this is his best-known work.

Most famous of all abolitionists, Garrison (1805–1879) was born in Newburyport. Indentured to a printer, he quickly rose to compositor and then contributor. Rejecting then-current ideas of gradual emancipation and colonization of former slaves elsewhere, Garrison demanded immediate emancipation and the rights of citizens for slaves. Without subscribers or capital, Garrison and a friend founded in Boston the *Liberator*, which became a powerful voice for abolition. Not all fellow Bostonians sympathized; in 1835 Garrison was mobbed there and had to be jailed for his own safety until he could escape the city. The *Liberator* also opposed war, alcohol, tobacco, freemasonry, capital punishment, and imprisonment for debt. Garrison's pro-feminist views led him to insist on equal participation by women in the anti-slavery movement.

WALL RELIEF.
Coast Guard Station.
Adio di Biccari (*See* Boston [Boston Common]: *Parkman Plaza*).

SEA GRASS IN THE WIND, 1990. Cast glass, 12′ × 16′ × 2′.
Main stairway, second floor, Newburyport District Courthouse, Rte. 1 and State St.
Dan Dailey (*see* Boston [Fenway] [Children's Hospital]: *Rain on Water*).
Funded by Massachusetts 1% for Art.

NEWTON

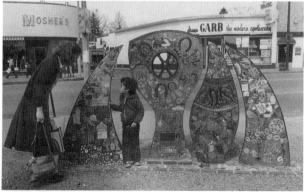

MARVIN ROSENBERG PHOTO

ROSENBERG, FIVE CONCRETE MOSAIC SCULPTURES

FIVE CONCRETE MOSAIC SCULPTURES, 1980–83. Five units, h. 3'–7'.
Newton Centre at Centre and Langley Sts.
Lilli Ann Killen Rosenberg (1924–   ).

A resident of Newton, Rosenberg has produced a number of community art projects and public ceramic murals (*see* Boston [South End/Rox-
bury]: *Betances Mural* and MBTA [Park St.]: *Celebration of the
Underground*). Trained in architecture, sculpture, and ceramics, she
was educated at Los Angeles City College, Cooper Union, the Art Students League in New York City, and at Cranbrook Academy of Art in
Michigan. For eighteen years she was director of the art department at
the Henry Street Settlement in New York, and in the 1960s, under a
Rockefeller grant, she was assigned by the New York City housing authority to humanize public spaces through participatory art projects.
With her husband, Marvin, she has created public murals in Philadelphia, Wilmington, Del., New York City, and Montgomery County, Md.
She is the author of *Children Make Murals and Sculpture: Experiences
in Community Art Projects*.

Over a three-year period, more than 200 Newton residents—from
the mayor to small children—trooped through Rosenberg's ceramics
studios, making the clay pieces that compose this work into a kind of
community autobiography. Sponsored by the Arts in the Park program
of the Newton Parks and Recreation Department; funded by a grant
from the Massachusetts Council on the Arts and Humanities.

JOHNNY KELLEY, 1993. Bronze, h. 8'.
Commonwealth Ave. and Walnut St.
Rich Muno (1939–   ).

Rich Muno, born in Arapaho, Okla., began whittling wood sculptures
when he was a 9-year-old farm boy. He attended Oklahoma State University School of Technical Training, and for twenty years he was director of the National Cowboy Hall of Fame in Oklahoma City. His heroic
figures include explorer Zebulon Pike in Colorado Springs, a pioneer
man in Clinton, Okla., a rancher on horseback in Pampa, Tex., square
dancers in Oklahoma City, and others.

Of all the athletic legends in sports-crazy Boston, marathoner Johnny
Kelley, a local boy from Medford, can claim the longest active career.
Three times an Olympian, he was national champion eleven times at
four different distances. He ran sixty-one Boston Marathons, beginning
in 1928 when he was 20 (and failed to finish) and ending in 1992 when
he was 84 (finishing with a time of 5:42:54). Although he announced
his retirement after the 1992 race, Kelley toyed with the idea of starting
the '93 Marathon if his doctors would let him. He won the race in 1935
and 1945, finished second seven times, and was in the top ten on nine
other occasions. This site, five miles from the tape, is at the bottom of
"Heartbreak Hill," so named by a sportswriter because Kelley habitually
started at a reckless pace and ran out of gas on the hills. Kelley found
this location for his statue appropriate because, he said, "I think I've
spent more than half my life running on Commonwealth Ave."

Dr. Wayman R. Spence, a Waco, Tex., physician and entrepreneur,
founded several medical and publishing companies, such as Spenco.
An art collector who himself has run the Boston Marathon three times,

Spence awoke one morning after a vivid dream about Johnny Kelley, then 81, running hand in hand with his youthful self. Spence commissioned friend and artist Muno to sculpt such an image, and then lobbied the Boston Athletic Association and the city of Newton to place the double statue on the racecourse. It was dedicated the day before running of the 1993 Marathon, and on Marathon day Kelley ran the five miles from the statue to the finish line. Funded by WRS Group, Inc. and by sales of ninety-nine maquettes of the sculpture.

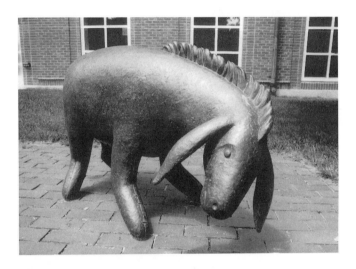

EEYORE, 1991. Bronze, h. 28″.
Children's Garden, Newton Free Library, Walnut and Homer Sts.
Nancy Schön (*see* Boston [Public Garden]: *Make Way for Ducklings*).

Eeyore the donkey, the pessimist among Winnie-the-Pooh's friends, is modeled on the decorations drawn by Ernest H. Shepard for A. A. Milne's children's classics. Funded by private donation.

THE 14 VILLAGES OF NEWTON, 1983. Quilt, 9′ × 12′.
In City Hall, left of entrance.

Fifty quilters worked for a year to produce this work to mark the founding of the Fund for the Arts in Newton. Community history and activities are included, from John Eliot, an early preacher to the Indians, to the Boston Marathon, which wends its way through the heart of the city every April. Sponsored by Honeywell Corp.

CHILDREN'S MURALS, 1978–80. Ceramic mosaic, eight units, various sizes.
Lobbies, Administration Bldg., Newton Board of Education, 100 Walnut St.
Lilli Ann Killen Rosenberg (*see Five Concrete Mosaic Sculptures* above).

GALLERY: Newton Art Center, 61 Washington Park.

THE MINISTRY OF THE WHOLE PEOPLE OF GOD, 1983. Ceramic bas-relief, 5′ × 5′.
Andover-Newton Theological Seminary, 210 Herrick Rd. In Worcester Hall.
John Moakley (*see* East Bridgewater: *Mural*) and Sonni Waldo (*see* Scituate: *The Heritage of Freedom by the Sea*).

GALLERY: Boston Sculptors at Chapel Gallery, 60 Highland St., at Second Church in Newton—only Greater Boston gallery devoted exclusively to sculpture.

At Boston College:

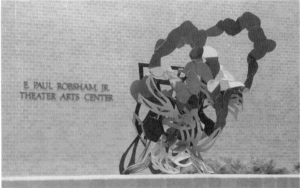

PHOTO COURTESY BOSTON COLLEGE ART COLLECTION

CONCORD, 1983. Painted metal, h. 8′ × 7½′ × 4′.
★ George Sugarman (1912–   ).

Born in the Bronx, Sugarman was the son of an Oriental-rug dealer; he says that his aesthetic mindset was influenced by the patterns and colors of Persian and Turkish carpets. After military service, Sugarman used his G.I. Bill benefits to graduate from City College of New York and then to study in Paris from 1951 to 1955. Returning to New York from Paris, he was struck by the "conglomerate but somehow cohesive structure of the city," the energy generated by its unplanned variety. His work is designed to create unity out of disparity, reflecting a reality that is changing and open-ended. His early work consisted of complex, sprawling constructions in laminated wood; in the late 1960s he began to simplify his forms and to design large-scale works to be fabricated in metal. These recent works, which he calls "field" sculptures, reflect his interest in physics and his attempts to unify its conflicting and unlike component theories. Sugarman has taught at Hunter and Bard Colleges, has been a visiting professor at Yale, and has held grants from the National Council on the Arts, the Longview Foundation, and the Ford Foundation.

EAGLE, date unknown, installed 1957. Bronze, larger than life.
    In front of Gasson Hall.
    Japanese, artist unknown.

   The B.C. eagle displayed at the entrance to the campus is more
than a standard college mascot. It was brought back from Japan by
Larz Anderson after his service there as ambassador and was part of
the estate he bequeathed to the town of Brookline. Arthur O'Shea,
town administrator, saw the bronze bird while touring the estate prior to
the town's acceptance of it and asked the executor whether Boston College might have the eagle. The column and base used to be in front of
South Station, supporting a bust of Admiral Dewey.

GALLERY: Boston College Gallery, in Devlin Hall.

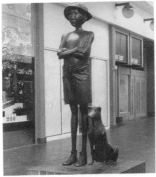

ED MACKINNON PHOTO COURTESY C&R CORP.

LOST BOY WITH DOG, 1975. Bronze, life-size.
    In The Mall at Chestnut Hill.
    Cornelius Zitman.
    Commissioned by C&R Management Corp.

LES GIRLS, 1975. Bronze, life-size.
    In The Mall at Chestnut Hill.
    Cornelius Zitman.
    Commissioned by C&R Management Corp.

THE SUN, ca. 1970. Mural on brick, h. 30′ × 60′.
    On Wasserman Bldg., 271 Auburn St., Auburndale, visible from Mass.
    Pike east of Weston interchange.
    Artist unknown.

   This mural was the subject of a civil suit when it was begun. The
block of stores has been owned by the Wasserman family for some
sixty years; in the late 1960s Ronnie Brooker (since deceased) had a
gift shop called The Ends of the Earth in the south end of the block.
She commissioned the mural, but neighbors objected to it, claiming (although the mural was unrelated to the shop's logo) that it was an adver-
tisement. The artist's work was halted for a time by court order. The
Wasserman family took the case to the state Supreme Judicial Court,
contending it was a work of art, and won.

NORTH ANDOVER

PHILLIPS BROOKS, 1916. Bronze, larger than life.
  Academy and Great Pond Rds., on Old Andover Common, opposite Merri-
  mack Valley Textile Museum.
  Bela Pratt (*see* Malden: *The Flag Defenders*).
  For Phillips Brooks' biography, see Boston [Back Bay].

SOLDIERS MONUMENT, 1913. Bronze, larger than life.
  In front of police station, Osgood St. near Massachusetts Ave.
  Theo Alice Ruggles Kitson (*see* Malden: *The Hiker*).

SHEEP-SHEARING ON NORTH ANDOVER COMMON, 1985. Acrylic on
  plaster, h. 6′ × 14′.
  Senior Center, Main St.
  Linda Aubry (1954–   ).

  Aubry sought a degree in music before turning to painting, attending
the Philadelphia College of Art, Berklee School of Music, and the Boston Conservatory before taking an M.F.A. at Bennington College. She
paints murals as a profession. The mural depicts an annual North Andover tradition on the old common. Commissioned by North Andover Arts
Council.

NORTON

At Wheaton College:

HEBE, 1983 recasting of original ca. 1840. Bronze, h. 4½′.
  Courtyard between Killam and Metcalf halls.
  Bertel Thorwaldsen (1770–1844).

  Thorwaldsen, a Dane, has been called the most successful imitator
of Classical sculpture. The original of this statue was given by Eliza
Wheaton, the college's founder, to mark Wheaton's fiftieth anniversary
in 1884. Made of lead and painted white, the figure suffered enough
damage that it was recast in bronze a century later. Goddess of youth,
daughter of Zeus and Hera, Hebe sometimes (as here) appears as cup-
bearer to the gods instead of the better-known Ganymede. In legend,
she became the bride of Hercules after the end of his mortal life. Her
presence here illustrates Wheaton's motto: "Who sips" (from the cup of
knowledge) "will thirst for more."

DIRECTIONAL NO. 4, 1966. Bronze, h. 39″ × 31″.
  Hood Court, behind Watson Fine Arts Bldg.
  Paul Von Ringelheim.

  Von Ringelheim is an Austrian-born American sculptor. Anonymous
gift to the college.

GALLERY: in Watson Fine Arts Center on Rte. 140 (Taunton Ave.), one block east of junction with Rte. 123. Rotating exhibits include works from the permanent collection, student work, and traveling exhibitions.

NORWOOD

PROTECTORS OF THE AMERICAN WAY, 1991. Bronze and granite, h. 18′.
  Town common, Washington and Nahatan Sts.
  Robert Shure (*see* Boston [Back Bay]: *Teddy Bear*).
  Moise Altshuler (1922–   ).

  Born in Moscow, Altshuler studied sculpture at Moscow Institute of Sculpture and Academy of Fine Arts. He now lives in Brookline and works for Shure at Skylight Studios in Woburn. Granite construction is by Monti Granite (*see* Quincy: *Constitution Common Sculpture*).
  Except for World War II combat gear worn by the figures, this heroic grouping in neo-modern style could date from the 1930s rather than the 1990s. Norwood businessman Frank Simoni, a veteran of two wars, commissioned the monument to honor "the protectors of the American family way of life."

PEABODY

SOLDIERS AND SAILORS MONUMENT, 1881. Granite and bronze, h. 50′.
  In Peabody Sq.
  After Thomas Crawford (*see* Cambridge [Harvard University]: *James Otis*).

  Among America's early expatriate sculptors in Rome, Crawford re-crossed the Atlantic several times to seek commissions. In 1853 his dreams were realized with a request to sculpt the pediment figures for the U.S. Senate. He accomplished this monumental work at the same time as *Armed Freedom* and a huge statue of James Otis (now at Harvard), although he had begun to suffer from the tumor behind his left eye which ended his life at the age of forty-four. Friends saw to it that *Armed Freedom* was cast during the Civil War; it was hoisted atop the Capitol, to the accompaniment of cannon salutes, in 1863.
  The figure crowning the obelisk here is modeled, with some modifications, on Crawford's *Armed Freedom*. The changes, which contemporary accounts say the committee "thought an improvement," substituted a broken shackle for the coat of arms in Freedom's left hand, and changed the angle of the sword in the right. The monument is dedicated to the fallen from Danvers (now Peabody) during the Civil War.

QUEEN VICTORIA, 1867. Enamel on porcelain, 14″ × 10″.
  In Peabody Library.
  F. A. Tilt.

Largest miniature portrait in history at the time it was painted, this work was commissioned especially for presentation from Queen Victoria to George Peabody (1795–1869), American-born financier, for his philanthropies for the workers of London. Born in the part of Danvers that is now Peabody, he was apprenticed to a merchant and, after volunteering in the War of 1812, formed a dry-goods partnership. By 1830 he found himself the head of one of the largest mercantile concerns in the world. He increased his fortune by buying up American state securities following the panic of 1837; then, establishing himself in London, he became one of the first Americans in international banking. His philanthropies encompassed scientific research, education, and low-income housing which still flourishes in London. The Queen offered him a baronetcy, which he declined because it would require loss of his American citizenship; this portrait, in her robes of state, is a substitute.

PLYMOUTH

MASSASOIT, 1921. Bronze, heroic size.
Coles Hill, Water St., directly across from Plymouth Rock.
★ Cyrus E. Dallin (see Arlington: *Indian Hunter*).

The survival of the band of settlers from the *Mayflower* was made possible principally by the friendship of Massasoit (ca. 1580–1661), chief of the Wampanoags. His tribe of several thousand had been all but wiped out by an epidemic, thought to be yellow fever, just prior to the arrival of the Pilgrims. Samoset, an Indian who had contact with Europeans and spoke a little English, arranged a meeting in the spring of 1621 between Massasoit and Governor Bradford; the two signed a peace treaty which lasted until 1675.

WILLIAM BRADFORD, 1976. Bronze, life-size.
Water St., just south of Plymouth Rock.
★ Cyrus E. Dallin (see Arlington: *Indian Hunter*).

This portrait of the leader of the Plymouth colony, intended to mark the tercentenary of the historic town, was modeled in 1920. The committee ran out of money, however, and the model was not cast. In 1976, as part of the United States Bicentennial celebration, the Plymouth Bicentennial Commission raised funds to cast and erect the statue.

Second governor of Plymouth Colony, Bradford (1590–1657) was elected in 1621 after the death of John Carver and served, with an occasional hiatus, for about thirty years. He was born in Yorkshire of well-to-do parents, joined the Separatists, was imprisoned briefly before emigrating to Holland in 1608, and was among the band of colonists arriving here aboard the *Mayflower*. Biographers credit the success and prosperity of Plymouth Colony in large part to his firm and judicious rule. His *History of Plymouth Plantation* (until 1646) is the major source of information about the colony's settlement and growth. Funded by public subscription.

THE PILGRIM MOTHER, 1920. Fountain and stone figure, larger than life.
    Water and North Sts.
    C. P. Jennewein (1890–1978).

    Born in Germany, Carl Paul Jennewein was brought to the U.S. in
1907; he studied at the Art Students League in New York and at the
American Academy in Rome. The federal buildings in Washington,
D.C., bear many of his marble carvings. His work is owned by the Metropolitan Museum of Art in New York and by the art museums of Baltimore and Philadelphia.

★ THE PILGRIM MAIDEN, 1924.
    Bronze, h. 8½'.
    West end of Brewster Park,
    Water and Leyden Sts., half a
    block south of Gov. Bradford's
    statue.
    Henry Hudson Kitson (*see*
    Lexington: *The Minuteman*).
    Commissioned by National
    Society of New England
    Women.

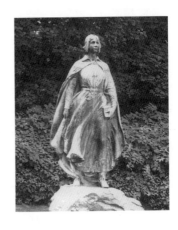

NATIONAL MONUMENT TO THE FOREFATHERS, 1889. Granite and
    marble, h. 81'.
    Allerton St.
    Hammatt Billings (1818–1874), William Rimmer (*see* Boston [Common-
    wealth Avenue]: *Hamilton*), and others.

    Charles Howland Hammatt Billings was born in Milton and educated
in Boston public schools and at the workshop of Abel Bowen, Boston's
first wood engraver. By the 1840s he was a jack-of-all-arts, turning his
hand to architecture, painting, sculpture, landscape design, decorative
arts, funerary monuments, fireworks design, and magazine and book illustration—his drawings are associated with such nineteenth-century
classics as the works of Louisa May Alcott and Harriet Beecher Stowe.
    Billings was responsible for both the design and the fund-raising for
this work. Dr. Rimmer made the nine-foot model of Faith, based on the
Venus de Milo, but the stonecutter who quadrupled its size for the monument replaced Rimmer's delicate drapery with quantities of material.
In an effort to make it a truly national monument, sculptors from elsewhere were engaged to carve the various figures and plaques: Alexander Doyle of New York did Education; Karl Conrad, Morality; J. H.
Mahoney, Freedom and Law. Although Billings designed the monument
in 1853, it was not completed until 1889.
    A typically Victorian work, this mammoth allegorical group represents
the virtues of the Pilgrims. Atop the central pedestal, her arm pointed
heavenward, is Faith; she is surrounded by Morality (flanked by a

prophet and an evangelist), Law (flanked by Justice and Mercy), Education (flanked by Wisdom and Youth), and Liberty (flanked by Peace and Tyranny overthrown). Four alto-relief carvings on the base depict the departure of the colonists from Delft Haven, Holland, the signing of the Mayflower Compact, the landing of the Pilgrims, and the treaty with the Indian chief Massasoit. At the time of its erection *Faith* was said to be the largest granite statue in the world. Statements that it is 216 times life size refer to its volume (6^3), a grandiose method of calculation. By the usual standard, *Faith* is roughly six times as large as life, her height (for instance) being thirty-six feet, her nose sixteen inches long. Sponsored by the Pilgrim Society; funded by public subscription.

TRAIL OF TEARS, ca. 1984.
    Wood, h. approx. 20′.
    At Tourist Information bureau,
    Exit 5 off Rte. 3.
    Peter Toth (1947–   ).

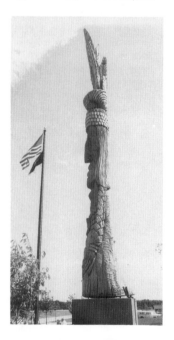

    Peter Toth was eleven when his family emigrated from revolt-torn Hungary to Ohio. Deeply empathetic with the Amerindian, Toth abandoned his college studies in 1970 and began carving monumental works in stone and wood to honor America's indigenous peoples and to protest their treatment. Traveling across the nation, the sculptor creates his works from materials found wherever he may be. Toth's goal is to place a sculpture from this series in each of the fifty states, all gifts of the artist.

MUSEUM: Pilgrim Hall Museum, 75 Court St. Although it is a historical museum, Pilgrim Hall contains some important works of art: the only known portrait of a Mayflower Pilgrim (Edward Winslow), three other seventeenth-century portraits of Massachusettsians, the original painting for the Pilgrim mural by Robert Weir in the Capitol in Washington, D.C., and paintings of the landing of the Pilgrims by Henry Sargent and Michel Corné.

QUINCY

CONSTITUTION COMMON SCULPTURE, 1980. Granite, h. 8′.
    At City Hall annex, Hancock and Temple Sts.
    Edward P. Monti (1927–   ).

Descended from a line of stoneworkers from northern Italy, Ed Monti owns the granite monument company which his father founded in Quincy after immigrating from Italy. After apprenticing with his father and serving in World War II, Monti graduated from the Barre School of Design in Vermont, then studied with animal sculptor Bonnie Boranda. Experimenting with ways to accelerate the process of stone carving, Monti settled on the quarryman's jet torch, a tool that burns a kerosene-oxygen mixture at 3600 degrees; it forces the stone to spall, or flake off the block, in controllable ways. With this technique Monti has produced fountains, waterfalls, animals, and abstract sculpture for malls, parks, and business complexes on the Eastern Seaboard, in the Virgin Islands, and in Europe.

To commemorate the bicentennial of the drafting of the Massachusetts Constitution, this massive work of Quincy granite was erected in 1980. Oldest democratic constitution in use today and the model for the federal Constitution, the document was written in the Quincy law offices of John Adams by the Adams cousins (John and Samuel) and James Bowdoin. The three major granite forms represent the three patriot/authors; the interplay of shapes and spaces echoes the interchange of ideas. The monument bears quotations from the document. Commissioned by the City of Quincy.

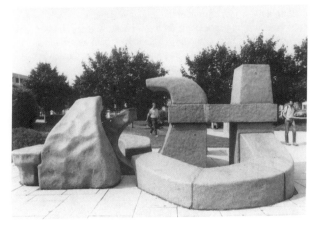

THE DOUGHBOY, 1924. Bronze, larger than life.
  At Adams Academy (Quincy Historical Society), Hancock and
  Granite Sts.
  Bruce Wilder Saville (1893–1939).

Quincy-born, Saville studied in Boston under Cyrus Dallin and in the Quincy studio of Theo Alice Ruggles Kitson. After service during World War I, he set up a studio in Quincy, then at the age of twenty-eight was appointed head of the art department of Ohio State University. Within four years he returned to Boston, planning to devote full time to sculpture, but in 1932 he moved to Santa Fe, N.M., for his health, and died there of influenza at the age of forty-six.

This soldier is a casting of a work Saville created as the central figure of a war memorial for Columbus, Ohio; the City chose it to honor the men of Quincy who served in the First World War.

JOHN HANCOCK, ca. 1900. Gilded bronze bust, h. 5'.
Artist unknown. Casting attributed to Gorham Co., Providence, R.I.
At Adams Academy.

This megascale portrait marks the site of the birthplace of John Hancock (1737–1793), president of the Continental Congress 1775–77, first signer of the Declaration of Independence, and legendary for declaring that he signed "large enough for King George to read it without his spectacles." Hancock was adopted by his childless merchant uncle, Thomas Hancock of Boston, and fell heir to a fortune and a prospering business. With Samuel Adams, he was a "most-wanted man" during the agitation that led to the Revolution; the King's troops marching to Lexington and Concord on April 19, 1775, sought to capture him and Adams as well as to destroy rebel arms. Never really a leader (although he was a militia major general and repeatedly governor), he was a flamboyant and expansive man and a popular public figure.

This bust was designed to stand over the entrance of a John Hancock Co. building on Federal Street early in this century. In 1922 the company moved, placed the bust in storage, and never found it had a location for it again. When the company built Boston's first skyscraper in 1949, a full-length portrait of the patriot was commissioned for its lobby (*see* Boston [Back Bay]: *John Hancock*). At that point the company offered this bust to the city of Hancock's birth, which funded a base of Quincy granite for it. Presented to the City of Quincy in 1951 by the John Hancock Life Insurance Co.

ROBERT BURNS, 1925. Granite, life-size.
Junction of Burgin Pkwy. and Granite St.
Gerald T. Horrigan (1903–   ).

Son of sculptor-stonecutter John Horrigan, Gerald Horrigan studied at the Boston Museum School. Like his father, he frequently assumed a craftsman's role as master stonecutter, translating to stone works designed in clay by other sculptors; John cut major work for Loredo Taft, and father and son both executed large-scale works for the sculptor Grace Vanderbilt Whitney.

In this case the statue, designed by Gerald, was cut by his father. Presented to the City of Quincy by the Burns Memorial Association. Rededicated 1971.

RIVETERS and GRANITE. Bas-relief panels, stone.
CRANES. Bas-relief pediment carving, stone.
Entrance to Thomas Crane Library, Washington and Coddington Sts.
Joseph Coletti (*see* East Boston, Logan Airport: *General Logan*).

WINGED MIGRATION #2, 1980–81. Steel, h. 13'.
Outside offices of National Fire Protection Association, Batterymarch Park, off Granite St.
Dennis Kowal (*see* Wellesley [Babson College]: *Ominous Icon #6* and *Yaddo Study*).
Commissioned by National Fire Protection Association.

RANDOLPH

CIVIL WAR MEMORIAL, no date. Bronze, larger than life.
  In front of Stetson Hall, North Main and Union Sts.
  F. Kohlhagen.

REVERE

CHRISTOPHER COLUMBUS, 1892. Bronze, larger than life.
  At St. Anthony's Church, 250 Revere St.
  Alois G. Buyens.

  Ceremoniously presented to the Cathedral of the Holy Cross in the
South End of Boston, this huge statue overpowered its site; in the
1920s it was discreetly relocated here at St. Anthony's Church to balance an equally large St. Anthony. Commissioned by the Knights of
Columbus.

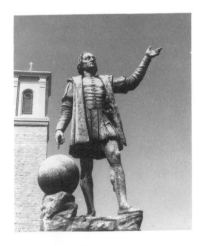

TREE OF LIFE, 1978. Stainless steel, diffraction grating, h. 9′.
  At Hebrew Rehabilitation Center for the Aged.
  William Wainwright (*see* East Boston, Logan Airport: *Windwheels*).

SPANISH WAR MEMORIAL, 1931. Bronze, approximately life-size.
  Broadway and Hyde St., south of City Hall.
  M. H. Mosman (*see* Saugus: *Civil War Memorial*).

  Apparently created specifically for Revere, this briskly marching soldier departs from the generic Kitson statue replicated in many other
towns. Commissioned by City of Revere.

CIVIL WAR MEMORIAL, 1931. Bronze, larger than life.
Broadway and Hyde St., south of City Hall.

The Boston foundry of McGann and Sons cast this work in the style of Martin Milmore (see Framingham: *Civil War Memorial*). Vandals have bent the soldier's bayonet. Erected by City of Revere.

ROCKLAND

ART IN THE LANDSCAPE, 1989. Painted galvanized steel, h. 12′.
Ten99 Hingham Street, junction Rtes. 228 and 3.
Mary Smith (1944–   ).

Landscape architect/artist Smith received a degree in English literature in 1966 from Boston College, turned to studies in fine arts and landscape architecture, earned a master's from Harvard Graduate School of Design, and established her firm in Quincy in 1982.

Smith's work here is an example of the blurring of boundaries between environmental art and landscape design. Her playful sculptural poles function as address signposts, and by day they evoke Maypoles, ribbon, ticker tape. Lighted from within at night, they become a grove of tree branches. Combined with pastel-painted fencing, they won the 1991 prize for landscape art from Boston Society of Landscape Architects. Commissioned by Morton Grossman.

ROCKPORT

SCENES OF ROCKPORT. Mural in gilded steel, h. 4′ × 30′.
At Granite Savings Bank.
C. Fayette Taylor (see Boston [Government Center]: *Upward Bound*).

GALLERY: Rockport Art Association, 12 Main St. Three exhibition spaces, more than fifty exhibitions a year.

SALEM

★ HAWTHORNE, 1925. Bronze, larger than life.
Hawthorne Blvd., near Essex St.
Bela L. Pratt (see Malden: *The Flag Defenders*).

Nathaniel Hawthorne (1804–1864), sometimes called the most distinguished craftsman of the New England school of letters, was a native of Salem and periodically returned here to live. Hawthorne's father died when he was small, leaving him, his mother, and his sisters in a household of genteel poverty and grim Puritanical gloom. Aloof and a loner, he graduated from Bowdoin College and returned to Salem to spend twelve solitary years mastering the craft of self-taught authorship. After

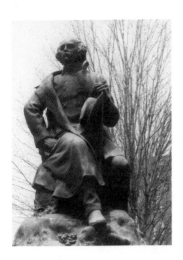

some meager literary success he married a Salem woman, Sophia Peabody; their marriage is one of New England's enduring love stories. Her sister Elizabeth, involved in all the causes of the day, introduced Nathaniel to the great figures of Transcendentalism. For a few years Hawthorne worked unhappily in the customs house in Salem, until *The Scarlet Letter* brought him popular success at the age of forty-six. It was followed by *The House of Seven Gables*, set in a house Hawthorne knew in Salem (now a museum open to the public). Descendant of generations of sea captains, the novelist is depicted hat in hand, gazing toward the sea. Funded by the Nathaniel Hawthorne Memorial Association.

★ WITCH MEMORIAL, 1992. Granite, twenty benches, paving, plantings.
Charter St., behind Old Burying Ground.
James Cutler and Maggie Smith.

This collaborative design between architect Cutler and artist Smith, both of Winslow, Wash., was selected from among 246 entries for a memorial to mark the 300th anniversary of the infamous Salem witch trials.

One of the darkest episodes in American history was the witch hysteria here in 1692, in which prepubescent girls claimed to be victims of witchcraft practiced by an ever-expanding number of people. Nineteen were hanged and one pressed to death before reason prevailed. Each bench bears a name, along with the date and manner of execution; declarations of innocence from the accused are engraved on paving stones. Because those executed were buried in shallow unmarked graves near Gallows Hill, these stones are intended to double as tombstones. The Boston Society of Architects in 1993 gave this project top honors for artist/architect collaboration. Commissioned by the Salem Witchcraft Tercentenary Committee.

FOUNTAIN, 1977. Stone.
East India Sq.
John Collins.

The pool is designed to display graphically the changes in Salem's topography as the old seaport has experienced dredging and filling. Dry stepping-stone cobbles replicate the original land masses;

submerged cobbles trace today's vastly enlarged dry ground. Collins, the designer, is a member of Delta Group of Philadelphia.

ROGER CONANT, 1911. Bronze, larger than life.
Brown St. at Washington Sq.
Henry Hudson Kitson (*see* Lexington: *The Minuteman*).

Roger Conant would be distressed to learn that many visitors mistake his figure for a witch, or at least a warlock, because of his seventeenth-century garb, swirling cloak and tall hat. The fact that he stands in front of the Witch Museum does nothing to dispel the notion. In reality, Conant was the first settler of Salem. The statue has been vandalized by what appear to be bullet holes. Funded by the Conant Family Association.

MOURNING VICTORY, 1947. Marble, h. 30′.
Lafayette and Washington Sts.
Joseph A. Coletti (*see* East Boston, Logan Airport: *General Logan*).

This art deco shaft commemorates the dead of the two World Wars.

CHOATE MONUMENT.
West End of Essex St.
J. Massey Rhind (1860–1936).

Rhind was born in Edinburgh, Scotland, son and student of John Rhind of the Royal Scottish Academy. He came to this country in 1889 and won a gold medal at the St. Louis Exposition in 1904. His best-known work is an equestrian Washington in Newark; other works are located in Pennsylvania, Ohio, and elsewhere in New Jersey.

A Parisian-style allegorical monument, this work honors Judge Joseph Hodges Choate (1832–1917), lawyer and diplomat, instrumental in breaking up the Tweed Ring, ambassador to Great Britain, and delegate to the first International Peace Conference in The Hague in 1907. The figure is Liberty in a mobcap, seated, holding up a laurel wreath. A medallion portrait of Judge Choate is affixed to the pedestal. Donated by Henry Clay Frick.

FATHER THEOBALD MATHEW, 1887. Stone, life-size.
Hawthorne Blvd. and Derby St.
Artist unknown.

Father Theobald was an early temperance advocate.

SAUGUS

CIVIL WAR MEMORIAL, 1875. Stone and bronze, larger than life.
Main and Central Sts.
M. H. Mosman.

Although the allegorical War, in stone atop the monument, is different, the sailor and soldier appear to be duplicates of two of the figures on the Civil War monument in Wakefield. Mosman was a Chicopee sculptor. Gift of Henry E. Homer.

SCITUATE

THE HERITAGE OF FREEDOM BY THE SEA, 1986. Glazed ceramic on steel-reinforced concrete, h. 8'.
At Town Hall, Rte. 3A and First Parish Rd.
Sonni Waldo (1938–   ).

Born in Philadelphia, Sonni Waldo studied sculpture there under Frank Gasparro, and later under John Moakley (*see* East Bridgewater: *Mural*); she subsequently earned a degree at the Boston Museum School. She and Moakley have also created a ceramic wall for Andover-Newton Theological Seminary.

Incorporating images from Scituate's history, this work was commissioned to commemorate the town's 350th anniversary. Funded by Scituate Arts Council, the 350th anniversary commission, Scituate Historical Society, and private donations.

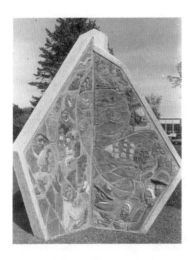

SHARON

DEBORAH SAMPSON GANNETT, 1989. Bronze, life-size.
At Sharon Public Library, Main and Depot Sts.
Lu Stubbs (*see* Brookline: *Three Women*).

Deborah Sampson (1760–1827) disguised herself as a man and served for seventeen months as a common soldier in the Revolutionary

War. Wounded twice, she pulled the bullet out of her leg herself the first time. Her second wound resulted in a fever; doctors treated her; her gender was discovered and she was mustered out. After the war she married a Sharon farmer, Benjamin Gannett, and lived the rest of her life here as a conventional early American woman.

In the only extant portrait Gannett appears most unattractive, and critics have complained that Stubbs portrayed the heroine as "too pretty." The sculptor retorts that the portrait was painted by an ill-trained itinerant painter and Gannett's descendants are quite attractive. Commissioned by townspeople of Sharon.

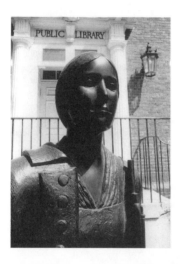

SHERBORN

MEMORY, 1923. Bronze war memorial, larger than life.
    Rte. 27 and Rte. 16 west (Main and Washington Sts.).
    Cyrus E. Dallin (*see* Arlington: *Indian Hunter*).

SOMERVILLE

FOSS PARK MURAL, 1992. Acrylic, h. 8′ × 36′.
    Broadway and McGrath Hwy.
    Be Allen (*see Flag* below), David Fichter (*see* Boston [Chinatown]: *Unity-Community*), and Clint Antar, Nicole Gonzales, Nicole Green, Gerry Lorenzo, Gamiel Pinto, and Gloria Pinto, all teenagers from the community.

    For this poolside mural, the artists incorporated sports themes and ethnic patterns drawn from the cultures of the neighborhood. Somerville Arts Council summer project in collaboration with The Partnership and Employment Resources, Inc.

CIVIL WAR MEMORIAL, 1908. Bronze, heroic size.
Highland St., west of library.
Augustus Lukeman (b. 1872).

Henry Augustus Lukeman was born in West Virginia, studied with
Daniel Chester French and then in Paris at the Ecole des Beaux Arts.
His name is associated with Augustus Saint-Gaudens, appearing sometimes as assistant and sometimes as competitor. The Angel of Victory
here owes its pose to a similar angel Saint-Gaudens created in 1903
for the *Sherman* monument in New York.

SPANISH WAR MEMORIAL, 1929. Bronze, two figures, life-size.
In front of library, Walnut and Highland Sts.
Raymond A. Porter (1883–1949).

Born in Mt. Herman, N.Y., Porter taught in the 1920s at Massachusetts Normal Art School, now Massachusetts College of Art. He also
sculpted the Henry Cabot Lodge portrait at the State House.

FOUR ORDINARY PARK BENCHES WITH THREE MAPLE TREES ON A
BLUESTONE CARPET, 1992. Wood, welded steel, stone, 15′ × 20′.
Union Sq., Highland Ave. and Walnut St.
Ross Miller (*see* Boston [Downtown]: *Dancing Trellis*).

Miller envisioned this usable work of art as counterpoint to the war
memorials nearby. They evoke the past; this work is "in the present
tense, in present life." Commissioned by Somerville Arts Council.

FLAG, 1985. Phenolic plastic, painted. Mobile screens, three units, each
12′ × 15′.
Overhead, lobby, Public Safety Bldg., Washington and Merriam Sts.
Be Allen (1940–   ).

Somerville artist Be Allen, born in New York City, attended the Boston Museum School and the San Francisco Art Institute.
This building, an MBTA car barn newly converted to a police/fire station, offered a vast open space in its entry lobby. Here Allen's mobile
screens, hanging from the skylights, refer in a delicate and fragmented
way to the colors and configurations of the American flag. Funded by a
Community Development grant.

SEVEN HILLS PARK, 1990. High-density foam, acrylic paint, steel, alumi-
num, brick, granite, h. 28′–50′.
Davis Sq., Holland St. and Buena Vista Rd.
Clifford Selbert (1953–   ).

A graphic designer and landscape architect, Selbert is particularly interested in what he calls "environmental graphics"—elements that help
people find their way around. He holds degrees in fine arts (1975) and
landscape architecture (1976) from Rhode Island School of Design; for
a time he was landscape architect for the city of Providence. He has
participated in the design of such environments as Boston's Harborwalk, the Blackstone River Valley National Heritage Park, and the Alle-
gheny Ridge Industrial Park. He has offices in Cambridge.

Six sculptures and a clock rise from brick bases commemorating the seven hills on which Somerville was built: Winter, Walnut, Spring, Cobble, Clarendon, Ploughed, and Prospect. The works depict two historic houses, a fort, a cow, a tree, and a fish—an alewife, for which the brook at the base of Ploughed Hill was named. Commissioned by the City of Somerville.

THE GREAT SOMERVILLE MURAL PROJECT, 1992. Acrylic, h. 10′ × one block long.
   Davis Sq., near 167 Holland St.
   Be Allen (*see Flag* above).

To commemorate the 150th anniversary of Somerville's separation from Charlestown, Be Allen solicited time-related drawings from the community and incorporated them into this megamural. Commissioned by Somerville Arts Council.

UNTITLED, 1984. Cast cement statues, life-size.
   Davis Sq., Highland St. and College Ave.
   James Tyler.

Tyler has studied at Hampshire College, Nasson College (Maine), and at St. Mary's College and Herron Art College (both Indiana). The figures, representing actual local residents, are cast from fondu cement. Tyler has moved to New York.

PANELS, 1989. Precast concrete, thirty units.
   Facade, between second and third stories, all sides, Davis Square Bldg., 18–48 Holland St.
   Syma (*see* Boston [Back Bay]: *Winged Caryatids*).

Eight interchangeable templates are rearranged into four distinct designs. Commissioned by Strekalovsky & Hoyt.

STONEHAM

AERIAL SCULPTURE, 1982.
   Interior, Flynn Rink.
   Linda DeHart (*see* Lexington: *Aerial Sculptures*).
   Funded by MDC 1% for Art.

SPANISH WAR MEMORIAL. Bronze, larger than life.
   Central and Common Sts.
   Joseph Pollia.
   Erected by the Town of Stoneham.

SUDBURY

MENORAH, 1974. Stainless steel, bronze, h. 6′.
   At Congregation Beth El, Hudson Rd.
   Barry Marchette (1939–   ).

Formerly on the faculty of the Art Institute of Boston, Lowell native Barry Marchette studied art at California College of Arts and Crafts and at Massachusetts College of Art. He held CETA grants in 1979–80 for environmental study and creation of a cultural community. In 1980 Marchette and a friend began making and marketing his recipes for hommus (chickpea spread) in the Beth El kitchen with a borrowed food processor; he is now a partner in the successful Hommus Factory, Inc. Commissioned by Congregation Beth El.

BUDDY DOG, 1977. Granite, h. 8′.
At Buddy Dog Humane Society, 151 Boston Post Rd.
John Weidman.

Weidman is an East Pepperell sculptor.

TEWKSBURY

★ WATER, 1985. Bronze, larger than life.
Town Hall grounds.
Mico Kaufman (*see* Lowell: *Homage to Women*).

This work is a memorial to Anne Sullivan, teacher of Helen Keller. It captures the moment that the teacher finally penetrated the closed world of the deaf-and-blind Helen, helping her understand the relationship between the word "water" and its physical presence. It is placed here because Sullivan, at a dark period in her life, was at the Tewksbury State Hospital. Erected by citizens of Tewksbury.

WAMESIT INDIAN, 1989. Bronze, h. 7′.
Main St., a quarter-mile south of I-495 interchange.
Mico Kaufman (*see* Lowell: *Homage to Women*).

When Tewksbury broke away from Billerica and incorporated in 1731, townspeople considered naming it "Wamesit" after the small subgroup of Passaconaway Indians who had a settlement near this spot. Town historians say Wamesit blood has descended to several current-day citizens of Tewksbury. Funded by public subscription conducted by Committee of Interested Citizens, Inc.

THE MUSTER FOUNTAIN, 1992. Bronze, h. 15′.
Edward Bowley Park, Main and South Sts., next to South Tewksbury firehouse.
Mico Kaufman (*see* Lowell: *Homage to Women*).

Cartoons in bronze figurative sculpture are rare; here is one. Funded by Committee of Interested Citizens, Inc.

TOUCHING SOULS, 1993. Bronze, life-size.
At United Methodist Church, Main and South Sts.
Mico Kaufman (*see* Lowell: *Homage to Women*).
Gift of the sculptor.

TOPSFIELD

THE WOUNDED COLOR SERGEANT, ca. 1921. Bronze, larger than life.
    On the common, across from library.
    Theo Alice Ruggles Kitson (*see* Malden: *The Hiker*).

      The statue commemorates Topsfield citizens who served in World
War I. Gift of Justin Allen, M.D.

WAKEFIELD

THE HIKER. Bronze, larger than life.
    Main and Common Sts.
    Theo Alice Ruggles Kitson (*see* Malden: *The Hiker*).

      Wakefield's casting of *The Hiker* lacks the usual platform base; his
feet are affixed directly to rock. Backed by a fountain, he enjoys one of
the prettier settings in Greater Boston.

CIVIL WAR MEMORIAL, 1902. Stone, h. approx. 30'.
    Main and Salem Sts.
    Sculptor unknown; design by Van Am Ringe Granite Corp.

      Although Wakefield's records fail to show the sculptor's name, it was
most likely M. H. Mosman of Chicopee. Two of the figures, the sailor
with his cutlass and the infantryman leaning on his rifle, are identical to
figures by Mosman in Saugus. Gift of Harriet Newell Flint.

WALPOLE

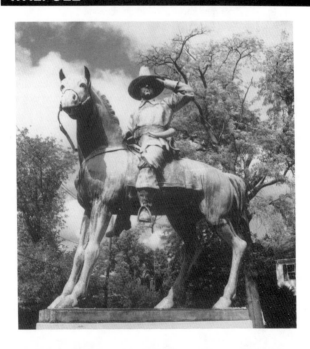

LIEUTENANT LEWIS MONUMENT, 1911. Bronze, life-size.
East and Plimpton Sts.
S. Barnicoat.

Lieut. Bachariah Lewis was one of this region's most involved citizens during his lifetime, 1663–1710. Surveyor, tax collector, tithingman, he served as an officer in the Wars of King William and Queen Anne (conflicts between the French and English colonies in North America, reflecting the hostilities of those two countries between 1689 and 1713). His aspect here is typical; astride his horse he explored and laid out roads in the area between Roxbury and Wrentham. Commissioned by his descendants, Isaac N. and Mary F. Lewis.

WALTHAM

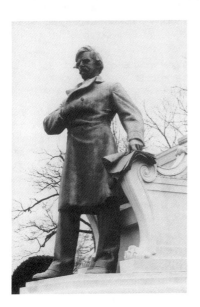

★ NATHANIEL PRENTISS BANKS, 1908. Bronze, larger than life.
Waltham city square, Moody and Main Sts.
Henry Hudson Kitson (*see* Lexington: *The Minuteman*).

Born in Waltham, Banks was speaker of the U.S. House of Representatives from 1856 to 1858, governor of Massachusetts, 1858–61, and major-general of U.S. Volunteers during the Civil War. This statue, once one of several behind the State House in Boston, was displaced by a parking lot and moved to the city of Banks' birth in 1950. Funded by appropriation of the Commonwealth.

THE HIKER MONUMENT, 1928. Bronze, larger than life.
  Waltham city square, Moody and Main Sts.
  Theo Alice Ruggles Kitson (*see* Malden: *The Hiker*).

  This monument is dedicated to Waltham's veterans of the Spanish-American War, 1898. Erected by the City of Waltham and James M. Dermody Camp No. 5 Spanish War Veterans.

At Bentley College:

★ PORTAL, 1979. Stone, h. 9'.
  Carlos Dorrien (1948–   ).

  Argentine-born, Carlos Dorrien is now an associate professor of art at Wellesley College. His simple but monumental stone carvings and portals are widely placed in the Boston area (*see* Cambridge [Harvard Square]: *Quiet Stone* and East Boston: *Portal*). Dorrien was sculptor-in-residence at Bentley in 1978–79. He has trained at Universidad de la Plata in Argentina, and in this country at Lowell Technological Institute, Montserrat College of Art, and Massachusetts College of Art.

★ WALL SCULPTURE, 1963. Copper with patina, h. 50' × 32' × 1½'.
  Atrium, Wyman St. Bldg., 275 Wyman St.
  Michio Ihara (*see* Lowell: *Pawtucket Prism*).

  "In sculpture I am concerned above all with two things," Michio Ihara has written; "time as a creative element which allows change and motion; and nature, combining forces of light, wind, heat and manpower for constructive ends." Ihara's wall sculpture here is designed to take advantage of the changing light streaming through the atrium skylight. One-foot copper squares are set at angles engineered so that shadow patterns, integral to the visual impact, vary as the sun moves. The copper is colored with heat and flux, a chemical that aids brazing. Vertical grooves in the sandblasted concrete wall are part of Ihara's design.

At Brandeis University:

A partial listing follows:

NEON FOR THE ROSE ART MUSEUM, 1985. Neon.
  Exterior, Rose Art Museum.
  Stephen Antonakos (1926–   ).

  A native of Greece, Antonakos came to this country at an early age and graduated from Brooklyn Community College. He was an early experimenter with neon as an art form; his work is owned by the Museum of Modern Art, the Whitney Museum, and others. He has taught at Yale, the University of North Carolina, and Brooklyn College. Museum purchase.

HORIZON, 1966. Bronze.
  Rose Art Museum portico.
    ★ Anthony Caro (1924–   ).

Caro was for two years in the early 1950s an assistant to England's great sculptor, Henry Moore. London-born, Caro as a teenager apprenticed to another English sculptor, Charles Wheeler, and later studied under him at the Royal Academy. Caro's abstract bolted and welded works first appeared in the late 1950s. Gift of Mr. and Mrs. Max Wasserstein.

END FREE SERIES XV, 1971. Welded steel.
  At right of Rose Art Museum facade.
  ★ Alexander Liberman (1912–   ).

Born in Kiev, Russia, Liberman came to the U.S. in 1941 and joined the staff of *Vogue* magazine. He swiftly rose to art director and then to editorial director of Condé Nast Publications. His steel abstractions are owned by the Museum of Modern Art, the Metropolitan Museum, the Whitney Museum, DeCordova Museum, Storm King Art Center, and many others.

PEGASUS (BIRTH OF THE MUSES), 1971. Bronze relief.
  Facade of Pollack Fine Arts Teaching Center.
  ★ Jacques Lipchitz (*see* Cambridge [M.I.T.]: *The Bather*).
  Funded by Lester Avner Foundation and the Jack I. and Lilian L. Poses Foundation.

ISTRA. Mixed media architectural structure.
  In wooded area to right of Rose Art Museum.
  Ed Rothberg.
  New Works Program, Massachusetts Council on Arts and Humanities.

WAND OF INQUIRY, 1983. Stainless steel, h. 15'.
  In front of Rosenstiel Basic Medical Sciences Research Center.
  Lila Katzen (1932–   ).
  Rosenstiel Foundation.

STUDENT, 1986. Bronze and stone, life-size.
  Outside Farber Library.
  Penelope Jencks (*see* Chelsea: *Chelsea Conversation*).

LOUIS B. BRANDEIS, 1957. Bronze.
  Fellows Garden.
  Robert Berks (1922–   ).

Born in Boston and educated at Harvard, Berks is best known for his huge bust of John F. Kennedy at Kennedy Center and for his portrait of Einstein, both in Washington, D.C. Berks now lives on Long Island.
  Justice Brandeis (1856–1941), first Jewish member of the U.S. Supreme Court, was born in Kentucky of Jewish immigrant parents who had prospered here. At the age of eighteen he entered Harvard Law School, without any undergraduate education, and graduated with honors in two years. Forming a law partnership in Boston, he found himself probing economic and social issues behind the legal issues of the day. Woodrow Wilson appointed him to the Supreme Court in 1916. His image as a dissenter stems from his ability to "state the law as it was to

be interpreted in the future," biographers write. He favored economic regulation to meet changing social and economic needs, but opposed curbs on thought, speech, or the press. Of 528 opinions he wrote, however, only forty-four were in dissent. The university named in his honor was founded in 1948. Commissioned, to commemorate the 100th anniversary of Brandeis' birth, by Lawrence E. Wien, trustee of the university.

MUSEUM: Rose Art Gallery hosts bi-monthly rotating exhibitions.

AERIAL SCULPTURE, 1981. Fabric, plexiglass, h. 3 stories.
Atrium, 204 Second Ave.
Linda DeHart (*see* Lexington: *Aerial Sculptures*).
Commissioned by Boston Properties Inc.

204 SECOND AVE., 1981. Graphic wall collage, silkscreen on plexiglass, fabric, h. 2′ × 8′.
Lobby, 204 Second Ave.
Linda DeHart (*see* Lexington: *Aerial Sculptures*).
Commissioned by Boston Properties Inc.

WATERTOWN

SIR RICHARD SALTONSTALL, 1926.
Charles River Rd. near Watertown Sq.
Henry Hudson Kitson (*see* Lexington: *The Minuteman*).
Theo Alice Ruggles Kitson (*see* Malden: *The Hiker*).

The Kitsons collaborated on several memorial sculptures (*see* Commonwealth Avenue: *Collins Memorial*) in addition to their independent pieces. Although they were said to have separated about 1909, contemporary accounts list them as collaborators on this work.

Sir Richard Saltonstall led the colony from England that founded Watertown in 1630. This monument commemorates the event that established the principle of "no taxation without representation." A tax of eight pounds had been levied toward the building of a stockade at New Towne (Cambridge); the freemen of Watertown objected. Here, in the bas-relief on the right, the Rev. George Phillips and Elder Richard Browne address them, contending that "English freemen cannot rightfully be taxed save by their own consent." The result was that each town was asked to send two deputies to a General Court, the origin of the Massachusetts legislative body. At left, a colonist and friendly Indians exchange fish and bread. Funded by public subscription.

WATERTOWN PAST AND PRESENT, 1983. Mural.
Merchants Row, off Main St.
Elizabeth Carter (*see* Cambridge [Central Square]: *Floating Down Mass. Avenue*).

MURAL II, 1984. Ceramic, h. 30′.
  Exterior wall, Metco Tile Corp., 291 Arsenal St.
  Lilli Ann Killen Rosenberg (*see* Newton: *Five Concrete Mosaic Sculptures*).

WATERTOWN PUBLIC LIBRARY owns a number of works by Harriet
  Goodhue Hosmer (1830–1908), Watertown native and member of the
  American artists' colony in Rome in the 1850s.

WAYLAND

THE WORLD OF WAYLAND MIDDLE SCHOOL, 1991. Acrylic, h. 32′ × 78′.
  Wayland Middle School, 201 N. Main St.
  David Fichter (*see* Lawrence: *Bread and Roses Mural*), students, teachers, and parents of Wayland Middle School.

  A specialist in collaborative school murals, Fichter has overseen
more than thirty in the Greater Boston area. Portraits of biologist
Rachel (*Silent Spring*) Carson, naturalist author Henry David Thoreau,
and inspirational black activist Martin Luther King, Jr. contribute to the
theme of the mural: the school in the environment and the larger world.
Commissioned by the Cultural Educational Cooperative with funding
from Massachusetts Cultural Council.

WELLESLEY

DAVID CARAS © PHOTO

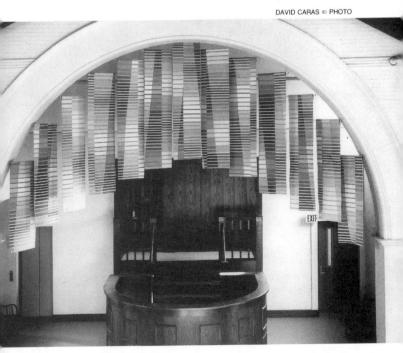

WELLESLEY BIRTHDAY QUILT, 1991. Fabric, thirteen panels, each 20″×
4.5′–7′.
Great Hall, Wellesley Town Hall.
Carol Keller (1951–   ).

Keller's fabric art has been shown nationwide in juried shows, and
her quilts have twice been used as textbook covers. Born in Wilmington, Del., she studied at Rhode Island School of Design (B.F.A., 1974)
and at Moore College of Art in Philadelphia. She now lives in Somerville. Commissioned by Wellesley Arts Council for the Wellesley bicentennial celebration.

At Babson College:

SQUARE THROATED ELBOW. Cor-ten steel, h. 30″.
In front of Horn Library.
David Kibbey (*see* Charles River Esplanade: *Trimbloid X*).

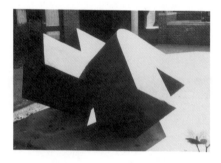

OMINOUS ICON #6, 1976. Cor-ten steel, h. 6′.
YADDO STUDY, ca. 1970. Cor-ten steel, h. 4′.
Between Horn Library and Kriebel Hall.
Dennis Kowal (1938–   ).

Boston sculptor Dennis Kowal maintains his studio in Cohasset on
the South Shore. A native of Illinois, he studied at the Art Institute of
Chicago, University of Illinois, and at Southern Illinois University under
Buckminster Fuller. He received an M.F.A. in 1962. Kowal came East
to accept a fellowship at the MacDowell Colony in Peterborough, N.H.,
and remained in New England. He has taught at University of Southern
Illinois and been artist-in-residence at the MacDowell and Yaddo colonies, Dartmouth and Amherst colleges, Milton Academy, DeCordova
Museum, University of Georgia, and others. Kowal's training in engineering and design led him to experiment with carved acrylic and steel.
Of his twenty-two major public commissions, nine are in the Boston
area.

GALLERY: The Gallery at Horn, to the right of Horn Library entrance. Monthly exhibitions of work by contemporary artists, theme shows about the college, or exhibitions arranged by Smithsonian Institute's SITES program. Horn Library also contains works from the college's collection on permanent display.

APPLES OF YOUTH, 1988. Bronze, h. $64'' \times 43'' \times 7''$.
Computer Center.
Judith Shah (1942–   ).

Shah earned a B.F.A. and an M.F.A. (1975) at Boston University, then undertook intensive non-degree studio work at Wellesley College and Mass/Art. Turning to printmaking, she was awarded a scholarship to study at the Hand Graphics Atelier in Santa Fe, N.M.; she has also been a guest artist at the Experimental Etching Studio in Boston.

At Wellesley College:

★ WALKING MAN, 1876. Bronze, h. 7' (*see* picture on page 160).
Academic Quadrangle.
   ★ Auguste Rodin (1840–1917).

Born in Paris, Rodin early in his studies displayed the creative non-conformity that made him the bane of academicians and, eventually, the towering figure of nineteenth-century sculpture. The uninhibited, almost savage, modeling of his late works paved the road for modernism in this century.

Rodin's first major figure had been so masterly that critics accused him of casting his forms directly from the body of the live model. In response, he tried to create his second, *St. John the Baptist Preaching*, in a pose that would be impossible to cast. The *Walking Man*, originally modeled at half scale, was a study for St. John. Rodin wanted to render the progressive development of movement, as if the figure were pushing off the left leg and then transferring weight to the right; thus both feet are solidly planted. *St. John* was completed in 1880; it was not until twenty-five years later that Rodin saw the sketch as a work in its own right. In 1912 it was given to the French embassy in Rome, where its fragmentary nature made it the butt of jokes: Rodin himself said, "A man without a head is the perfect symbol of our diplomacy." This example is from a series of twelve cast in 1969, from Rodin's original 1907 model, by the Georges Rudier Foundry in Paris.

LONG SPREAD, 1973. Steel.
   ★ Michael Steiner (*see* Cambridge [M.I.T.]: *Niagara*).

SCHECHINAH TEMPTATIONS, 1976. Steel.
   ★ Jules Olitski (1922–   ).

Olitski is credited with the first thoroughgoing attempt to make a painting out of nothing but pure color. Brought to the U.S. from Russia at the age of two, Olitski served in the U.S. Army, attended various art institutes in New York and Paris, earned a B.A. and a master's at New York University, and taught at Bennington, C. W. Post College, and

State University of New York at New Paltz. A first prize at the Corcoran Biennial in 1967 solidified his reputation. He turned for a time to sculpture; this is one of several examples.

★ UNTITLED (Filagreed Steel Line for Wellesley College), 1979–80.
North of Lake Waban, near college library.
Robert Irwin (1928–   ).

California Robert Irwin started out as a painter of poetic, reductive works. Interested in psychological sensory research, he began to create installations in which space was delineated merely with tape, string, or scrim. He is credited with invention of the terms "site-dominant" and so forth (*see* Introduction) to describe the relationship of works of art to their environment. Here Irwin walked the campus and mused for two days before designing the work, which surely qualifies as "site-determined," responding to the site and visually woven into it. Both this work and *Wild Spot*, below, were installed as part of a group of environmental siteworks.

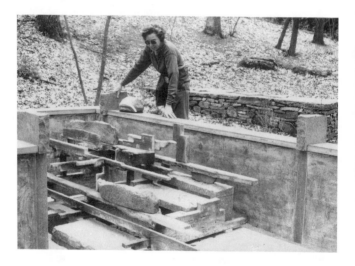

★ UNTITLED SITEWORK, 1992. Schist, granite, and bronze, h. 2' × 17.5' × 13'.
West shore of Lake Waban.
Michael McKinnell (1936–   ), Michael Singer (1946–   ).

McKinnell is an architect, a partner in the Boston firm Kallmann, McKinnell & Wood, designers of such civic landmarks as Boston City Hall and Back Bay station. Born in Manchester, England, he studied art and architecture in England, then attended Columbia University. He has taught at Harvard Graduate School of Design.

Singer, a sculptor, divides his time between Vermont and New York. His *Ritual Series*, subtle nature-based sculpture created in remote places of reeds, willow wands, saplings, and stone, has received wide critical acclaim. Singer's work has appeared at the Guggenheim Museum and at the most prestigious international art exhibitions of recent decades, including the Whitney Biennial, the Venice Biennale, the German Documenta, and the Biennial de São Paolo, Brazil.

This work was erected under a National Endowment for the Arts program to encourage collaborations among artists, architects, and landscape designers. "The idea is to design a *place* rather than an artwork," an NEA official explains. Singer and McKinnell have evoked the stone walls and cellar holes often found in New England woods, the weathered boards and beams of abandoned farms. Respect for the natural site, indigenous mosses and bushes, is implicit. Funded by Design Arts/Visual Arts special initiative, NEA.

★ WILD SPOT, 1979–80. Wrought iron, h. 10′.
North of Whitin Observatory.
Nancy Holt (1938–   ).

All Holt's work is involved in site, time, and orientation in space, often astronomical orientation. Born in Worcester and educated at Jackson College (now Tufts), Holt deals in film, video, and large-scale sculpture and installations. She has held Guggenheim and NEA grants. She was married to Robert Smithson, environmental earthworks artist who was killed in an airplane crash in 1973.

Wild Spot creates a demarcation of the landscape, fencing a tiny wildplant garden, inviting the viewer into its space to view framed vertical slices of the environs. Much of Holt's site-specific work has been done in the West; this more confined piece seems well suited to the less open, more constricted woods of the Eastern Seaboard.

GALLERY: Jewett Arts Center.

At Wellesley Office Park (Rte. 128 and William St.):

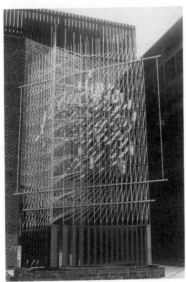

IHARA, WIND SCULPTURE

★ WIND SCULPTURE, 1973. Stainless steel, h. 25′ × 20′ × 8′.
At Bldg. #5.
Michio Ihara (*see* Lowell: *Pawtucket Prism*).

3-D HANGING, M3D6/A, 1979. Textile, h. two stories.
Lobby, 45 William St.
Peter Collingwood.

CASCADE OF CUBES, 1972. Aluminum, h. 20′.
Atrium, 40 William St.
William Wainwright (*see* East Boston, Logan Airport: *Windwheels*).

WESTFORD

BICENTENNIAL TRIBUTE, 1992. Granite, four 3.5′ cubes.
At Westford Academy, Patten Rd.
Mary Stanton (1973–   ).
Carolyn Tetrev (1974–   ).

Lowell native Carolyn Tetrev, a junior at Westford Academy when
these blocks were designed, decided to be an artist as the result of this
experience and enrolled at Columbus (Ohio) College of Art and Design.
Senior Mary Stanton, born in Dayton, Ohio, went on to the University of
New Hampshire.

As part of DeCordova Museum's Public Art Program, visiting artist
Ralph Helmick (*see* Boston [Charles River Esplanade]: *Arthur Fiedler*)
led Westford High School students through a six-week process of designing a public work. Dozens of student designs were juried and the
Stanton-Tetrev concept selected for execution in local Chelmsford granite. The work is particularly appropriate because, at the time of its design, this public high school was occupied by both high schoolers and
kindergarteners. Erected to mark the 200th anniversary of the founding
of the school; funded by Massachusetts Cultural Council as administered by DeCordova Museum, Westford Academy Art Club, Westford
Academy Trustees, and Westford Arts Lottery.

CIVIL WAR MEMORIAL, 1910. Bronze, larger than life.
Boston Rd. and Main St.
Artist unknown.

Dedicated on Memorial Day, 1910, this figure was a gift to the town
from Edwin D. Metcalf in honor of his father, Lt. William Metcalf.

WESTON

THE WESTON LIBRARY SCULPTURE SITE (planned for 1995).
School St., near Alphabet Lane.

In erecting its new public library, Weston has provided an outdoor
spot for display of large-scale contemporary sculpture. Works on exhibi-

tion will change every year or two. Project of Weston Library Art and Exhibitions Committee.

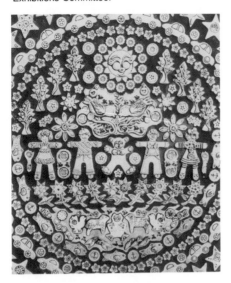

TAVERNSIDE PARK MOSAIC, 1986. Ceramic, h. 3′ × 3′.
In Tavernside Park, Boston Post Rd., south of town green.
Phyllis Biegun (1947–   ).

A native of Boston who lives and teaches in Weston, Biegun earned a bachelor of fine arts degree from Cornell and a master's degree in art education from Rochester Institute of Technology. She instructed in a Buffalo-area high school, and has since taught on many levels from boys' clubs to adult education.

Biegun's mosaic is another example of art designed to reflect the uses of a specific site. For this children's play area, the ceramicist cut the components from clay with cookie cutters: stars, flowers, toy cars, gingerbread children, and even (very central) a teddy bear. Matching pairs can be discovered among the forms. Biegun is impatient with art that looks difficult to kids: "I wanted children to look at this and say, 'I could do that.'" Funded by Weston Arts Council and Weston Children's Community Association.

WESTWOOD

★ IN THE DENSE WORDS, 1988. Laminated books, chain-sawed, five units, 30″ × 24″ × 24″ to 105″ × 48″ × 48″.
Faxon Co., 15 Southeast Park.
Mags Harries (*see* Chelsea: *Bellingham Square*).

Because it is a library subscription service, Faxon Co.'s clients are librarians and publishers. Instead of turning tree trunks into books, Harries here turns books back into tree trunks. Commissioned by Richard R. Rowe.

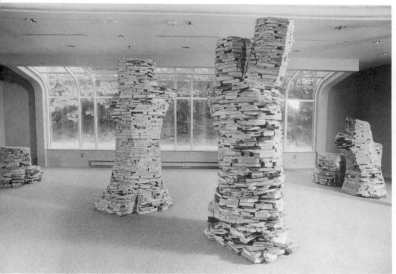

HARRIES, IN THE DENSE WORDS   KATHY CHAPMAN PHOTO

WEYMOUTH

RAINBOW CASCADE, 1986. Diffraction grating, h. 70′.
  Atrium, Stetson Place, 541 Main St.
  William Wainwright (*see* East Boston, Logan Airport: *Windwheels*).
  Commissioned by H.J. Davis Co.

WILMINGTON

BALDWIN APPLE MONUMENT, ca. 1895. Granite, h. approx. 7′.
  Chestnut St., near Butters Row.
  Sculptor unknown.

Although Col. Loammi Baldwin (*see* Woburn) is often credited with
discovering the Baldwin apple, Wilmington tradition has it that the fruit
was merely named in his honor. The famous apple is said to have
been found about 1789 during the surveying of the Middlesex Canal,
and the progenitor tree was cultivated by the Butters family, who had a
farm here. Its admirers believe this monument is one of only two in the
world dedicated to apples (the other is in Baltimore). Erected by the
Count Rumford Association, which maintains Rumford's birthplace in
Woburn.

WINCHESTER

★ WAR MEMORIAL, 1927. Bronze, larger than life.
Main St. and Mystic Valley Pkwy.
Herbert Adams (*see* Woburn: *Col. Loammi Baldwin*).

WINTHROP

WORLD WAR I MEMORIAL, ca. 1927. Stone, approximately life-size.
1 Metcalf Sq., between library and Town Hall.
Gerald T. Horrigan (*see* Quincy: *Robert Burns*).

WOBURN

COL. LOAMMI BALDWIN, 1917. Bronze, life-size.
Jct. Main and Elm Sts.
★ Herbert Adams (1858–1945).

Herbert Adams attended school in Fitchburg, and at Worcester Institute of Technology, Massachusetts Normal Art School, and the Ecole des Beaux Arts in Paris. He gained contemporary fame with his marble portrait busts of women to which he added tints of color, a style that seems gauche today. Teaching at Pratt Institute in Brooklyn, he was selected to complete the bronze doors of the Library of Congress after Olin Warner's death, and shortly thereafter had to give up teaching to attend to his many commissions. Among his works are the *Channing* on Boston Common, *William Cullen Bryant* at New York Public Library, and *Joseph Henry* in Washington.

Soldier and civic leader, Baldwin (1745–1807) is immortalized by the Baldwin apple, which was discovered growing wild on a tree a mile or so from this spot. Sometimes regarded as America's first engineer, Baldwin as a young man attended science lectures at Harvard with his precocious neighbor Benjamin Thompson (*see Count Rumford* below). A participant in the battles of Lexington and Concord, Baldwin became a colonel in the Continental Army and saw action at New York and Trenton. Donated by his descendants.

CIVIL WAR MEMORIAL, 1869. Bronze, larger than life.
Main and Pleasant Sts.
Martin Milmore (*see* Framingham: *Civil War Memorial*).

THE HIKER, 1934. Bronze, larger than life.
Main and Common Sts.
Theo Alice Ruggles Kitson (*see* Malden: *The Hiker*).
Presented by Charles H. Moloy Camp 42, Spanish-American War Veterans.

COUNT RUMFORD, 1899. Bronze, heroic size (*see* picture on page 162).
  In front of library, Pleasant and Federal Sts.
  Caspar Zumbusch.

   Benjamin Thompson Count Rumford (1753–1814) was born in Woburn of a prosperous farming family and went on to a multi-faceted career that included distinction in science, progressive social ideas, high posts in the governments of England and Bavaria, a knighthood from George III, and a title from Maximilian of Bavaria. Precocious at fourteen, he was able enough in astronomy and higher mathematics to calculate a solar eclipse within four seconds of accuracy. At nineteen he married a wealthy widow fourteen years his senior and became a major of local militia. For a time he lived in what is now Concord, then called Rumford, N.H. When the Revolution broke out he was suspected (correctly) of Tory sympathies, embarked for London, and shortly found a post in the department of state, where he rose steadily in rank. His scientific pursuits, meanwhile, earned him membership in the Royal Society. The American war having ended, he decided to join the Austrian army; true to form, he promptly became minister of war, minister of police, and grand chamberlain. In a pioneering workfare experiment, he removed 2,600 beggars from the streets of Munich. His experiments with firearms led him to a theory that heat is motion, not, as was then believed, a substance, and he had an inkling of what is today called the law of conservation of energy. A casting of a statue whose original was in Munich, this one was given to Woburn by Marshall Tidd.

SUSPENDED SCULPTURE, 1985. Stainless steel, gold-plated brass, aluminum, h. $33' \times 11' \times 9'$.
  Atrium, Bldg. 600, Unicorn Office Park.
  Michio Ihara (*see* Lowell: *Pawtucket Prism*).

INDEX OF ARTISTS